Tools for Learning

A Guide to Teaching Study Skills

M.D. Gall

Joyce P. Gall

Dennis R. Jacobsen

Terry L. Bullock

Association for Supervision and Curriculum Development
Alexandria, Virginia

About the Authors

M. D. Gall is Professor, College of Education, University of Oregon, Eugene, Oregon.

Joyce P. Gall is President, M. Damien Educational Services, Eugene, Oregon.

Dennis R. Jacobsen is Assistant Professor, School of Education, California State Polytechnic University, Pomona, California.

Terry L. Bullock is Associate Professor, University College, University of Cincinnati, Cincinnati, Ohio.

Printed in the United States of America.
The type for this book was set using Xerox Ventura Publisher 2.0.
Cover designed by Simeon Montesa.

Ronald S. Brandt, *Executive Editor*
Nancy Modrak, *Managing Editor, Books*
Julie Houtz, *Associate Editor*
Al Way, *Manager, Design Services*
Simeon Montesa, *Graphic Designer*
Valerie Sprague, *Desktop Consulting Specialist*

$13.95
ISBN: 0-87120-170-4
Stock Number: 611-90086

Library of Congress Cataloging-in-Publication Data

Tools for learning: a guide to teaching study skills / M.D. Gall . . .
[et al.].
    p. cm.
  Includes bibliographical references and index.
  ISBN 0–87120–170–4
  1. Study, Method of.   I. Gall, Meredith D., 1942–
  II. Association for Supervision and Curriculum Development.
LB1049.T64   1990
371.3'028'1—dc20
                                 90–36146
                                   CIP

Contents

Acknowledgments

We wish to acknowledge the researchers and practitioners who have contributed to the large and growing literature on study skills instruction. This book is largely a synthesis of their work. We hope that we represented it fairly and accurately.

Many colleagues have supported our study skills work in schools, the development of our ideas and materials, and the writing of this book. We thank them all, with special acknowledgements to: Carol Acklin, Bandon School District; Margaret Artero, University of Guam; Ron Brandt, ASCD; Megan Clark, Lowell School District; Glenn Hogen, Sylvan Learning Corporation; Reneé Jacobsen; Peter Taylor, Tigard School District; Ione Wolfe and Dottie Winterrle, Guam Department of Education.

Foreword

For many educators, study skills is a topic that lacks the pop and sizzle of other classroom activities. Perhaps that is why I have no recollection of learning how to study. Somehow, though, I did learn; had I not, I would have been denied access to the meat and potatoes of my education. Many students, however, are educationally shortchanged simply because they have never been taught the basic skills involved in learning. In fact, researchers have observed that successful and unsuccessful students differ greatly in their use of study skills. The differences go beyond motivation, genetic potential, and learning style preferences; many are *learned behaviors* that directly affect academic performance. It is these learned—and changeable—behaviors that are discussed in this book.

Although scholars may disagree about the specific skills that should be included under the rubric of study skills, most agree that learning how to learn is as essential as learning the content of individual disciplines. In a world of rapid changes and exponential increases in available information, lifelong learning is inevitable, and the teacher-as-facilitator plays a critical role in the development of the lifelong learner. *Tools for Learning: A Guide to Teaching Study Skills* gives teachers the resources they need to fill this role.

We must equip all students with the tools for continued learning. It is no longer in this nation's best interest for schools to perform a sifting and sorting function; our human resources are too limited. If we want to be pacesetters in a global economy, we must become a total learning society, valuing and educating every individual, developing and sharpening every person's skills.

ASCD believes that schools should teach students how to learn and that students should eventually become responsible for their own learning. As educational leaders, we must ensure this. Learning how to learn cannot be left to students. It must be taught.

Donna Jean Carter
ASCD President, 1990-1991

1
The Case for Study Skills Instruction

We have written this book with two main goals in mind. Our first goal is to make the case for providing study skills instruction at the elementary and secondary school levels. Study skills instruction, at this time, is not part of the standard curriculum; it should be among the *basic* skills that all schools teach.

Most of the book concerns our second goal, which is to identify important study skills and how to teach them. Chapter 3 describes how to go about starting a study skills program in your school or district. The remaining chapters discuss the basic study skills needed for managing one's study behavior (Chapter 4), participating in class (Chapter 5), reading textbooks (Chapter 6), writing papers (Chapter 7), and taking tests (Chapter 8). We also describe methods for teaching each of the skills and summarize research on various aspects of study skills instruction. Much of the recent research is based on cognitive learning theory, which is explained in Chapter 2. We have drawn from our own experience as teachers and teacher educators, each of us having taught study skills to students and trained teachers in methods of study skills instruction.

Why Teach Study Skills?

The Importance of Study Skills

The importance of study skills can be demonstrated by a medical analogy. Until recently, most people placed their illnesses entirely in the hands of doctors. Illness was a mysterious thing that only doctors understood and only doctors could cure. The patient was viewed as a passive participant in the healing process.

That view is not held so widely today. Many people now see that they play an active role in keeping themselves healthy. If they become ill, they believe that they can affect their own healing process. Firsthand accounts of illnesses, such as Norman Cousins' best-seller, *Anatomy of an Illness*, have demonstrated that patients can do much to heal themselves. Doctors are no longer seen as all-knowing, godlike persons. In the contemporary view of things, they are viewed as partners, working with patients, to bring about healing. In fact, doctors now realize that most common illnesses will go away of their own accord if the patient exercises effective health care practices.

A similar principle applies to the learning process. Traditionally, the teacher has been regarded as the most important element of instruction. But the teacher cannot learn for the student. Learning occurs inside the student's head, not the teacher's. The teacher can only provide the instructional conditions that facilitate learning; the rest is up to the student. The student must use appropriate skills for learning—study skills—or learning will not occur. An obvious example involves the study skill of attending to instruction. If a student does not pay attention, learning is impossible.

Many students are not aware that they use such skills to help themselves learn, but that doesn't make the skills any less important. Just as patients can prevent illnesses or speed their recovery by working in partnership with their doctor, students can improve their academic performance by using study skills that support their teacher's instructional efforts.

To put it simply, study skills are important because they help students learn. They also help students meet the school's expectation that students become increasingly independent learners. Primary grade teachers structure much of their students' learning time, knowing that young children possess too few study skills to take much responsibility for their own learning. College professors, however, provide little structure for the learning process because they assume that college students have the appropriate study skills to learn independently.

Unless students develop good study skills, they will be unable to respond to expectations at each grade level for greater self-motivation, self-structuring, and self-monitoring of the learning process. Thomas and Rohwer (1986) make the point this way:

> Instructors in early grades usually inform students about what they are supposed to do when studying and about what they are supposed to know or be able to do for a test. With the transition to high school and beyond, however, the criteria for studying become increasingly shrouded in secrecy. Thus, studying can become sophisticated detective work for a small number of "cue seekers," but it can constitute guesswork or blind routinized behavior for the majority (p. 21).

The eventual result of guesswork or blind routinized behavior (poor study skills) is academic failure or the need to select a watered-down academic program that minimizes independent learning.

Above all, study skills are important because they are *lifelong* skills. They are critical for success in the workplace and in our lives. Consider the skill of organizing study materials so that they are easily accessible. We advocate teaching students to keep their lecture notes, study notes, and teacher handouts in a three-ring binder. Is this organizational skill useful only in school? Certainly not. Most people will handle information recorded on paper throughout their lives. If they cannot keep this paper organized and accessible, they will not cope well with the demands of work and home.

Consider also the study skill of generating questions about textbook content or other school material. This skill helps students to think carefully about the material they are studying and to reflect on what the teacher might consider important enough to ask on a test or other assignment. This ability to reflect on what another person considers important is also useful in later life.

In fact, the distinction between "school" and "life after school" is becoming increasingly blurred. The "lifelong learner" has become a household term in our generation. Many adults go back to school to learn skills for a second, or even a third, career, while others return to learn new skills for their current job or to enhance effectiveness. Study skills are essential to get the most from these experiences.

The Importance of Study Skills Instruction

Most educators agree that study skills are important. They do not agree, however, on how to teach these skills. The public school curriculum is crowded, and some critics argue that it should be reduced, not expanded, to a common core that emphasizes the academic disciplines (e.g., Sizer 1984). In addition, developing and implementing new instruction is often difficult, expensive, and time-consuming. To overcome these serious obstacles to making study skills instruction part of the core curriculum, educators must look at the research on how students learn study skills.

Evidence shows that most students will not learn study skills unless they receive explicit instruction in their use. Some educators, however, believe that study skills are a natural by-product of maturation and schooling. In fact, most students *do* become more efficient learners as they progress through school. The same learning tasks that are difficult for young children are easy for most adolescents, who can concentrate for longer periods of time and perform each learning task more quickly and effectively (Rohwer 1973).

On the other hand, this argument does not take into account the nature of the learning task. Adolescents may perform well on learning tasks that would challenge a younger student, but how well do they perform on learning tasks of greater complexity? Many teachers have told us that they have to water down their instruction to accommodate deficiencies in students' study skills and attitudes. Some say they cannot assign homework, even though they would like to, because students won't do it. Nor can they assign papers longer than a paragraph or a page because students will be overwhelmed.

In addition, Thomas and Rohwer (1986) found that some study skills improve over time, but not others. As shown in Table 1.1, taking notes in class is a skill that naturally increases with use. Generating questions and making visual representations of ideas, however, do not show natural increases in use over time, even though these are important study skills. Systematic instruction is necessary if students are to learn and use these skills.

Table 1.1

Use of Study Skills by Middle- to High-ability Students at Different Levels of Schooling (Thomas and Rohwer 1986)

| Study Skill | Percentage of Students Using Skill | | |
	Junior High School	Senior High School	College
Taking notes on assigned readings	31%	40%	43%
Taking notes when teacher emphasizes point in class	50%	71%	92%
Making up questions to guide reading	15%	5%	3%
Making charts, graphs, or other pictures to represent important ideas or events	8%	9%	9%

What kind of instruction ensures that students develop effective study skills? Armbruster and Anderson (1981) state, "A . . . major conclusion from the research on study techniques is that students often have to be carefully trained to use a technique to advantage" (p. 155). Training means more than *telling* students to use a particular study skill. For example, Anderson and Armbruster (1984) reviewed research on the effectiveness of outlining as a study skill for comprehending textbook material. Two studies found that outlining was effective, but four other studies found that it was no more effective than other strategies, including repetitive reading. The two studies with positive results involved training students extensively in outlining skills. One study, for example, consisted of a 30-lesson training program (Salisbury 1935). In the four studies that found no effect, the only intervention was telling students that they should outline the text. No training was involved.

The need for systematic instruction in study skills becomes even more compelling when we consider the characteristics of today's students. Harold Hodgkinson, former U.S. Commissioner of Education, has documented that an increasing percentage of students are from disadvantaged, ethnic minority backgrounds (Hodgkinson 1985). Many are ill-equipped for the demands of conventional schools, which are primarily oriented to white, middle-class values and behavior patterns. If educators are to serve these students effectively, they must teach them study skills and habits; they cannot assume that these students already have them.

Hodgkinson (1983, 1985) also points out that because of these population changes and the lack of study skills instruction in schools, colleges face a declining pool of well-qualified applicants in the 1990s. The immediate economic survival of many colleges will depend on their ability to work with poorly qualified applicants, which means that colleges will probably have to lower academic standards or provide remedial instruction. We must ask ourselves, however, whether this is the proper role of "higher education." Instituting effective study skills programs in grades K–12 would ensure that colleges do not become forever saddled with the inappropriate task of remedial education.

The Status of Study Skills Instruction

Elementary and Secondary Schools

When conducting study skills workshops for educators and the general public, we usually show participants a list of study skills. After defining and explaining the skills, we ask, "How many of you were taught these skills while you were going to school?" Virtually no one raises a hand. At best, some of their teachers mentioned a few skills; some have even taught a few skills, such as how to search for main ideas and how to take notes. Our impression, however, is that efforts to teach study skills have been neither systematic nor sustained, and thus have had few lasting effects on students.

This impression is supported by research. Durkin (1979) directly observed the reading lessons of a sample of intermediate grade teachers. One purpose of her observations was to record the amount of time that teachers taught such study skills as outlining textbooks and looking up information in an encyclopedia. She observed 4,469 minutes of reading instruction, but did not record a single incidence in which study skills were directly taught or reviewed. The same result was obtained in observing 2,775 minutes of social studies instruction. Nonetheless, teachers in both types of lessons expected students to apply these study skills in performing assigned learning tasks.

Policymakers also have raised concerns about the haphazard teaching of study skills in American schools. The most visible expressions of these concerns are the widely circulated report *A Nation at Risk* and the reports of other school reform commissions in the early 1980s (Felt 1985). Nearly all of these commissions came to the same conclusion: schools need to take more responsibility for teaching study skills to the nation's youth. Three recent developments in education support this conclusion.

One development is the dramatic advances that have occurred in cognitive psychology. Within just the past decade or so, researchers have learned a great deal about the cognitive processes involved in learning. As a result, educators are seeing more clearly than ever that the student is not a passive recipient of the teacher's instruction, but an active participant in it. Educators are beginning to see that it might be desirable to have students learn about their own cognitive processes and how to use them in particular ways to facilitate learning. That, in effect, is what study skills instruction is all about.

Another development has been society's renewed concern for the at-risk student. In the 1960s and 1970s, early childhood programs such as Head Start and Follow Through were developed to better prepare disadvantaged children for public school. Despite the success of these programs, too many students still drop out of school. The national dropout rate is approximately 25 percent, and in some school districts it is 50 percent or higher (Baker and Ogle 1989).

Obviously, the positive effects of these early childhood interventions are not sustained through the middle-school years when students usually first exhibit symptoms of dropping out. New types of programs are needed at all levels of education. Because at-risk students usually have poor study skills and attitudes, these programs should include a study skills component.

Also, because at-risk students are unlikely to get support at home for studying, these programs might show parents how they can support their children's homework behavior and their attitudes toward studying and school.

The third development influencing the current interest in study skills instruction is the push for higher standards of performance for the nation's youth. A variety of societal changes, including students' declining SAT scores and the United States' perceived decline as a global political and economic power, have prompted movements for school reform on many levels. For example, Coleman, Hoffer, and Kilgore (1982) conducted an influential study in which they compared education in public and private schools. They found that private school students have higher academic achievement and more rigorous homework requirements.

Although these results do not demonstrate a direct cause-and-effect relationship between homework and academic achievement, some educators have made this interpretation. In response, they have advocated increasing the amount of homework given to students, not only because of its presumed effectiveness, but also because of their own desire to show that public school education is comparable in quality to private school education.

With this pressure for more homework have come the broader demands for a more rigorous high school curriculum (e.g., Sizer 1984; Adler 1982) and higher graduation standards for all students.

Study skills instruction is essential to the success of any of these school reform efforts. As the school day becomes more demanding, students will need more sophisticated study strategies to succeed. Unless our nation's students receive study skills instruction, many are likely to be overwhelmed and achieve even less than they do now.

But the good news is that many teachers and administrators *are* showing greater interest in study skills programs. The growing body of research on study skills and several large-scale projects to develop study skills materials have given educators more information on how such a program might work.

The most visible of these projects is the work of the National Association of Secondary School Principals (NASSP) and the National Association of Elementary School Principals (NAESP) in developing and distributing the *hm Study Skills Program*, which includes a comprehensive set of workbooks for a wide range of grade levels and subjects. NASSP and NAESP have sponsored workshops across the country to help school districts implement the program.

Many school districts are currently using the *hm* program. Its availability has significantly increased educators' awareness of study skills instruction and its importance in the elementary and secondary curriculum.

Several additional programs are being developed or are now available (see Chapter 2). They should further raise educators' awareness.

Despite this progress, study skills instruction is not yet a priority for many school districts. Some districts have formed committees to plan a study skills curriculum, while others have implemented small-scale programs. At the individual level, many teachers, school librarians, and reading specialists are taking the initiative to teach study skills to their classes. Overall, however, study skills instruction in elementary and secondary schools is characterized by increasing interest but rather limited implementation.

Higher Education

Study skills courses have been taught at the college level since at least the early 1920s (Krumboltz and Farquhar 1957). The popularity of these courses and related services grew rapidly in the late 1960s when many students with poor academic preparation were admitted to college. Now most colleges have a staff of instructors who specialize in working with students having academic difficulties or wishing to improve their academic effectiveness. They often work in a special college unit called a learning assistance center or similar name. Even elite institutions of higher education such as Harvard and Stanford have learning assistance centers to serve the needs of their students (Walker 1980).

Study skills instruction in learning assistance centers usually emphasizes time management, note taking in lectures, textbook reading, test taking, and library research. Assistance with writing problems is usually relegated to the English Department, where it is a major enterprise. It is remarkable, indeed, that so many students come to college without the study skills needed to write acceptable papers.

A new service, typically called "developmental education," is appearing on many college campuses. Its goal is to help high school graduates who are unable to cope with the academic demands of college by providing a "sheltered workshop" environment in which these students can acquire necessary study skills and gradually make the transition to regular college work.

Although the main reason for the rapid growth of study skills instruction in higher education is that many students are unprepared for its academic demands, this has always been the case. In the past, it was not uncommon for half the freshman class to drop out after a term or two, usually due to academic failure. Why the current concern about their academic success?

The answer to this question can be found in the demographic shifts in the student population that we noted earlier. Colleges cannot ignore the shrinking pool of high school graduates and the increasing numbers of disadvantaged students that make up the pre-college student pool. Rather than close their doors, most colleges are choosing to lower entrance standards and provide study skills instruction. Unfortunately, many students will receive the benefits of a college education only if colleges agree to provide remedial services; otherwise, they will be among those who drop out of the educational mainstream and perpetuate the cycle of poverty. Until elementary and secondary schools teach all students to use study skills effectively, college-level remedial instruction will undoubtedly thrive.

The Private Sector

Many private companies offer various types of study skills instruction. Most prominent are the companies that teach students specialized study skills, such as how to take tests that are required for admission to college and professional schools—the Scholastic Aptitude Test, the Medical College Admission Test, and the Law School Admission Test. Some of these companies, such as Princeton Review Inc. and the Stanley H. Kaplan Educational Center, are multi-million-dollar national operations. Other companies, such as Evelyn Wood Reading Dynamics, train students in effective reading techniques, especially techniques of "speed reading."

Some companies provide a full program of instruction in study skills. For example, the Sylvan Learning Corporation, the nation's largest private tutoring service, has developed a study skills program that is appropriate for elementary and secondary students.

Another source of private sector activity is the publishing of study skills books for the general public. Many bookstores have a section entitled "Study Aids" that includes such books.

The private sector would not provide these services and materials unless it perceived a need for them. We think that the private sector will become even more active in study skills instruction in the coming years. If so, public school educators are likely to respond by launching their own study skills programs.

How Study Skills Instruction Relates to Other Aspects of Schooling

Defining Study Skills

We define study skills as *the effective use of appropriate techniques for completing a learning task*. In other words, a student who has good study skills can successfully carry out a learning task (e.g., participating in class) by using appropriate techniques (e.g., taking notes that paraphrase what the teacher has said) in an effective manner. A student with poor study skills may carry out the same learning task using inappropriate techniques or using appropriate techniques in an ineffective manner.

The notion of "learning task" is central to our definition of study skills. Simply stated, a learning task is an activity that is designed to help students achieve an instructional objective. The usual learning tasks in school settings are:

1. Managing time, materials, and self
2. Listening and taking notes in class
3. Answering teacher questions and participating in class activities
4. Reading textbooks and other materials
5. Writing papers
6. Preparing for and taking tests.

These learning tasks cut across subject areas and grade levels; therefore, teaching students to perform one of these tasks effectively should help them in most or all of their courses and throughout their academic career.

Test preparation and test taking may not seem at first glance to fit the definition of learning tasks. This is because testing is intended to determine how much learning has been acquired rather than to facilitate the acquisition of new knowledge. But testing, especially the preparation phase, often stimulates students to engage in new learning and to consolidate what they have already learned by reorganizing it for easy retrieval.

We distinguish between "study skills" and "study techniques." A study technique is a particular procedure used to perform a learning task. A study skill is the ability to use that technique appropriately and efficiently. We use the term "study skill" most often in this book in order to emphasize the importance of appropriate, efficient use of study techniques.

We also distinguish between "study skill" and "study strategy." A study skill refers to just one aspect of a study process, whereas a study strategy refers to the total study process. For example, writing a school paper requires the use of many study skills—identifying an appropriate topic, brainstorming ideas, outlining, researching, and so forth. The use of all these skills in an appropriate sequence constitutes a study strategy. Some educators use the term "study method" in the sense that we use "study strategy."

In working with students, we sometimes find it helpful to use the terms "plan" and "steps" instead of "strategy." For example, we tell students that they should learn and follow a "plan" for writing school papers, reading a textbook chapter, or preparing for a test. The "steps" in the plan constitute particular study skills used in a particular sequence.

"Study attitudes" and "study motivation" are often discussed in the literature on studying. Attitudes and motivation refer to students' *desire* to use particular study techniques rather than their skill in using the techniques effectively. For example, students can have poor note-taking skills, but be very conscientious about applying them to the best of their ability. Other students may have good note-taking skills but not apply them because of indifference or laziness.

Study Skills and Independent Learning

Learning tasks usually are assigned by the teacher, but students sometimes set their own learning tasks, as when they choose to do an independent learning project. Although this book primarily concerns learning tasks specified by the teacher and the study skills needed to complete them effectively, the same study skills, used to different degrees, are appropriate for independent learning. For example, test-taking skills are usually not very important in independent learning projects, but self-management skills are critical. Because students must choose both the learning tasks and the study skills needed to complete them, successful independent learning is usually more difficult for students than teacher-directed learning. Independent learning projects done outside the classroom are especially demanding and require a repertoire of study skills for success.

Homework is a modified form of independent learning. Although the teacher has specified the tasks to be completed outside the classroom, students must determine, without the teacher's ready assistance, what study skills to use. Without study skills instruction, however, students use few well-defined study skills and rely primarily on their own natural study abilities, which are likely to be inadequate. We must equip students with the tools that are necessary for successful learning in and out of the classroom. Strong study skills are valuable wherever they are used, but for work done outside the classroom, they are essential.

Study Skills and Learning Strategies

The term "learning strategies" appears increasingly in education journals and books (e.g., Weinstein and Mayer 1986; Thomas and Rohwer 1986; Nisbet and Shucksmith 1986). It is used primarily by cognitive psychologists who study the learning process—how information is attended to, stored in memory, and retrieved from memory. A learning strategy is any technique that facilitates this process, as Weinstein and Mayer (1986) explain:

> [Learning strategies] . . . can be defined as behaviors and thoughts that a learner engages in during learning and that are intended to influence the learner's encoding process. . . . For example, in preparing a learning situation, a learner may use positive self-talk to reduce feelings of anxiety; in learning paired-associates, a learner may form a mental image to help associate the objects represented by the members of each pair; in learning from an expository passage, a learner may generate summaries for each section; in learning about a scientific concept, a learner may take notes about the material. Each of these activities—coaching, imaging, summarizing, and notetaking—are examples of learned strategies (p. 315).

Weinstein and Mayer's definition of learning strategies is similar to what we mean by the term "study skills." We prefer the latter term because it is more commonly used by educators and is better understood by the general public. We wish to emphasize, however, that research done under the label of "learning strategies" is important to study skills instruction. This line of research is discussed extensively throughout the book.

Study Skills and Learning Styles

Students have different learning styles, and their academic performance generally improves if they are allowed to study using their preferred style (Dunn and Dunn 1987). The Dunns have found that:

1. Some students learn better when studying with music, whereas others require silence.

2. Some students learn better if they sit on couches, pillows, or other informal furniture. Other students are unaffected by sitting surfaces, or they do better with formal types of seating.

3. Students differ in the time of day that they experience energy peaks. They learn better if allowed to study at the time of day that their energy is at its peak.

4. Some students learn better in isolation, whereas others learn better when working with peers or adults in teams or pairs.

If teachers wish, they can adjust their study skills instruction so that it is sensitive to students' learning styles, although they may not be able to arrange the classroom environment to accommodate every student. Students, however, can adjust their study environment at home. Teachers should encourage students to experiment with different noise and light levels, furniture, study hours, and other factors to establish their own optimal conditions for home studying.

Teachers also need to keep in mind that some students develop learning styles that are detrimental to their academic performance. We've seen many students who carry their school papers loosely gathered in such organizers as file folders, pee-chees, or Trapper Keepers, even though these devices make it difficult for them to locate needed materials. Many students like to study with the TV or radio on, even when the noise or visual images distract them from their work. Marton (1988) found that some students prefer a "surface" approach to reading in which the emphasis is on verbatim recall. This learning style is less adaptive than the "deep" approach, which emphasizes extracting personal meaning from the text.

Thus, teachers should sensitize students to the advantages and disadvantages of their preferred learning styles, and to learning styles that may be more effective. A useful resource for this purpose is the workbook *No Sweat! How to Use Your Learning Style to Be a Better Student* (Tobias and Guild 1986). It provides exercises that help students discover whether their learning style is global or analytic. Later in the workbook, Tobias and Guild discuss the strengths and weaknesses of each learning style. They also describe techniques of studying that work well for students with a global style and techniques that work well for students with an analytic style.

Teachers also should consider their own needs and preferences when teaching study skills. Most teachers would find it overwhelming to try to teach each student a personal method of studying. To make instruction manageable, most teachers need to teach one note-taking method, for instance, to the entire class. This makes it possible for the teacher to hold students accountable for learning and using note-taking skills. Once students have mastered the study method taught in class, they can adapt it, with the teacher's blessing, to fit their preferred learning style.

Study Skills Instruction and Other School Instruction

Many schools these days are introducing thinking skills instruction into the curriculum and debating whether to develop separate curriculums for study skills and thinking skills or whether the two curriculums can dovetail in some way.

Our view is that study skills instruction and thinking skills instruction have largely different objectives. The purpose of a typical thinking skills program is to develop generic thinking skills such as planning, categorizing, analyzing, and problem solving that apply across subject areas. In contrast, study skills programs develop thinking skills that apply specifically to the performance of learning tasks. For example, an important study skill is to break a large assignment into small tasks to be completed over a period of days or weeks. This study skill involves the thinking skills of planning, analyzing, and problem solving in the context of a specific learning task.

Some students may be able to learn a generic thinking skill and use it to improve their performance in a variety of subjects, including the study process; however, many students would find this difficult. A program of thinking skills instruction can reinforce a program of study skills instruction, but the former cannot substitute for the latter.

Some study skills programs teach more skills or skills other than those presented in this book, for instance, library skills. This may be appropriate, depending on your definition of study skills. We see a need for caution, however, when teaching students how to use a library as part of study skills instruction. The problem is that students can learn a lot about a library—the Dewey classification system, the library's catalog system, types of reference sources—and still not be able to study effectively. That is why we stress *the ability to perform learning tasks* as the primary objective of study skills instruction.

We recommend that a study skills program teach students about the use of the library, but only as an aid to the completion of learning tasks. We would teach students how a library could be helpful in writing a school paper or for learning more about a topic when the assigned textbook's treatment of that topic is unclear or incomplete. Specific skills for using a library also should be taught, but as part of library instruction rather than a standard component of a study skills program.

Our analysis of the relationship between library instruction and study skills instruction extends to other school subjects as well. For example, procedures for solving math word problems, for doing arithmetic computations, for determining the plot and theme of a story, for doing science lab experiments, and so on, are, in a sense, study skills. But they are tied too closely to specific content. Students do not have the opportunity to focus their attention on study skills per se.

We can clarify this point with an example. It is possible to teach students (1) general study skills for taking notes, or (2) specific study skills for taking notes on a particular textbook in a chemistry class. The advantage of the former approach is that it focuses students' attention entirely on note taking—how note taking promotes the learning process, the skills of note taking, and the improvement of the students' note-taking ability. Thus, students have an opportunity to develop a deep understanding of the studying process, a particular type of learning task (i.e., learning from textbooks), and skills for performing that task. The advantage of the latter approach is that students learn how to perform a very specific task (i.e., learning from a particular chemistry textbook); the disadvantage is that this is all they learn.

Students need to know more than how to do a few very specific tasks, however. The ability to quickly learn new information, new technology, new ways of doing almost anything will be one of the most valuable commodities of the future. General study skills can help students learn—no matter what the subject, no matter what the environment. In a world of rapid change, teaching students how to help themselves learn throughout life is the most valuable service our schools can perform.

References

Adler, M. (1982). *The Paideia Proposal: An Educational Manifesto.* New York: Macmillan.

Anderson, T. H., and B. B. Armbruster. (1984). "Studying." In *Handbook of Reading Research,* edited by P.D. Pearson, R. Barr, M. L. Kamil, and P. Mosenthal. New York: Longman.

Armbruster, B. B., and T. H. Anderson. (1981). "Research Synthesis on Study Skills." *Educational Leadership* 39, 2: 154–56.

Baker, C. O., and L. T. Ogle, eds. (1989). *The Condition of Education, 1989. Vol 1. Elementary and Secondary Education.* Washington, D.C.: U.S. Department of Education.

Coleman, J. S., T. Hoffer, and S. Kilgore. (1982). *High School Achievement.* New York: Basic Books.

Dunn, K., and R. Dunn. (1987). "Dispelling Outmoded Beliefs about Student Learning." *Educational Leadership* 44, 6: 55–61.

Durkin, D. (1979). "What Classroom Observations Reveal about Reading Comprehension Instruction." *Reading Research Quarterly* 14: 481–533.

Felt, M. C. (1985). *Improving Our Schools: Thirty-three Studies That Inform Local Action.* Newton, Mass.: Education Development Center.

Hodgkinson, H. L. (1985). "The Changing Face of Tomorrow's Student." *Change* 17: 38–39.

Hodgkinson, H. L. (1983). "College Students in the 1990s: A Demographic Portrait." *Education Digest* 49: 28–31.

Krumboltz, J. D., and W. F. Farquhar. (1957). "The Effect of Three Teaching Methods on Achievement and Motivational Outcomes in a How-to-Study Course." *Psychological Monograph* 71: 443.

Marton, F. (1988). "Describing and Improving Learning." In *Learning Strategies and Learning Styles,* edited by R. R. Schmeck. New York: Plenum.

Nisbet, J., and J. Shucksmith. (1986). *Learning Strategies.* London: Routledge and Kegan Paul.

Rohwer, W. D., Jr. (1973). "Elaboration and Learning in Childhood and Adolescence." In *Advances in Child Development and Behavior,* Vol. 8, edited by H. H. Reese. New York: Academic Press.

Salisbury, R. (1935). "Some Effects of Training in Outlining." *English Journal* 24: 111–116.

Sizer, T. (1984). *Horace's Compromise: The Dilemma of the American High School.* Boston: Houghton Mifflin.

Thomas, J. W., and W. D. Rohwer, Jr. (1986). "Academic Studying: The Role of Learning Strategies." *Educational Psychologist* 21: 19–41.

Tobias, C. U., and P. Guild. (1986). *No Sweat! How to Use Your Learning Style to Be a Better Student.* Seattle, Wash.: The Teaching Advisory (P.O. Box 99131, Seattle, WA 98199).

Walker, C. (1980). *The Learning Assistance Center in a Selective Institution.* San Francisco: Jossey-Bass.

Weinstein, C. F., and R. F. Mayer. (1986). "The Teaching of Learning Strategies." In *Handbook of Research on Teaching.* 3rd edition, edited by M. C. Wittrock. New York: Macmillan.

2
Theory and Research

Theories of Studying

Basic Cognitive Processes

Cognitive psychologists specialize in the study of cognitive processes involved in learning, thinking, and motivation. Their theories (summarized in Gellathy 1986 and Gagn 1985) are being used by researchers and educators to develop more effective methods of study skills instruction. Figure 2.1 presents a simple model of how cognitive psychologists currently conceptualize the learning process. The basic cognitive processes involved in learning are listed sequentially in column 1 of the figure.

Attending to incoming information is the first step in learning something new. Students, like anyone else, are exposed to an enormous amount of incoming stimuli; they cannot possibly attend to all of it. Cognitive psychologists, therefore, stress the importance of selective attention. They recommend teaching students that they can and should use varying degrees of attentiveness, from focused attention for important information to relaxed alertness for less important or already-known information. Of course, students must then be taught how to judge the importance of incoming information.

Cognitive psychologists claim that importance should be judged at least partly by the nature of the criterion task (Thomas and Rohwer 1986; Armbruster and Anderson 1981). Suppose that an instructor typically includes definitions of technical terms on tests. Knowing this, students can pay special attention when they come across a new technical term in class or in doing homework.

Once information has been attended to, it enters memory. Cognitive psychologists theorize that there are two types of memory, possibly corresponding to different brain structures. Information is first stored in *short-term memory*; however, only a small amount can be stored there, and it is quickly forgotten. The classic example of this phenomenon is looking up a telephone number. We read the number, remember it long enough to dial it, and then quickly forget it, immediately making room in short-term memory for the next bit of new information.

Figure 2.1
A Cognitive Learning Model of Studying

Basic Cognitive Processes	Metacognitive Processes	Cognitive-Motivational Processes
Attending to incoming information	Knowing your learning processes	Making causal attributions
Getting information into short-term memory	Selecting appropriate learning strategies	Developing expectations for success
Getting information into long-term memory	Monitoring how learning strategy is working	Recalling positive models
Retrieving information from long-term memory		

Many students believe that if they listen in class or read their textbook with good comprehension, they will learn. Their model of learning is something like osmosis. Unfortunately, most of the incoming information actually goes into and out of short-term memory. Psychologists believe that permanent learning requires transfer of information from short-term memory to *long-term memory*. In fact, effective studying can be viewed as the process of moving information from short-term memory to long-term memory. Much of the recent research by cognitive psychologists has focused on how this process occurs and how it can be enhanced. They have found that students must act upon information in some way in order to store it in long-term memory. The more deeply information is processed, the better it is stored in long-term memory and the more easily it is retrieved (Craik and Lockhart 1972; Mayer 1984).

For example, suppose students were trying to learn the meaning of the word *photosynthesis*. A textbook definition might state that it is "a process by which green plants combine energy from light with water and carbon dioxide to make food." A student could try to understand this definition by analyzing the word photosynthesis. Her train of thinking might be as follows: "The word has two parts—*photo* and *synthesis* . . . Photographs are made by using the light that bounces off objects, so *photo* probably has something to do with light . . . *Synthesis* means to bring together, which makes sense here because plants make food by bringing together several things—light, water, and carbon dioxide . . . so analyzing the word *photosynthesis* will help me remember what it means." This is an example of deep processing. If she merely read the textbook definition or repeated it several times, her cognitive processing would be superficial and, consequently, the information would be less securely stored in long-term memory.

Entwistle (1988) reviewed research on how students differ in their approach to processing information in order to learn it. He and a colleague (Entwistle and Ramsden 1983) found that some college students have a "meaning orientation," as indicated by their positive responses to such questionnaire items as:

- I usually set out to understand thoroughly the meaning of what I am asked to read.
- I try to relate ideas in one subject to those in others, whenever possible.
- When I'm reading an article or research report, I generally examine the evidence carefully to decide whether the conclusion is justified.

Other college students have a "reproducing orientation," as indicated by their positive response to such questionnaire items as:

- I find I have to concentrate on memorizing a good deal of what we have to learn.
- I generally prefer to tackle each part of a topic or problem in order, working out one at a time.
- Although I generally remember facts and details, I find it difficult to fit them together into an overall picture.

The reproducing and meaning orientations correspond to the cognitive-psychological concepts of superficial and deep processing, respectively.

Entwistle and Kozeki (1985) investigated whether the two orientations are associated with academic achievement. In a sample of British and Hungarian high school students, they found that a meaning orientation was associated with higher academic achievement, and a reproducing orientation with lower academic achievement.

This analysis of short-term memory and long-term memory helps to explain why certain types of study skills are important to academic success. Because new information is usually presented quickly in the classroom, students need to transfer information into a format that allows them to return to it later. Note-taking skills are useful for this purpose. To move information into long-term memory, deep-processing skills, such as relating new knowledge to prior knowledge (Wittrock 1981) and generating and answering questions about text (Palincsar and Brown 1984) are important.

The fact that information has been stored in long-term memory does not mean that it is readily accessible, however. Learners must organize information and occasionally rehearse it so that it can be retrieved when desired. Retrieving information from long-term memory is the last basic process of learning.

Information retrieval is affected by the principle of encoding specificity, which states that the way in which information is stored in long-term memory affects the retrieval cues that students can use to recall it (Tulving and Thomson 1973). For example, suppose a student is learning Spanish vocabulary. For each Spanish word, he memorizes the English equivalent (e.g., casa = house). His processing strategy for getting this type of information into long-term memory is to rehearse by looking at each Spanish word and trying to recall the English equivalent until he can do so quickly and without error. On a test, he should be able to do well in stating the correct *English* equivalent for each Spanish word on the test.

Suppose, however, that the test assesses the student's ability to recall the *Spanish* equivalent for each English term, or to spell the Spanish word correctly when the teacher says it aloud. The student may do poorly on this test because he did not memorize (i.e., encode) the information this way. In other words, information processing (encoding) tends only to facilitate a specific kind of retrieval. For this reason, it is helpful for students to know how they eventually will need to remember and use the information. They can help themselves remember what they have studied by using encoding techniques appropriate to the anticipated use of the information.

The preceding example demonstrates that a particular strategy for processing new information is not necessarily effective or ineffective. Its effectiveness depends on the student's goals or the criterion tasks that will be used to evaluate his learning. This dependency has been termed "transfer-appropriate processing" by Morris, Bransford, and Franks (1977). Transfer-appropriate processing implies, for example, that deep processing may be effective in some situations and ineffective in others. Similarly, shallow processing may be effective under certain circumstances. Therefore, in teaching study skills, teachers must teach not only the skills, but the learning tasks for which they are appropriate.

Other theorists have developed different versions of the cognitive model of learning described above. For example, Weinstein and Mayer (1986) divide the learning process into four components:

• *Selection*. The learner actively pays attention to some of the information that is impinging on the sense receptors, and transfers this information into working memory (or "active consciousness").

• *Acquisition*. The learner actively transfers the information from working memory into long-term memory for permanent storage.

• *Construction*. The learner actively builds connections between ideas in the information that have reached working memory. This building of internal connections . . . involves the development of a coherent outline organization or schema . . . that holds the information together.

• *Integration*. The learner actively searches for prior knowledge in long-term memory and transfers this knowledge to working memory. The learner may then build external connections . . . between the incoming information and prior knowledge (p. 317).

Selection is similar to the attending and short-term memory steps of the model in Figure 2.1, while acquisition is similar to the long-term memory step. Construction and integration also parallel the long-term memory step, but emphasize specific kinds of deep-processing activities that help information become stored in long-term memory. The main difference between these two models is that the first emphasizes retrieval as a separate step in the learning process. This step reminds us that information, even if stored in long-term memory, can become inaccessible unless it is well organized and reviewed continually.

Thomas and Rohwer's (1986) cognitive model of learning has five elements similar to those in Weinstein and Mayer's model and the model in Figure 2.1:

• *Selection*. Differentiating among and within sources of information according to importance and criterion relevance; identifying and eliciting cues regarding criterion-relevant information.

• *Comprehension*. Enhancing understanding; alleviating failures of understanding.

• *Memory*. Enhancing storage; enhancing retrieval.

• *Integration*. Constructing relationships among items to be learned; constructing relationships between items to be learned and other information.

• *Cognitive monitoring.* Assessing the need for cognitive transformational activities; assessing the adequacy of cognitive transformational activities (p. 24).

Rohwer and Thomas's model includes additional elements that we categorize below as metacognitive processes.

Metacognitive Processes

Cognitive psychologists theorize that additional cognitive processes, beyond those listed in column 1 of Figure 2.1, are involved in learning. Flavell (1976) labels these processes "metacognition," which Jones (1986) defines as "thinking about what one knows and how to control one's learning process" (p. 9). Baker and Brown (1984) identify several metacognitive abilities involved in reading that are consistent with Jones' definition: (1) knowledge about one's own study skills and habits, (2) ability to monitor the success of one's study behavior, and (3) inclination to use compensatory strategies when studying is not successful.

Drawing on these different views of metacognition, we list three metacognitive processes in column 2 of Figure 2.1. First is knowledge of one's learning processes, which might take the form of such self-statements as "I have trouble paying attention in this class" or "I had better start reviewing at least three days before this test if I want to do well." This type of personal knowledge is probably fostered by teaching students a model of the learning process (e.g., the model in column 1 of Figure 2.1). A model gives students a basis for understanding their personal learning process and its strengths and weaknesses.

The second important metacognitive process is selecting an appropriate learning strategy for a particular study task. (Keep in mind that a learning strategy is similar to a study skill.) For example, if students decide that something the teacher has said is important, they should hold the information briefly in short-term memory while they choose a learning strategy for committing it to long-term memory. In this instance, they may choose to make a written note of the information and decide that a paraphrase rather than a verbatim recording of what the teacher said is sufficient.

The third metacognitive process is monitoring the use of a learning strategy to determine how well it is working. This judgment requires the use of criteria of effectiveness. Using "immediate comprehension" as one criterion, students might ask themselves, "Do I understand what I'm hearing or reading?" For the criterion of long-term retention, students might ask a question like "Will what I'm doing help me remember what I'm hearing or reading so that I can review it for a test or use it in a term paper?" Students' answers to such questions determine whether they should continue using a particular learning strategy or switch to an alternative strategy.

Students who have a limited repertoire of learning strategies may continue to use an ineffective strategy simply because they do not know an alternative strategy. This is why it is so important to teach students multiple learning strategies.

Cognitive psychologists have studied whether students' learning improves when they are taught these metacognitive processes. Meichenbaum and Asarnow (1979) found that instruction in metacognitive skills does improve student learning, although students sometimes have difficulty generalizing the use of skills across learning tasks. Instruction typically involves training students to make certain kinds of covert statements (i.e., metacognitions) to guide their learning: self-interrogations (e.g., "What is it I have to do?"); self-reinforcements (e.g., "Good, I'm doing fine"); and coping remarks (e.g., "I made an error, but if I take my time, I can correct it").

Motivational Processes

The motivational processes involved in studying are just as important as the cognitive processes, if not more so. A survey of Arizona educators (Rickman 1981) found support for this view:

> Many respondents would like to acquire more skills to enhance their teaching of study skills, . . . particularly motivational skills. A respondent asked for "more motivational skills to excite students about particular subjects, school, and life." Another said, "It seems to me that [study] skills are secondary to motivation. I find very few students coming to high school who are interested in doing anything. It takes ages to get most to even read a book" (p. 364).

If teachers can find a way to increase students' motivation, students will put more effort into studying, which in turn is likely to lead to higher academic achievement. It is important, therefore, to identify the factors that motivate students to put effort into studying.

Behavioral psychologists emphasize the importance of external factors as motivators of behavior. In their view, students' desire to study is determined primarily by the external rewards and punishments that follow studying. If students receive rewards for studying, they are likely to put more effort into it.

In contrast, cognitive psychologists emphasize the importance of internal factors—cognitions—as motivators of behavior. One of their theories, called attribution theory (Weiner 1980), relates students' motivation and academic performance to two types of cognition: causal attributions and expectations for success. These cognitions, and one other, are listed in column 3 of Figure 2.1.

Causal attributions are the reasons students give for success and failure, and they generally fall into four categories: ability, luck, effort, and difficulty of the task. Cognitive psychologists have found that these attributions for success and failure affect students' emotions, persistence at learning tasks, and expectations for success. Effort and ability appear to be the most critical attributions: Students who attribute success and failure to *effort* are more likely to experience positive emotions, greater task persistence, and higher success expectations, while students who attribute success or failure to *ability* are less likely to have these experiences.

Social learning theorists have identified another type of cognition that affects study motivation. They hypothesize that we learn by observing other people's actions and their consequences (Bandura 1977). Subsequent recall of these actions and consequences (a cognition) can motivate our own behavior. For instance, suppose that students observe someone struggle with a math problem and eventually solve it. In a similar situation later, students may persist in the task because they remember the success they saw earlier. Their motivation is strongly affected by the study behaviors they observed.

Attribution theory and social learning theory remind us that teaching learning strategies is not enough to help students become more effective learners. Changing students' cognitions—teaching them to attribute academic success and failure to effort, rather than ability, for instance—is just as important. Educators need to show students examples of effective study behaviors and their positive results so that students will be motivated to emulate these behaviors.

In addition, educators should try to keep abreast of psychologists' discoveries about the cognitive processes involved in learning and studying. New knowledge about basic learning processes can be used to enhance current models of study skills instruction or to develop even more effective methods of instruction.

Models for Study Skills Instruction

The Teacher-as-Mediator Model

One of the most basic models for instruction is the teacher-as-mediator model, shown in Figure 2.2. Although it is only a partial model, it highlights a critical element of successful learning: the relationship between teacher and student. In the diagram, the arrow from teacher to curriculum indicates that teachers *mediate* the curriculum; they determine what is important for students to learn and how learning is demonstrated on tests, homework assignments, and class projects. Teachers also specify the criteria for grading student performance.

The arrow from student to curriculum indicates that students attend school to *master* the curriculum. Students have a second task, however, as indicated by the arrow from student to teacher: students must figure out what the teacher wants them to learn about the curriculum and what the teacher's criteria are for assigning grades. In other words, students must study the teacher as well as the curriculum. By learning the teacher's priorities and expectations, students can study effectively and efficiently.

We are not arguing that students should study only those parts of the curriculum that the teacher considers important; students should also study the curriculum for intrinsic reasons. It would be misleading, however, to encourage students to approach the curriculum any way they wish. Schools are formal organizations guided by persons in positions of authority—teachers, curriculum directors, and administrators—who create a curriculum and set expectations. To succeed in school, students must learn the "rules of the game." We recommend that teachers use the model in Figure 2.2 to introduce students to study skills instruction.

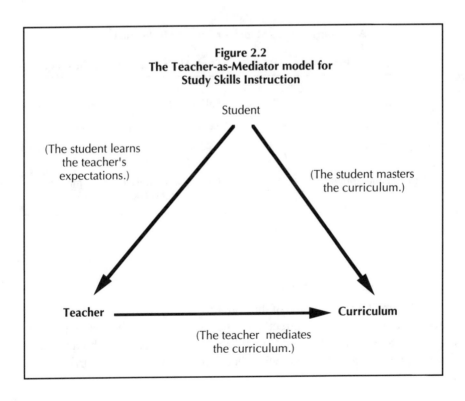

Figure 2.2
The Teacher-as-Mediator model for
Study Skills Instruction

Student

(The student learns the teacher's expectations.)

(The student masters the curriculum.)

Teacher

Curriculum

(The teacher mediates the curriculum.)

A Cognitive-Psychological Model

The model shown in Figure 2.3 highlights the *learning process* as conceptualized by cognitive psychologists in recent years. It represents the sequence of the four major processes involved in learning new information: (1) attending to information; (2) storing information initially in short-term memory; (3) transferring information permanently to long-term memory; and (4) retrieving information for various applications, such as taking a test, writing a paper, or creating an artistic product.

The cognitive-psychological model suggests that the goal of study skills instruction is to teach students the skills needed to effectively execute each of the four learning processes. Examples of study skills that researchers (e.g., Weinstein and Mayer 1986) have identified and validated as facilitators of various steps in the learning process are shown in column 2 of Figure 2.3. Educators can draw on such research to develop a study skills curriculum. Although this model is valuable because it can focus attention on the process of learning, it is still removed from the everyday world of school and studying.

Figure 2.3
A Learning Process Model for Study Skills Instruction

Major Learning Processes	Study Skills that Facilitate the Process
Attending	Self-Monitoring, time management
Short-term memory	Repeated rehearsal of the information
Long-term memory	Taking notes, generating questions, making visual presentations
Retrieval and application	Organization into schemas, mnemonics, production and feedback

A Learning Task Model

Figure 2.4 is our model of the domain of study skills instruction, which we developed to relate directly to the tasks that teachers and students perform every day (Gall and Gall 1988). The teachers with whom we have worked often use this model when building their study skills curriculum.

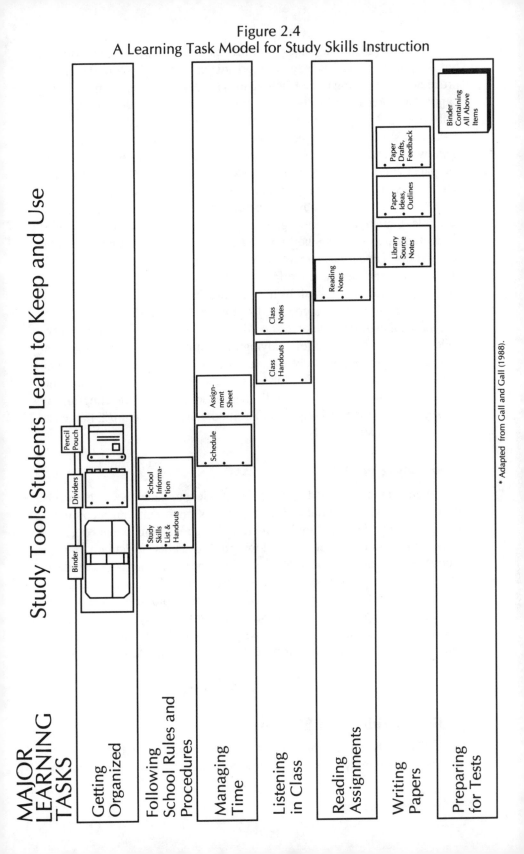

Figure 2.4
A Learning Task Model for Study Skills Instruction

Study Tools Students Learn to Keep and Use

MAJOR
LEARNING
TASKS

Getting Organized

Binder — Dividers — Pencil Pouch

Following School Rules and Procedures

Study Skills List & Handouts — School Information

Managing Time

Schedule — Assignment Sheet

Listening in Class

Class Handouts — Class Notes

Reading Assignments

Reading Notes

Writing Papers

Library Source Notes — Paper Ideas, Outlines — Paper Drafts, Feedback

Preparing for Tests

Binder Containing All Above Items

* Adapted from Gall and Gall (1988).

The model lists the major *learning tasks* that confront students at all but the lowest grade levels: getting organized, following school rules and procedures, managing time, listening in class, reading assignments, writing papers, and preparing for tests. The *study tools* in the model are the study skills essential for performing each of the learning tasks effectively. These tasks and skills are arranged around the theme of organizing and using paperwork. Of course, there is more to studying and academic success than the paper and binder icons in this model, but the icons *do* represent basic study skills that need to be taught in a study skills curriculum.

This model also has obvious instructional implications. It suggests, for example, that study skills for getting organized should be taught early. If students are unorganized, they will find it difficult to learn and practice other study skills. Time management skills are important for a similar reason: if students manage their time ineffectively, they will have insufficient time to practice and use the study skills they are taught.

The last four tasks in column 1 of Figure 2.4 do not have to be taught in a particular order. Students should be shown, however, that the tasks follow a logical sequence for studying new information: (1) hearing about it in class, (2) reading about it in a textbook, (3) applying it in written homework, and (4) preparing for a test to measure mastery of it. Students should be taught a set of study skills that carries them in a meaningful way through this instructional sequence. The model shown in Figure 2.4 suggests one such set of study skills.

Choosing a Model

None of the three models above is sufficient to guide the development of a study skills curriculum. Each represents important, but incomplete, insights about effective studying; therefore, we recommend that educators draw from all three models in developing a study skills curriculum for their students. The teacher-as-mediator model can be used to introduce students to their role in the classroom; the learning task model to teach students the nuts and bolts of studying; and the cognitive-psychological model to help students develop a deeper understanding of the study process and of themselves as learners. The study skills and teaching methods discussed later in this book are derived from research on these models.

Study Skills Research

Indirect Evidence of Effectiveness

The likely benefits of study skills instruction can be determined by comparing the study skills of high-performing and low-performing students. If the groups differ in their use of particular study skills, we can conclude that the use of these skills is at least partially responsible for the success of high-performing students and the lack of success of low-performing students. We can also assume that training students, especially low-performing students, in these skills *probably* will improve their academic success. There is a possibility, however, that these cause-and-effect inferences are spurious because the research design was nonexperimental.

Using nonexperimental designs is common in other professions, especially medicine. A classic example is the finding that lung cancer patients are more likely to be cigarette smokers than nonsmokers. Because the finding resulted from a nonexperimental research design, it does not prove that cigarette smoking causes lung cancer or that not smoking will decrease the risk of lung cancer. It only provides indirect evidence of cause-and-effect relationships.

In the research literature on study skills, there is much indirect evidence of a link between study skills and school achievement. For example, Zimmerman and Pons (1986) studied two groups of high school sophomores. One group of 40 students was in an advanced achievement track because of their high entrance test scores, GPA prior to high school, and teachers' and counselors' recommendations. The other group of 40 students was in the lower achievement tracks because of low performance on the same criteria.

Zimmerman and Pons interviewed students individually to determine how often they used "self-regulated learning strategies" (i.e., study skills) in six different school contexts: (1) in classroom situations, (2) at home, (3) when completing writing assignments outside class, (4) when completing math assignments outside class, (5) when preparing for and taking tests, and (6) when poorly motivated. They analyzed students' responses to determine which of 14 different self-regulated learning strategies they used in each context. The 14 strategies and their definitions are listed in Figure 2.5. Also shown is a measure of the average use of each strategy by high- and low-achieving students. This measure is the number of contexts (0 to 6) in which students said that they used a particular strategy multiplied by students' estimate of how often they use that strategy. Estimates could range from "seldom" (1) to "most of the time" (4).

The results shown in Figure 2.5 demonstrate that high-achieving students made substantially greater use of each of the self-regulated learning strategies than did the low-achieving students. Zimmerman and Pons further analyzed the interview data and discovered that low-achieving students were more likely than high-achieving students to make use of a "willpower strategy," which consists of "simple statements of resolve such as 'If I'm having difficulty motivating myself to complete my homework, I just work

Figure 2.5

Use of Self-Regulated Learning Strategies by High- and Low-Achieving High School Students

Type of Learning Strategy	High-Achieving Students	Low-Achieving Students
1. Self-Evaluation. Student-initiated evaluations of the quality or progress of their work. (e.g., "I check over my work to make sure I did it right.")	.97	.78
2. Organizing and Transforming. Student-initiated overt or covert rearrangement of instructional materials to improve learning. (e.g., "I make an outline before I write my paper.")	3.86	1.18
3. Goal Setting and Planning. Student setting of educational goals or subgoals and planning for sequencing, time, and completing activities related to those goals. (e.g., "First, I start studying two weeks before exams, and I pace myself.")	3.03	1.55
4. Seeking Information. Student-initiated efforts to secure further task information from nonsocial sources when undertaking an assignment. (e.g., "Before beginning to write the paper, I go to the library to get as much information as possible about the topic.")	4.40	1.41
5. Keeping Records and Monitoring. Student-initiated efforts to record events or results. (e.g., "I took notes of the class discussion.")	3.98	1.65
6. Environmental Structuring. Student-initiated efforts to select or arrange the physical setting to make learning easier. (e.g., "I isolate myself from anything that distracts me.")	1.90	.97
7. Self-Consequences. Student arrangement or imagination of rewards or punishment for success or failure. (e.g., "If I do well on a test, I treat myself to a movie.")	1.70	.30
8. Rehearsing and Memorizing. Student-initiated efforts to memorize material by overt or covert practice. (e.g., "In preparing for a math test, I keep writing the formula until I memorize it.")	2.27	.98

(continued)

9. Asking Peers for Help. (e.g., "If I have problems with math assignments, I ask a friend for help.")	1.75	.57
10. Asking Teachers for Help. (e.g., "If I don't understand how to complete an assignment, I ask the teacher for more information.")	2.25	.67
11. Asking Adults for Help. (e.g., "When I write speeches for class, I ask my parents to be my audience so I can practice.")	1.10	.17
12. Reviewing Tests. (e.g., "After I've answered all the questions on a test, I go over them to make sure that I've done my best.")	1.05	.40
13. Reviewing Textbooks. (e.g., "When I read, I highlight important information and then go through the chapter again and reread that information.")	4.65	2.48
14. Systematically Reviewing All Materials to Prepare for Special Projects or Tests. (e.g., "When I study for final exams, I review my textbook, handouts, and notes.")	2.85	1.05
15. Other. Learning behavior that is initiated by other persons, such as teachers or parents, and all unclear verbal responses. (e.g., "I just do what the teacher says.")	1.17	2.21

Note: All differences between the high-achieving and low-achieving groups are statistically significant, except for learning strategy 1 (self-evaluation).

Source: Adapted from Zimmerman and Pons 1986.

harder' " (Zimmerman and Pons 1986, p. 623). These findings suggest that the systematic use of particular study skills, rather than willpower, is responsible for the success of high-achieving students.

Much of the research on study skills has been done using the Survey of Study Habits and Attitudes, commonly called the SSHA (Brown and Holtzman 1967). This self-report instrument contains four scales that measure how students function in four areas of study behavior:

• The Delay Avoidance Scale (DA) measures the extent to which students avoid delay and distraction.

- The Work Methods Scale (WM) measures how effectively students organize their study behavior.
- The Teacher Approval Scale (TA) measures students' attitude toward their teacher.
- The Education Acceptance Scale (EA) measures students' agreement with the expressed goals of education.

The DA and WM scales assess study habits, whereas the TA and EM scales assess study-related attitudes.

Researchers have found that SSHA scores correlate positively with grades in both high school and college, with the correlation coefficients generally ranging between .36 and .49 (Shay 1972). These statistical results mean that students with better study skills and attitudes, as measured by the SSHA, tend to have better school grades than students with poorer study skills and attitudes. Because these are correlational results, they do not prove that study skills and attitudes *cause* students to have better school grades; the results only suggest this.

SSHA scores also consistently correlate with school grades independent of students' academic aptitude (Shay 1972). In other words, if two students have the same academic aptitude, the student with better study skills and attitudes—as measured by the SSHA—is likely to have better grades. This finding suggests that academic success is not just a function of ability; study skills and attitudes also contribute.

Measures similar to the SSHA have been developed and tested to determine whether they differentiate between students with high GPAs and students with low GPAs (e.g., Gibson 1983; Houston 1987). Research findings using these measures are generally consistent with those of studies using the SSHA. In addition, other researchers have investigated study behaviors and attitudes that are more specific than those measured by the SSHA and similar instruments. Their research is reviewed later in the book, when we discuss specific study skills, but the evidence from these varied lines of research does show that high-performing and low-performing students differ significantly in their approach to studying.

Direct Evidence of Effectiveness—College Students

Researchers have done many experiments to determine whether study skills instruction has a positive effect on students' academic performance. Because study skills instruction has been primarily a college phenomenon until recently, most experiments have involved study skills instruction for college students. Research findings provide clues, however, to whether study skills instruction will work at lower grade levels and whether some forms of study skills instruction are more effective than others. Much of the college-level research involves two types of students: freshmen, who are usually similar in many respects to students still in high school, and students at risk of failing their courses, who are similar to the population of low-performing, at-risk students in elementary and high school for whom study skills programs recently have become a high priority.

Thirty years ago, Entwistle (1960) reviewed 19 investigations of the effectiveness of study skills instruction, some dating back to the 1930s. She concluded that "some kind of improvement following a study-skills course seems to be the rule, although the improvement varies from a very slight amount . . . to a considerable amount" (p. 248).

Bednar and Weinberg (1970) reviewed 23 studies that evaluated the effectiveness of different programs for low-ability and underachieving college students. The programs investigated were quite varied. Some involved academic or personal counseling, others involved study skills instruction, and still others involved a combination of both methods. Not all approaches were found to be equally effective, but the majority of the programs had positive effects on students' GPA. The effects were statistically significant in 13 of the studies, and in another 6 studies the effects were positive but not statistically significant. Of the studies reporting positive effects, nine followed students' academic performance for three months to a year after the treatment. Only three of these studies reported positive effects. In other words, the programs generally were effective in improving students' GPA, but the improvement tended to be short-lived.

More recently, Kirschenbaum and Perri (1982) reviewed 33 studies of programs designed to improve college students' academic competence. The studies were published between 1974 and 1978, and the programs evaluated in the studies included four main types of intervention: behavioral (i.e., behavior modification or behavior therapy); general counseling to enhance students' personal adjustment; training in self-control techniques (e.g., planning, self-monitoring, self-reward/punishment); and study skills instruction. The programs that involved just one of these types of intervention were called "single-component programs"; those that involved two or three of the interventions were called "multi-component programs."

The studies investigated the effectiveness of the various programs in improving students' performance on four outcomes: GPA, grades in specific courses, anxiety, and study attitudes. Not all studies investigated all criteria. The procedure for determining the effectiveness of a program in improving students' performance on a particular outcome was to compare the performance of a group of students who participated in the program with that of a control group that did not participate in it.

One of Kirschenbaum and Perri's major findings was that multi-component interventions generally were superior to single-component interventions. This was true regardless of the outcome investigated and whether the studies examined short-term or long-term program effects. Multi-component interventions that included study skills instruction and either behavioral or self-control training were particularly effective.

After reviewing all 33 studies, Kirschenbaum and Perri did a special review of a subset of the studies that employed rigorous research methodology. They concluded that "the results of more than a dozen well-controlled investigations justify genuine optimism, especially with regard to the effectiveness of structured multicomponent interventions focused on improving study and self-regulatory skills" (Kirschenbaum and Perri 1983, p. 90).

Bednar and Weinberg (1970) reached the same conclusion about the greater effectiveness of multi-component programs:

> When the treatment consists of some form of counseling, the higher the therapeutic conditions (empathy, warmth, genuineness), the more effective the treatment. . . . However, counseling, either individual or group, aimed at the dynamics of underachievement and used in conjunction with an academic studies course seems the most potent of all treatment options (p. 6).

The similarity of conclusions is all the more remarkable in that Bednar and Weinberg reviewed only pre-1970 studies, with several dating back to the 1920s, and Kirschenbaum and Perri reviewed a different set of studies dating back only to 1974.

Why are multi-component programs more effective? Rothkopf (1988) writes that

> study skills training is like information about birth control. General educational programs produce results, but a substantial number of unwanted conceptions persist that are not due to deficiencies of method, or lack of knowledge or skill, but, simply, from failure of use. . . . We are concerned not only with whether students know how to study effectively but also whether they are willing or disposed to do so (p. 276).

The implication of the research findings and Rothkopf's comment is that the effectiveness of a study skills program depends on learner characteristics. If students are motivated, instruction can focus on teaching study skills for performing the learning tasks described earlier in the chapter—participating in class, reading textbook assignments, and so on. If students are unmotivated, however, instruction also must include a substantial component directed at students' personal needs and their motivation to attend school and to study.

The factor of study motivation may explain a conclusion that Entwistle (1960) reached in her research review:

Improvement is likely following many kinds of study-skills courses. The amount of improvement does seem related to whether the course is voluntary or required. . . . All the voluntary college-level courses report gains that are rather impressive, and in every case where follow-up results are available, the gains persist (p. 250).

Voluntary study skills courses probably attract a greater percentage of motivated students than do required courses. If so, voluntary courses that focus on the technical skills of studying would be sufficient to help students improve their academic performance. Required courses might cover the same technical skills, but be less effective because the unmotivated students in them would not apply the skills to improve their academic performance.

The factor of study motivation also would explain the impressive results of a brief study skills program that was evaluated by Prather (1983). The sample consisted of 24 cadets at the U.S. Air Force Academy who had the lowest GPAs (below 2.0) at the midpoint of their third semester on campus. Half of the cadets were randomly assigned to receive a study skills program and "directive counseling" from their class committee, squadron officer, and the Cadet Counseling Center. The other half of the cadets received only directive counseling.

The study skills program was remarkably short. Students received a 30-minute briefing that contained information about 12 different study techniques covering a wide range of learning tasks. Afterwards, students returned to the instructor every two weeks for a 10- to 15-minute session to review their implementation of the techniques. The typical student experienced four such sessions.

Prather found that the cadets who participated in the study skills program gained .54 points in their third-semester GPA from midterm to end-of-term, while the control group made virtually no gain (.02). These results raise the question of how so brief a study skills program could be so effective. The answer may well be that this population of students, USAF cadets, is very motivated to study, and when students are motivated, training in techniques to perform learning tasks effectively is likely to be sufficient to improve students' academic performance.

Direct Evidence of Effectiveness—High School Students

The review of research on study skills courses by Entwistle (1960) included three studies at the high school level. Positive effects on grades or achievement test scores were found in each study. In two of the studies, researchers found that students of intermediate ability profited the most from study skills instruction. These students are both motivated and in need of better study skills, whereas low-ability students often lack the motivation to learn and apply study skills, and high-ability students are able to meet the challenge of learning tasks without refining their study skills.

More recently, Wilson (1988) described the Learning Strategies/Study Skills Program, which he and others developed and implemented in a school district over a ten-year period. The program (described further in Chapter 3) is a required ninth grade course at each of the district's three high schools. Evaluations of the program yielded dramatic evidence of its effectiveness:

> A measurement of success of the program was demonstrated in the significant gains made on a nationally normed achievement test by the students participating in the program compared to those who did not participate. Local surveys were used to gather data from teachers, parents, and students. These results also showed strong support for the program. The SRA Achievement Test composite percentiles and growth scale values provided the most obvious measure of students' improved academic performance. Significant gains on these test scores were observed. The trend of declining test scores that existed for several years prior to the implementation of the learning strategies/study skills program was dramatically reversed for all levels of students (Wilson 1988, pp. 325–326).

More such evaluations of K–12 study skills programs are needed to determine whether Wilson's findings are generalizable.

Additional evidence of the effectiveness of study skills instruction comes from research involving the Learning Strategies Curriculum, a study skills program for mildly handicapped high school students that was developed by the University of Kansas Institute for Research in Learning Disabilities (further described in Chapter 3). Deshler and Schumaker (1986) do not report effects of the program on students' grades, but they do report effects on other aspects of academic performance:

> In all of the studies to date, once training in a strategy has been implemented, the students showed marked gains. For example, once students learned the Paraphrasing Strategy, their reading comprehension went from 48% to 84% on passages written at their current grade level. Mastery of the Error Monitoring Strategy reduced the number of errors that they made in written materials from 1 in every 4 words to 1 in every 33 words. Similar results have been found with each of the other strategies (p. 588).

Regardless of whether these outcomes lead to higher course grades, the Learning Strategies Curriculum shows that study skills instruction markedly affects student learning.

Summary of Research Findings

The evidence from the above research suggests that study skills instruction significantly improves the academic performance of high school and college students *under certain conditions*. The most important of these conditions involves students' motivation. If students are unmotivated, teaching them the technical skills of studying is unlikely to improve their academic performance. The content and method of study skills instruction also can enhance or weaken a program's effectiveness. A program can fail if the teacher uses poor teaching methods, covers inappropriate study skills, or rushes students through the program.

Through research and experimentation, study skills experts have developed a repertoire of strategies for teaching study skills. It's important for teachers to take advantage of their work and go into the classroom with a thorough understanding of what makes a study skills program successful. In this book, we specify conditions that support an effective study skills program, all of which involve basing the program content on research-validated study skills and using proven methods for teaching them to students.

References

Armbruster, B. B., and T. H. Anderson. (1981). "Research Synthesis on Study Skills." *Educational Leadership* 39, 2: 154–156.

Baker, L., and A. Brown. (1984). "Metacognitive Skills and Reading." In *Handbook of Reading Research*, edited by P. D. Pearson, R. Barr, M. L. Kamil, and P. Morenthal. New York: Longman.

Bandura, A. (1977). *Social Learning Theory*. Englewood Cliffs, N.J.: Prentice-Hall.

Bednar, R. L., and S. L. Weinberg. (1970). "Ingredients of Successful Treatment Programs for Underachievers." *Journal of Counseling Psychology* 17: 1–7.

Brown, W. F., and W. H. Holtzman. (1967). Forms C and H in *Survey of Study Habits and Attitudes*. New York: The Psychological Corporation.

Craik, F. I. M., and R. S. Lockhart. (1972). "Levels of Processing: Framework for Memory Research." *Journal of Verbal Learning and Verbal Behavior* 11: 671–684.

Deshler, D. D., and J. B. Schumaker. (1986). "Learning Strategies: An Instructional Alternative for Low-Achieving Adolescents." *Exceptional Children* 52: 583–590.

Entwistle, D. R. (1960). "Evaluations of Study-skills Courses: A Review." *Journal of Educational Research* 53: 243–251.

Entwistle, N. J. (1988). "Motivational Factors in Approaches to Learning." In *Learning Strategies and Learning Styles*, edited by R. R. Schmeck. New York: Plenum.

Entwistle, N. J., and B. Kozeki. (1985). "Relationships Between Student Motivation, Approaches to Studying, and Attainment Among British and Hungarian Adolescents." *British Journal of Educational Psychology* 55: 124–137.

Entwistle, N. J., and P. Ramsden. (1983). *Understanding Student Learning*. London: Croom Helm.

Flavell, J. H. (1976). "Metacognitive Aspects of Problem Solving." In *The Nature of Intelligence*, edited by L. B. Resnick. Hillsdale, N.J.: Erlbaum.

Gagn, E. D. (1985). *The Cognitive Psychology of School Learning*. Boston: Little, Brown.

Gall, M. D., and J. P. Gall. (1988). *Study for Success Teachers Manual*. 3rd ed. Eugene, Oreg.: M. Damien Publishers.

Gellathy, A., ed. (1986). *The Skillful Mind: An Introduction to Cognitive Psychology.* Philadelphia: Open University Press.

Gibson, E. E. (1983). "The Study Behavior of Community College Students." Doctoral diss., Northern Illinois University, 1983. *Dissertation Abstracts International* 44, 4: 956-A.

Houston, L. N. (1987). "The Predictive Validity of a Study Habits Inventory for First Semester Undergraduates." *Educational and Psychological Measurement* 47: 1025–1030.

Jones, B. F. (1986). "Quality and Equality Through Cognitive Instruction." *Educational Leadership* 43, 7: 4–11.

Kirschenbaum, D. S., and M. G. Perri. (1982) "Improving Academic Competence in Adults: "A Review of Recent Research." *Journal of Counseling Psychology* 29: 76–94.

Mayer, R. E. (1984). "Aids to Text Comprehension." *Educational Psychologist* 19: 30–42.

Meichenbaum, D., and J. Asarnow. (1979). "Cognitive-Behavior Modification and Metacognitive Development: Implications for the Classroom." In *Cognitive-Behavioral Intervention: Theory, Research, and Procedures,* edited by P. C. Kendall and S. D. Hollon. New York: Academic Press.

Morris, C. D., J. D. Bransford, and J. J. Franks. (1977). "Levels of Processing Versus Transfer Appropriate Processing." *Journal of Verbal Learning and Verbal Behavior* 16: 519–533.

Palincsar, A. S., and A. L. Brown. (1984) "Reciprocal Teaching of Comprehension-fostering and Comprehension- monitoring Activities." *Cognition and Instruction* 1: 117–175.

Prather, D. C. (1983). "A Behaviorally Oriented Study Skills Program." *Journal of Experimental Education* 51: 131–133.

Rickman, L. W. (1981). "Arizona Educators Assess the Teaching of Study Skills." *Clearing House* 3: 363–365.

Rothkopf, E. Z. (1988). "Perspectives on Study Skills Training in a Realistic Instructional Economy." In *Learning and Study Strategies,* edited by C. E. Weinstein, E. T. Goetz, and P. A. Alexander. San Diego: Academic Press.

Shay, C. B. (1972). "Review of the *Survey of Study Habits and Attitudes.*" In *Seventh Mental Measurements Yearbook,* edited by O. K Buros. Highland Park, N.J.: Gryphon Press.

Thomas, J. W., and W. D. Rohwer, Jr. (1986). "Academic Studying: The Role of Learning Strategies." *Educational Psychologist* 21: 19–41.

Tulving, E., and D. M. Thomson. (1973). "Encoding Specificity and Retrieval Processes in Episodic Memory." *Psychological Review* 80: 352–373.

Weiner, B. (1980). *Human Motivation.* New York: Holt, Rinehart and Winston.

Weinstein, C. F., and R. F. Mayer. (1986). "The Teaching of Learning Strategies." In *Handbook of Research on Teaching.* 3rd ed., edited by M. C. Wittrock. New York: Macmillan.

Wilson, J. E. (1988). "Implications of Learning Strategy Research and Training: What It Has to Say to the Practitioner." In *Learning and Study Strategies,* edited by C. E. Weinstein, E. T. Goetz, and P. A. Alexander. San Diego: Academic Press.

Wittrock, M. C. (1981). "Reading Comprehension." In *Neuropsychological and Cognitive Processes in Reading,* edited by F. J. Pirozzolo and M. C. Wittrock. New York: Academic Press.

Zimmerman, B. J., and M. M. Pons. (1986). "Development of a Structured Interview for Assessing Student Use of Self-Regulated Learning Strategies." *American Educational Research Journal* 23: 614–628

3
Planning for Study Skills Instruction

In most school districts, study skills instruction is not mandatory. It is usually initiated by teachers or administrators who see a need for it in their school, and their perception of the need generally depends on the school level they represent. Elementary educators, for instance, say that study skills instruction provides the foundation for students' continued academic success, while middle school educators contend that it eases students' transition from the sheltered learning environment of the elementary school to the independent learning environment of the high school. At the high school level, teachers are concerned about students who are doing poorly in their courses or thinking of dropping out of school, and they tend to view the need for such instruction as remedial: it compensates for the study skills instruction that students should have received at lower grade levels.

Whatever the perceived need for study skills instruction, it must be translated into a plan of action. If only one teacher decides to offer instruction, a simple, informal plan is sufficient. If study skills instruction is to be schoolwide or districtwide, however, a more formal, complex action plan is required.

The Study Skills Committee

Forming a study skills committee to develop a comprehensive action plan is the best way to ensure that the plan addresses the many needs of the school or district.

The committee should include several teachers and at least one administrator. If the school is departmentalized, the committee should include several department heads, and if the committee is to develop a districtwide program, each school level (i.e., elementary, middle, secondary) in the district should be represented so that the committee can develop an articulated K–12 curriculum. One or more of the committee members should have expertise in study skills instruction (e.g., teacher, librarian, counselor, curriculum coordinator, or outside consultant).

Our experience in working with schools to set up study skills programs has taught us that change doesn't happen overnight. Don't rush into a program. Through research on school improvement and curriculum implementation (Fullan 1982), we know that school change is slow and complicated. For many schools, this may mean taking a year or two just to initiate a program for teaching students a core set of self-management skills, such as using a three-ring binder, a weekly schedule, and an assignment sheet. Even these seemingly small changes require that the committee, in conjunction with the school faculty, take time to decide:

- who will teach the skills to students (all teachers? selected teachers?);
- when the skills will be taught (beginning of the school year? at teachers' discretion?);
- at what cost (should students purchase their own binders? should the school provide binders?);
- and with what consequences (should students' study skills be graded or ungraded?).

To answer such questions, the committee needs to set and carry out an agenda that culminates with the implementation of a study skills program. The agenda should include the following tasks:

1. Develop a scope and sequence.
2. Review the homework policy of the school or district.
3. Decide whether study skills instruction is to be infused into the curriculum or offered as a separate course.
4. Decide whether to offer separate study skills programs for different types of students—gifted, learning disabled, at-risk, and others.
5. Review available programs and materials for possible adoption or adaptation, or as a basis for a locally developed program.
6. Decide whether to include a parent involvement component.
7. Provide for staff development and program evaluation.

Step 1: Developing a Scope and Sequence

Determining what skills to teach, when to teach them, and in what order is the committee's first task. A scope-and-sequence chart can help the committee organize and clarify its ideas about what a study skills curriculum should include. Figure 3.1 is an example of a typical chart, concisely listing major instructional objectives and when students will be expected to meet them. Although this chart should not be viewed as authoritative, we recommend that the study skills committee use it to begin discussion on the goals of a study skills program. The nine objectives in this chart are based on the research reviewed in Chapter 2 and on our own experience in the field.

Figure 3.1
Scope-and-Sequence Chart for Study Skills Instruction

Major Objectives	K	Elementary					Middle			Secondary			
		1	2	3	4	5	6	7	8	9	10	11	12
The student will learn how to:													
1. Organize school papers.	X	X		X			R		R				
2. Organize a home study space.				X			R		R				
3. Follow school rules and procedures.	X	X		X			X		X				
4. Manage study time.				X			X		R				
5. Listen and participate in class.	X	X			X		X	R	R	R	R	R	R
6. Do reading assignments.					X		X	R	R	R	R	R	R
7. Write school papers.					X		X	R	R	R	R	R	R
8. Do school projects.	X	X					X	R	R	R	R	R	R
9. Prepare for and take tests.		X					X	R	R	R	R	R	X

X = Basic instruction relating to the objective
R = Review and refinement relating to the objective

While educators still have much to learn about what skills to teach and when and how to teach them, teachers generally believe that study skills instruction should start in the early grades. In Rickman's (1981) survey of approximately 150 Arizona educators, "many respondents mentioned that study skills must be introduced in the early grades and refined and enhanced throughout the school years. One teacher stressed, 'I truly believe that skills must be introduced early, on a simple level, then built to greater levels of complexity over a long period of time.' "

By teaching study skills early, we give students the opportunity to practice and refine their skills through their senior year of high school and better prepare themselves for the learning demands of college or the workplace. In fact, research on information processing suggests that repeated practice of skills leads to "automaticity"—completing tasks without thinking about the steps involved. Students who can *automatically* use study skills are able to concentrate on mastering the content of the curriculum, whereas students who have poor study skills fumble through lessons, worrying about studying or avoiding it entirely.

Early teaching also allows students to use study skills to achieve academic success during their formative school years. Success from the outset is clearly better for students than a history of failure or mediocre performance reversed through later study skills instruction or other interventions. Even when students acknowledge that new study methods are better, "unlearning" bad study habits is difficult. One of the primary advantages of early study skills instruction is that it can prevent students from forming bad study habits.

Early study skills instruction does not mean that all study skills should be taught during the first years of school. Study skills are most effective when taught *as they are needed*. Some study skills are used as early as kindergarten, others not until the upper elementary grades or even later. The *basic* study skills relating to each of the objectives in Figure 3.1 should not be delayed beyond the start of middle school.

As shown in Figure 3.1, study skills instruction is often most intense at certain grade levels. This is because the transition from one school level to the next usually represents a major shift in the study tasks that students must master. Many teachers say that teaching study skills is easier during these years because students enter a new school feeling out-of-place and vulnerable, so they readily accept guidance and instruction from teachers that they may not accept a year or two later, when they are more self-confident and committed to their own ways of doing things.

The transition from kindergarten to first grade marks the beginning of a new and substantially different level of schooling, so the objectives taught in kindergarten should be taught again in first grade. The move from elementary school to middle school is another step into a new and more challenging learning environment. Instruction generally is organized into subject matter courses—English, mathematics, science, and so on—and students need to fine-tune their general study skills and learn new skills to meet the particular requirements of each course. Systematic study skills instruction is important for students to successfully adapt to this new environment. Our experience suggests that there is more study skills instruction in the sixth grade than in any other grade in American schools.

By the time students enter middle school, they should have mastered the first two objectives in Figure 3.1—organizing school papers and organizing a home study space—so that in grade 6, teachers need only review related study skills. Other familiar skills need to be retaught and new skills introduced for each course so that students are equipped to handle the unfamiliar demands of the middle school.

Moving from middle school to high school is students' last major transition before graduation. In high school, students are expected to be independent learners; for instance, their homework requirements usually increase and teachers give them less assistance in completing assigned tasks. The study objectives of high school courses are similar to those of middle school courses, however, so teachers need only review and refine the study skills needed to meet these objectives. There are two exceptions: (1) following school rules and procedures and (2) preparing for and taking tests. If the high school has different rules and procedures than the middle school, rules need to be taught systematically. And because many high school students take major tests for admission to college or the military, instruction in test-taking skills during grade 11 or 12 is recommended. Evidence shows that such instruction helps students do better on these tests (see Chapter 8). Apart from these two areas, high school study skills instruction should concentrate on refining students' use of study skills. Of course, students who are severely deficient in their study skills will need basic instruction, not review and refinement, in all study skills.

Figure 3.1 represents an articulated K–12 study skills curriculum. Districtwide committees can plan such a curriculum, but committees working within a single school don't have the authority to dictate the study skills instruction that precedes or follows their own instruction. Yet instruction at these other school levels *will* affect their planning. Single-school committees can address this problem by interviewing teachers and administrators at other schools to determine whether a study skills program exists, what the nature of the program is, what study skills teachers expect students to have mastered when they enter the school, and what instructional changes are planned for the future. During these interviews, the committee should also examine relevant documents and materials. In time, this work may lead to an official collaboration to develop a scope and sequence that is well articulated both within and across the different levels of schooling in grades K–12.

Step 2: Reviewing the School or District's Homework Policy

Different environments make different demands on students' study skills, and studying done at home can be particularly difficult for students. The study skills committee should review typical homework assignments to determine what they require of students and how the study skills program can help students do their homework assignments effectively.

We've found that some teachers and even entire teaching faculties of some schools do not assign homework. Other teachers assign homework, but allow students to use seatwork time to complete as much of it as possible. In our view, completing learning tasks during class is not homework, even if labeled so by the teacher.

The number one reason teachers give for not assigning homework is that their students won't do it because they have poor study skills and habits. And parents may be uncooperative and even hostile to the idea of homework. With no homework assigned, students fail to develop good study habits. The study skills committee needs to break this unproductive cycle.

All students should be expected to do some homework, even in the early grades. A substantial body of research indicates that homework improves students' academic achievement (Walberg 1984, Cooper 1989). It is also essential if students are to acquire certain kinds of study skills. Consider the following differences in study skills demanded by homework and seatwork:

1. *Skills for managing school materials.* Students usually have everything they need to complete work at their desks. These materials are maintained for students. Homework, however, requires students to take responsibility for transporting their textbooks, handouts, assignment sheets, and so on from school to home and back again.

2. *Skills for maintaining a home study area.* Schools are responsible for providing each student with a work surface and chair for completing seatwork. Lighting and sound are also controlled so that students have a physical environment conducive to study. In contrast, students themselves are responsible for organizing their home environment for completing homework. Their parents may help them, but not as much at higher grade levels, when homework demands are increasing.

3. *Skills for following directions.* When the teacher gives directions for completing seatwork assignments, students can ask the teacher or another student to repeat the directions or clarify them. In order to complete their homework, however, students must accurately record the directions so that they can follow them once they're at home, working on their own. Older students have several teachers giving different homework assignments, so the difficulty of the task is compounded. Once students leave school, they can't ask teachers to clarify directions. They must either figure out the directions themselves or telephone a classmate for assistance.

4. *Time management skills.* Once students arrive at school, their time, including time for seatwork, is managed almost entirely by the school schedule. At home most students do not have a fixed time schedule to guide them. They must manage time on their own and learn how to allocate enough time to get the work done.

5. *Self-management skills.* The teacher is present during seatwork to monitor students' behavior and help them stay on task. Some parents may do this at home, but most students probably are on their own, so they need to develop self-management skills to ensure that they complete their homework assignments on time and in accordance with the teacher's directions.

Thus, homework makes more demands on students' study skills than does seatwork. As students progress through school, they will do increasingly more of their studying as homework and less of it as seatwork; therefore, it is essential for teachers to familiarize students with the demands of homework and to teach them requisite study skills.

If the study skills committee agrees that students should be assigned homework, it should consider the amount and type of homework to be assigned and how students will be motivated to complete it.

We've found through informal surveys that total daily homework averages approximately 15 minutes in the primary grades, 30 minutes in the upper elementary grades, 45 to 75 minutes in middle school, and 60 to 120 minutes in high school. There seems to be more variation in amount of homework in the upper grades. Teachers at these grade levels are inclined to give high-performing students substantially longer, more challenging homework assignments than low-performing students.

Too much homework is a common complaint of middle and high school students, but the complaint may be legitimate if each teacher assigns homework without considering the homework assigned by other teachers. The teaching faculty of a school should work together so that the total amount of homework assigned to students is reasonable. They should take care not to assign any homework for which students lack prerequisite study skills.

In addition, all homework should be graded. Rewarding students with points counted toward the total course grade when they complete homework is a popular method of grading. At the beginning of the term, teachers might also send parents a letter explaining the type of homework that will be assigned, its frequency, its importance to students' grades, and what parents can do to help. Parents can then become allies in getting students to complete their homework.

Step 3: Organizing Study Skills Instruction

Schools generally offer study skills instruction in a separate course or by infusing it into the existing curriculum. Which approach is better?

The Separate Course Approach

A separate course on study skills has several advantages. Recruiting a few volunteers to teach the course usually isn't difficult, and volunteer teachers are more likely to be enthusiastic about study skills instruction. These teachers can be given intensive staff development to plan a high-quality study skills course and to refine their instructional skills. Because resources are expended on just a few teachers who can plan and train to a high level of expertise, the staff development is cost-effective. Other teachers will often feel relieved that the burden of study skills instruction has been lifted from their shoulders and that students are learning study skills that will help them succeed in their classes.

Students clearly benefit by receiving study skills instruction from a specially trained and highly motivated teacher. In a study skills course, students can concentrate on learning a variety of study skills in depth and without the worry of learning graded subject matter content in the same class.

A study skills course also provides a clear signal to students, parents, and the community that the school believes study skills instruction is important and has made a commitment to it. And it is not likely to get lost in the curriculum. Teachers at all grade levels have a tremendous amount of content to cover, and if they feel pressed for time, they may skip certain topics, like study skills, even though they've made a commitment to teach them.

Good arguments can also be made against a separate course. For one, a separate study skills course is workable only in schools whose curriculum is organized into courses taught by different teachers. We have not found any instances in which elementary or primary students are taken from their regular classroom for special instruction from a study skills expert, although resource teachers in special education "pull out" classes do sometimes offer study skills instruction to help students meet the demands of their regular classes.

Scheduling is another problem. It is desirable for all students to receive study skills instruction whenever they move from one school level to another, but this practice places heavy demands on the few teachers who offer the study skills course. The course could be offered several times during the school year, but many students would have to wait and thus lose the benefits of early instruction.

The biggest disadvantage of the separate course approach is that students may not transfer the skills they have learned to their other classes. Study skills teachers tell us that they can get students to learn the skills, but many students don't use them in their regular classes. The breakdown in transfer can occur if the subject matter teachers don't require students to use the study skills, don't help students transfer the skills, or want students to use another approach.

For example, in a workshop for all teachers in a districtwide at-risk program, we recommended that teachers require students to use a binder to organize their school materials. All the teachers thought this was a good idea, with one exception. A science teacher objected to the binder, saying that she has always required students to keep their science notes in a spiral notebook. Thus, at-risk students, already having trouble in school, faced the task of learning two different approaches—one system for science and another system for their other classes. The science teacher acknowledged the problem, and we were able to find a solution: students would keep their notes in a *prepunched* spiral notebook that could be carried in the three-ring binder. Thus, the students would learn and implement a simple, consistent system of organization.

Anderson-Inman, Walker, and Purcell (1984) provide additional examples of the problems caused by inconsistent requirements across classes, especially those involving special education students, who find inconsistent requirements particularly disabling.

The Infusion Approach

The alternative to a separate course on study skills is the infusion approach, in which students learn a set of study skills that are consistent across all of their classes. They have ample opportunity to practice the skills and to be reinforced for using them. Infused study skills have credibility for the students because all their teachers endorse them and require their use.

At the elementary school level, infusion is easy because each teacher instructs a class of students in most or all subjects. The teacher can introduce a study skill and then show students how it can be used in all their subjects. It's a somewhat different matter in middle schools and high schools, where all teachers bear responsibility for infusing study skills into their courses. In practice, this responsibility usually is shared among departments. For example, the English department in a high school might teach writing skills; the science department, testing skills; homeroom teachers, study organization skills; and so forth. Implementation of this approach is preceded by extensive planning among the teachers to decide what study methods are to be used across the curriculum, who should teach them, and what procedures are to be used to ensure student compliance. The study skills committee can coordinate this planning.

The infusion approach does have several disadvantages. When all or many teachers are responsible for study skills instruction, no one is responsible. It's easy for study skills instruction to fall through the cracks. Also, it's necessary to provide extensive coordination and training of teachers. Infusion can cause many teachers to feel overworked and to see study skills instruction as one more "add on." Teachers who feel this way are unlikely to fulfill their responsibilities with much enthusiasm, and may even avoid them.

A Recommendation

Neither the separate study skills course nor the infusion approach has a clear advantage. We recommend a combination of both.

The planning committee should try to identify one or two teachers in a school who are enthusiastic about study skills instruction. These "lead" teachers should be given resources to plan, to get training for themselves, to purchase materials, and so forth. The lead teachers can then offer a course on study skills, or a unit of instruction ranging from a few days to a few weeks, to as many students in the school as possible. If resources and a schoolwide commitment are available, the lead teachers can work with other teachers so that they too can offer study skills instruction. The other teachers can reinforce and fine-tune the study skills taught in the lead teachers' classes and teach additional study skills.

Step 4: Individualizing Study Skills Instruction

The study skills committee should consider whether to offer the same study skills instruction to all students or adjust instruction to the needs of different learners. We believe that all students need to learn the same basic study skills. If resources are available, however, instruction should vary to meet the special needs of students at the extremes of learning ability—learning-disabled and gifted students.

Gifted Students

Many gifted students are in an accelerated academic program that challenges their ability to learn; therefore, they will need to master study skills for reading textbooks and writing school papers before their peers need to master them. In effect, they need an accelerated study skills program. If the school cannot provide such a program, students may be able to take a study skills class at a community college or at the study skills center of a college or university.

Gifted students often have the desire and capacity to develop study skills to a more sophisticated level than other students, and they need a learning environment that gives them this opportunity. Consider, for example, the study skill of determining the main idea of a reading passage. This is a difficult skill to master. Most students struggle just to learn how to make a statement that does not literally repeat the text, and their main ideas often express only part of the content. In contrast, gifted students have less difficulty learning how to use their own words to express an idea that captures the entire content of the passage. Their instruction is facilitated by being with other students who are generating good examples of main idea statements and by being with an instructor who can help them realize their full potential.

A common misconception is that gifted students do not need study skills instruction because, being gifted, they have a high natural ability to learn academic content. Gifted students, however, generally are not gifted in all academic areas. Most have difficulty in certain subjects, as Gall (1986) noted:

> Gifted students often must take difficult subjects in which they are *not* gifted in order to pursue their particular talents. For example, when I was in the doctoral psychology program at the University of California, Berkeley, I met many students who were brilliant theoreticians or clinicians. Many of these students had to struggle through statistics courses, not only to meet degree requirements but also because statistical analysis is an important part of the professional psychologist's role. To master such difficult subjects, gifted students need study skills, just like other students (p. 33).

Many instructors do not see the need for study skills instruction for young gifted students, who usually earn high grades with little effort because they are in classes that serve the general population of children. The level of challenge and competition for gifted children is likely to increase, however, as their talents are recognized and they participate in special classes with students who are similarly gifted. Eventually, they may attend a prestigious college whose entire study body is highly capable. Gifted students need to learn study skills not so much to succeed in the present, but to prepare for these future challenges. Gifted students who have experienced frequent, easy success in school can become threatened when they are tossed suddenly into a more competitive learning environment. Early study skills instruction can help them avoid this threat or at least cope effectively with it.

Learning-Disabled Students

Students classified as learning-disabled often receive special instruction to help them learn the curriculum and overcome learning deficits. This instruction sometimes is called a "pull-out" program, because it occurs outside the regular classroom. We recommend that the program include instruction in the same basic study skills that other students are expected to learn, but that it allow more time and special support.

Most learning-disabled adolescents have a history of academic failure. Teachers must take care that these students do not experience study skills instruction as just another defeat. It's important for students to see study skills as tools that will help them, not as something mysterious and difficult to master. Because learning-disabled students are less apt to be motivated by academic instruction, they can especially benefit from a two-pronged instructional approach that not only teaches study skills but motivates them to internalize and use the skills. We've also found that study skills instruction is likely to be more effective if it is supplemented by counseling and guidance that develop these students' motivation to study.

Deshler and Schumaker (1986) took into account these two characteristics of learning-disabled students—history of academic failure and low academic motivation—in designing their study skills program. They also considered the potential problem of transferring skills learned in a pull-out program to the regular classroom. Teachers in pull-out programs should provide additional instruction to ensure that transfer occurs. Deshler and Schumaker's program includes three steps to ensure that students will learn skills and apply them in their regular classes:

1. *Orientation.* Make students aware of the variety of contexts (different subject matter classes, the home, the workplace, etc.) in which each study skill can be used.

2. *Activation.* Provide students with ample opportunities to practice the study skills using a variety of materials and instructional settings.

3. *Maintenance.* Make periodic checks to determine whether students are continuing to use the study skills at an acceptable level of proficiency. Reteach, if necessary.

These procedures for promoting transfer have wider applicability than pull-out programs. They should be used whenever any group of students—learning-disabled, average, or gifted—learn study skills in one setting, but are expected to use them in other settings.

Step 5: Reviewing Available Programs and Materials for Study Skills Instruction

There is no need for a school system to develop a study skills program from scratch. A good selection of programs and materials is available to meet various needs and preferences, and part of the study skills committee's work is to review what is available. The programs and materials can be adopted as is, adapted to meet local conditions, or used as a basis for developing the school system's own program.

The following descriptions of study skills programs and materials are intended to facilitate the committee's work. The list is not exhaustive, but it does represent the range of what is available. Our definition of a program is an organized curriculum that includes a teacher's guide and student materials, and possibly a scope and sequence. A detailed curriculum guide also would qualify as a program. We have tried to include programs and materials that are widely used or exemplary.

Programs Developed by Associations

Cognitive Learning Strategies Project, published by the University of Texas at Austin (University Station, Austin, TX 78712). The staff of this project at the University of Texas at Austin have developed a three-credit course in study skills for college students (see Weinstein 1988). The course includes the following units: characteristics of successful students; a problem-solving model for dealing with school-related problems; cognitive learning strategies; strategies for concentrating; listening skills; selecting important ideas; note taking; text marking and outlining; pre-, during-, and post-reading strategies; reading comprehension strategies and comprehension monitoring strategies; stress reduction strategies; test-taking skills; and strategies for reducing test anxiety.

The hm Study Skills Program, published by the National Association of Secondary School Principals (P.O. Box 3250, Reston, VA 22090). This program, for grades 5 and higher, includes a student text, teacher's guide, and workshop kit for each of the following grade levels and topics:

- Level I: Grades 5–7
- Level II: Grades 8–10
- Level III: Grades 11–13
- Math Study Skills: Grades 6–10
- Science Study Skills: Grades 7–10
- GED/Adult learning.

The range of study skills in the materials is illustrated by the content of Level II: listening, vocabulary, note taking, reading textbooks, problem solving, study habits, memory, paragraph organization, preparing for tests, test taking, and use of time.

The hm Study Skills Program Level B, published by the National Association for Elementary School Principals (NAESP Educational Products Center, 1615 Duke Street, Alexandria, VA 22314-3483). This program includes a student text, teacher's guide, and workshop kit for grades 3–4. The study skills in Level B pertain to listening, observing, understanding, directions, categories, sequence, tables and graphs, visualizing, main idea, supporting details, and problem solving.

The hm Study Skills Program Newsletter, published by the hm Study Skills Group (84 Bowers Street, Newtonville, MA 02160).

Learning Strategies Curriculum, published by the University of Kansas Institute for Research in Learning Disabilities (University of Kansas,

Lawrence, KS 66045). Developed for use with learning-disabled high school students, the program (described further in Deshler and Schumaker 1986) consists of a set of instructional packets, each of which includes student materials and teaching procedures to train students in a particular study strategy. The strategies are organized into three strands: (1) acquisition, which includes study skills for acquiring information from written materials; (2) storage, which includes study skills for identifying and storing important information; and (3) expression and demonstration of competence, which includes study skills for doing written assignments and taking tests.

Study Power, published by the American College Testing Program (ACT Publications, P.O. Box 168, Iowa City, IA 52243). Developed for high school use, this program includes a leader's guide, six student workbooks, and two evaluative instruments (described below in the section on measures). Each workbook covers one major study skill: (1) managing time and environment, (2) reading textbooks, (3) taking class notes, (4) using resources, (5) preparing for tests, or (6) taking tests.

Programs Developed by School Districts

STEPS: Study Skills Scope and Sequence K–12, published by the Lowell School District (Moss Street, Lowell, OR 97452). This 1987 program includes a scope and sequence for a K–12 study skills curriculum. The curriculum focuses on study skills involved in time management, listening and note taking, the SQ3R reading method, written communication, interpretation of graphic aids, use of the library, and test taking. The materials include a teacher's guide, teacher checklists, an eighth grade competency test, and wall charts.

The Learning Strategies/Study Skills Program, developed by the Greenville Independent School District (Greenville, TX 75401). An evaluation of this program's effectiveness was discussed in Chapter 2. The program includes 13 units of study that cover the following topics: organizational skills; study/reading systems; objective-test preparation and test taking; essay test preparation and test taking; goal setting, attitude, and time management; vocabulary building; listening skills; memory and concentration techniques; basic reading skills; note taking; critical thinking/problem solving; library skills and research writing; and speed reading. A recent description of the program (see Wilson 1988) does not indicate whether the materials used in the program are generally available, but the description itself might be useful to school districts that are developing a scope and sequence for a study skills program.

Programs Developed by Private Publishers

Effective Study Strategies, published by Academic Resources Corporation (148 Great Road, P.O. Box 222, Acton, MA 01720). The materials emphasize note-taking and reading skills.

A Guidebook for Teaching Study Skills and Motivation. (2nd ed.), by Bernice Bragstad and Sharyn Stumpf (Needham Heights, Mass.: Allyn and Bacon, 1987). The 14 chapters cover the entire range of general and content-specific study skills, and procedures for developing a school study-skills program. Reproducible handouts are included.

Skills for School Success, by Anita Archer and Mary Gleason (North Billerica, Mass.: Curriculum Associates, 1988). The current program is for grades 3 and 4, but programs for other grades are being developed. The program includes a teacher's guide and student workbook and teaches study skills involved in doing homework assignments, managing time and materials, following directions, taking tests, reading textbooks, and using reference books.

Study for Success Teacher's Manual (3rd rev. ed.), by Meredith and Joyce Gall (M. Damien Publishers, 4810 Mahalo, Eugene, OR 97405). The manual includes 23 lesson plans and parent involvement activities organized into eight units: (1) assessment of study skills; (2) using a school binder; (3) survey of study skills; (4) self-management for effective study; (5) class participation; (6) active reading; (7) following a step-by-step writing plan; and (8) test taking. The lesson plans, parent involvement activities, and reproducible handouts can be used as is or adapted for use in grades K–12 and different content areas.

Teaching Study Skills: A Guide for Teachers (2nd ed.), by Thomas Devine (Newton, Mass.: Allyn and Bacon, 1987). This is a comprehensive textbook about study skills instruction.

Books About General Study Skills

Getting Smarter: Simple Strategies to Get Better Grades, by Lawrence Greene and Leigh Jones-Bamman (Belmont, Calif.: David S. Lake, 1985). Eleven chapters cover such topics as self-assessment of study skills, getting organized, scheduling time, active thinking, taking notes, and taking tests. The book is intended for students at the junior high, senior high, and community college levels. An instructor's manual is available to facilitate its use as a course text.

How To Study, by Kenneth Standley (Palo Alto, Calif: Dale Seymour, 1987). This book for high school and college students is organized into five sections: (1) how to manage time, (2) how to take notes in class, (3) how to study a textbook, (4) how to study for tests, and (5) how to take tests.

How to Study in College (4th ed.), by Walter Pauk (Boston: Houghton Mifflin, 1989). Originally published in 1962, this is one of the classic textbooks on study skills. It provides comprehensive coverage of general and content-specific study skills.

Making the Grade, by Meredith and Joyce Gall (Rocklin, Calif.: Prima, 1988). The book describes 80 specific study skills organized into 5 chapters: (1) getting started, (2) active participation and listening in class, (3) reading textbooks effectively, (4) writing school papers, and (5) taking tests. It is appropriate for students who can read at the eighth grade reading level.

Study Skills Strategies: Your Guide to Critical Thinking, by Uelaine Lengefeld (Los Altos, Calif.: Crisp, 1987). This brief text is organized into seven sections: (1) attitudes toward studying, (2) time control, (3) note-taking techniques, (4) critical reading skills, (5) memory training, (6) exam strategies, and (7) mathematics study skills. The book is intended for use in high school instruction, college preparatory courses, college freshmen orientation, and classes for reentry students.

Books About Particular Aspects of Studying

How to Get Control of Your Time and Your Life, by Alan Lakein (New York: Wyden, 1973). This is a classic text on how to manage time effectively and overcome procrastination. Although most of Lakein's examples are drawn from daily life and the world of work, his techniques are generally applicable to studying.

How to Read Faster and Better: The Evelyn Wood Reading Dynamics Program, by Franklin Agardy (New York: Simon and Schuster, 1986). This book describes the methods used in the Evelyn Wood Program to improve students' reading speed and comprehension.

The Memory Book, by Harry Lorayne and Jerry Lucas (New York: Ballantine, 1973). This is a classic text on mnemonic techniques for remembering different kinds of information, such as speeches, foreign and English vocabulary, and numbers.

Test-Taking Strategies, by Judi Kesselman-Turkel and Franklynn Peterson (Chicago: Contemporary Books, 1981). This book describes techniques for preparing for a test, dealing with test anxiety, and answering different types of test items (multiple-choice, true-false, essay, problem-solving, etc.).

Books for Parents

Many books have been written about techniques that parents can use to help their children with school. Educators can use these books to find ideas about how to involve parents as partners in teaching study skills to students and improving students' academic motivation. At PTA meetings or parent nights at school, educators might want to recommend these books as resources to parents who wish to support their children's education.

Between Parent and Child, by Haim Ginott (New York: Avon, 1969). This is a classic work on techniques that parents can use to build a child's self-esteem, responsibility, and independence. A related book by Ginott, *Between Parent and Teenager*, was published in 1971 by Avon.

Help Your Son or Daughter Study for Success: A Parent Guide, by Joyce and Meredith Gall (M. Damien Publishers, 4810 Mahalo, Eugene, OR 97405). This book presents 17 specific recommendations, based on the authors' research, on how parents can help their children study effectively and do well in school.

Measures of Study Behavior and Study Skills

Measures of study behavior and study skills can be used to diagnose the strengths and weaknesses of students' study habits. Teachers can use the results to focus study skills instruction on areas of particular need, which can be important if time for study skills instruction is limited.

Teachers can also administer one of the measures at the beginning and end of a study skills course to determine how much students have learned. This record of progress is useful to students as well.

In the last section of this chapter, we describe how these measures can be used for program evaluation.

Learning and Study Strategies Inventory (LASSI), by Claire Weinstein, Ann Schulte, and David Palmer (Clearwater, Fla.: H & H Publishing, 1987). This measure was developed for use with college students. It takes approximately 30 minutes to administer and yields scores on the following ten scales:

1. Anxiety about school, studying, and tests.
2. Interest in school and in doing well in school.
3. Ability to concentrate and listen.
4. Ability to process information by organizing it, relating it to what one already knows, and paraphrasing it.
5. Motivation to work hard in school and to be self-disciplined.
6. Ability to manage time effectively.
7. Ability to select main ideas in information read or heard.
8. Inclination to review regularly the information one has learned.
9. Inclination to use study aids, such as practice exercises, summary tables, and group review sessions.
10. Ability to prepare for and take tests.

The LASSI has good validity and reliability (Weinstein, Zimmerman, and Palmer 1988), but because this is a self-report measure, its results are only as valid as students' willingness to report their study behavior honestly.

A high school version of the LASSI recently has become available. Information about its characteristics and use can be obtained from the publisher.

Survey of Study Habits and Attitudes (SSHA), by William Brown and Wayne Holtzman (New York: Psychological Corporation, 1967). This probably has been the most widely used measure of study behavior since its publication. Two forms of the SSHA are available: Form H for grades 7–12, and Form C for grades 12–14. The SSHA is valid for some purposes, but like the LASSI, its validity depends on students' willingness to give honest responses.

The SSHA yields four basic scales:

1. Delay Avoidance—measures the extent to which students avoid delay and distraction
2. Work Methods—measures how effectively students organize their study behavior
3. Teacher Approval—measures students' attitude toward the teacher
4. Education Acceptance—measures students' agreement with the expressed goals of education.

Scores on the first two scales can be combined to yield a score called Study Habits. Scores on the last two scales can be combined to yield a score called Study Attitudes. The total score across all four scales is called Study Orientation.

Study Power Assessment, published by the American College Testing Program (ACT Publications, P.O. Box 168, Iowa City, IA 52243). This is a recently developed true-false test of knowledge about study skills. It includes six scales, each of which measures students' knowledge about a different set of study skills: (1) managing time and environment, (2) reading textbooks, (3) taking class notes, (4) using resources, (5) preparing for tests, and (6) taking tests. This test is suitable for use with high school students.

Because the Study Power Assessment is new, its validity and reliability are still being established. Inspection of the test items indicates that the test measures students' knowledge of study skills generally acknowledged as important.

Study Power Inventory, published by the American College Testing Program (ACT Publications, P.O. Box 168, Iowa City, IA 52243). This measure includes six scales with the same names as the scales of the Study Power Assessment, but the Study Power Inventory measures study behavior rather than knowledge about study skills. The validity of the scores, like the scores of the SSHA and LASSI, depends on students' willingness to give honest responses to the items.

Step 6: Providing for Parent Involvement

The study skills committee will need to decide whether and how to involve parents in the study skills program. Parents can help students develop good study habits by providing space and materials for homework, a quiet time free of distractions, and motivational support. Unless they receive information from the school, however, they may not be aware that they *can* do anything to help.

It's important that all teachers agree to whatever policy is adopted by the committee (especially if students have a different teacher for each subject) so that they don't communicate inconsistent information about homework expectations and the parents' role. A letter or newsletter sent home can alert parents to the goals of the study skills program and what parents can do to help. And a series of seminars at the school can give parents a real sense of involvement in the program, even if only a small percentage are able to attend. Or teachers might have students take home an assignment sheet each day for parents to review. All of these ideas ensure that parents know the school's expectations for homework.

Several of the programs and materials described in the preceding section include parent involvement activities that the study skills committee can review to help formulate a policy for parent involvement and specific procedures that can be implemented once the study skills program is initiated.

Teachers and administrators often worry that parents will not cooperate with school requests for involvement. Although these concerns usually have some basis in fact, they tend to be exaggerated. When asked to estimate the number of parents at their school who are totally uninvolved in their child's education, teachers generally say about 20 percent. Of course, these 20 percent can be so troublesome that they overshadow the 80 percent of parents who truly are concerned and involved. Nevertheless, teachers and administrators who have reached out to parents invariably report that their efforts were successful.

Step 7: Providing for Staff Development and Program Evaluation

Staff Development

Because most teachers do not receive preservice training on how to provide study skills instruction, the study skills committee needs to provide at least an orientation to the program that they expect teachers to implement. Committee members are good candidates for providing this orientation, because they were closest to the development of the program and understand its philosophy, objectives, materials, and teaching methods.

The study skills programs described earlier in the chapter generally include a manual that orients teachers to their use. In some programs, such as *Skills for School Success* and the *Study for Success Teacher's Manual*, the manual provides detailed lesson plans that teachers can implement without special training.

Program Evaluation

The evaluation of a study skills program does not need to be complex, but it should be done in a timely fashion, preferably during the first year of program implementation, so that problems can be identified and corrected quickly. If problems are left uncorrected, teachers are likely to become discouraged with the program.

One simple evaluation process involves recruiting a few persons, perhaps members of the study skills committee, to interview a few of the teachers and students who are using the program in order to identify the program's benefits and weaknesses and to solicit ideas for improvements.

If resources are available, the evaluation can include an assessment of students' gains in study skills. One or more of the measures described earlier in the chapter can be administered to a sample of students when they begin the program, and again when they complete it. In selecting a measure, you will need to decide whether to assess students' *use* of study skills, their *knowledge* of study skills, or both. For example, the *Study Power Inventory* assesses students' use of study skills, whereas its companion measure, the *Study Power Assessment*, assesses students' knowledge of study skills.

Another approach is to identify a sample of students and inspect their school binders, notebooks, or other organizers to determine whether papers are neatly organized; whether the students are using time management tools such as a weekly schedule and assignment sheet; and whether class notes, reading notes, and homework assignments are competently done. Of course, inspecting these materials makes sense only if they represent objectives of the study skills program. Any evaluation process should be directly linked to the stated objectives of the study skills program.

References

Anderson-Inman, L., H. M. Walker, and J. Purcell. (1984). "Promoting the Transfer of Skills Across Settings: Transenvironmental Programming for Handicapped Students in the Mainstream." In *Focus on Behavior Analysis in Education*, edited by W. L. Howard, T. E. Heron, D. S. Hill, and J. Trap-Porter. Columbus, Ohio: Charles E. Merrill.

Cooper, H. (1989). *Homework*. New York: Longman.

Deshler, D. D., and J. B. Schumaker. (1986). "Learning Strategies: An Instructional Alternative for Low-Achieving Adolescents." *Exceptional Children* 52: 583–590.

Fullan, M. (1982). *The Meaning of Educational Change*. New York: Teachers College Press.

Gall, J. P. (1986). "Study Skills Instruction for Gifted Students." *Illinois Council for the Gifted Journal* 5: 33–35.

Rickman, L. W. (1981). "Arizona Educators Assess the Teaching of Study Skills." *Clearing House* 3: 363–365.

Walberg, H. (1984). "Improving the Productivity of America's Schools." *Educational Leadership* 41, 8: 19–27.

Weinstein, C. E. (1988). "Assessment and Training of Student Learning Strategies." In *Learning Strategies and Learning Styles*, edited by R. R. Schmeck. New York: Plenum.

Weinstein, C. E., S. A. Zimmerman, and D. R. Palmer. (1988). "Assessing Learning Strategies: The Design and Development of the LASSI." In *Learning and Study Strategies: Issues in Assessment, Instruction, and Evaluation*, edited by C. E. Weinstein, E. T. Goetz, and P. A. Alexander. San Diego: Academic Press.

Wilson, J. E. (1988). "Implications of Learning Strategy Research and Training: What It Has to Say to the Practitioner." In *Learning and Study Strategies*, edited by C. E. Weinstein, E. T. Goetz, and P. A. Alexander. San Diego: Academic Press.

4

Self-Management

We use the term "self-management" to refer to skills that students use to monitor, reward, and direct their own study behavior. These are the skills that enable students to become independent learners who no longer need to rely on external supervision to guide their actions. In the past, such skills have been taught primarily to special populations, such as learning-disabled or at-risk students (Karoly and Kanfer 1982). All students, however, can benefit from self-management training.

When teaching self-management skills, teachers need to consider the demands of both the school and the home, since students need to learn to balance all their activities, not just their academic tasks.

In school, students need to learn how to handle:

1. *Restricted activity.* Students listen, speak, and move under adults' close supervision. Usually, they must ask for permission to talk or move around, and are punished if they do not.

2. *Time pressures.* Students attend school six or more hours a day, five days a week, for nine months or more each year. There are due dates for assignments, penalties for late work, and the attraction of sports and other extracurricular activities that compete for students' time.

3. *Independent study.* School activities are heavily teacher-structured in the early grades, but more independent study is required as students advance.

4. *Class rotation.* Beginning in middle or junior high, sometimes even earlier, students must learn to move from class to class on a fixed schedule and respond to the teaching styles and expectations of different teachers.

5. *Competition and evaluation.* Schools place students in competitive situations. Students are often encouraged to compete against a previously established standard of performance, and they are judged not only on the quality of their academic work, but also on their behavior.

6. *Social Interaction.* Complex social interactions occur among students in school. Shifting patterns of rivalry, friendship, romance, and cliques or gangs characterize students' social activity outside the classroom and also affect classroom atmosphere. At the same time, socialization during class

is often discouraged because social activity is not "the main business" of school.

The most pressing demands outside of school include:

1. *Home chores.* Most students are expected to help with work at home. Some have major responsibilities for cleaning, meal preparation, and care of younger siblings.

2. *Family changes.* Family changes such as divorce or serious illness place major demands on students. They may be living in a single-parent home or continually shifting residence from one parent's household to the other's.

3. *Jobs.* Many students, especially in the upper grades, do volunteer work or hold part-time jobs.

4. *Entertainment.* Students can be easily distracted from their responsibilities by television, movies, video games, music, and friends.

Out-of-school demands are not always negative influences. Jobs, home chores, family responsibilities, and entertainment help students become well-rounded adults. It is important, however, for students to learn how to put them in perspective so that they do not interfere with schoolwork.

Negative Responses to Demands

Many students are unable to cope with the demands described above. Alarming numbers of young people turn to escape/avoidance mechanisms, including drugs, alcohol, and irresponsible sexual behavior. Among high school seniors surveyed in 1984 by the Monitoring the Future project, 86 percent reported using alcohol and 40 percent reported using marijuana or hashish during the past year (Johnston and O'Malley 1986). Suicide is one of the leading causes of death among young people in the United States. And of the over one million American teenagers who become pregnant every year, nearly half become mothers (Planned Parenthood 1986). The overwhelming majority of these teenagers have poor basic skills and a pattern of academic failure and low self-esteem.

Self-management skills are students' weapons against these escape/avoidance behaviors.

Skills for Effective Self-Management

Students need a variety of self-management skills. We focus on skills for: (1) organizing materials and space, (2) managing time, (3) managing stress, and (4) getting help. We have chosen these aspects of self-management because of their underlying importance in carrying out any study task, and because students will need them once they leave school.

Figure 4.1 lists study skills that contribute to effective self-management. Each skill is listed only once, but some skills are useful for more than one type of self-management. For example, while setting goals is treated under time management, it also contributes to stress management.

Figure 4.1
Skills for Self-Management

ORGANIZING MATERIALS AND SPACE
1. Filing and transporting classroom materials
2. Organizing a home study space

MANAGING TIME
3. Organizing a schedule
4. Setting reasonable goals and timelines
5. Setting priorities
6. Breaking big tasks into subtasks and scheduling each subtask
7. Rewarding yourself after studying
8. Arriving on time
9. Completing assignments on time

MANAGING STRESS

Mental Alertness

10. Scheduling study time to fit your natural energy cycle
11. Getting enough sleep
12. Focusing on the task at hand

Anxiety Control

13. Using meditation techniques
14. Using progessive muscle relaxation

Physical Fitness

15. Getting enough exercise
16. Eating nutritious meals
17. Avoiding harmful substances

Positive Self-Concept

18. Accurate self-assessment
19. Taking responsibility for your learning
20. Positive thinking
21. Developing a spiritual-moral viewpoint

GETTING HELP

22. Assessing the need for help
23. Identifying sources of help
24. Initiating requests for help

Skills for Organizing Materials and Space

Experts agree that using the same supplies and studying in the same place helps students develop a regular study routine. Patton, Stinard, and Routh (1983) investigated the settings in which elementary and junior high school students reported they studied at home. Students tended to prefer quiet locations when reading, but preferred having the TV, a radio, or a stereo on when they were doing writing and mathematics work. Even though most students reported studying in a nonquiet setting most of the time, a majority said that they would select a quiet setting if they wanted to do their "best" studying.

Zimmerman and Pons (1986) interviewed 80 high- and low-achieving high school students about their use of self-regulated learning strategies in various contexts. One of the 14 strategies in which responses were coded was "environmental structuring," which was defined as student-initiated efforts to arrange the physical setting to make learning easier. High-achieving students reported significantly more use of this learning strategy than low-achieving students. Examples of their environmental restructuring were: "I isolate myself from anything that distracts me," and "I turn off the radio so I can concentrate on what I am doing." Most of these high achievers learned such strategies on their own, through trial and error. Training students, beginning in the early grades, to organize their materials and space would enable more students to structure their environment to support study efforts.

STUDY SKILL 1
Filing and Transporting Classroom Materials

Organizing classroom materials such as handouts, notes, assignments, and pencils is important. A binder can help students get organized because different kinds of materials can be stored in it and because it's easy to carry from class to class.

Binders fill up as the school year progresses, so students also need to be taught how to weed out what they don't need. Older students may need to hold on to some material in order to do term projects or prepare for final exams, so they need to be taught how to set up a filing system to store papers that no longer fit in the binder.

Organizing a Home Study Space

Educators agree that a home study space should be well lit, have a good writing surface, and be removed from noise and other distractions (Duckett 1983; Gall and Gall 1988b).

Although parents may help set up a study area, students need to keep the space organized. They need to assess what "equipment" they need—a typewriter or computer, pencils, scissors, paper clips—and make sure that this equipment is easily accessible and neatly arranged. When projects are completed or interests change, they must file or discard materials they don't need. And they must find space to store materials for new projects.

Skills for Managing Time

As students advance through the grades, they face increasing demands on their time. Delucchi, Rohwer, and Thomas (1987) investigated the amount of time students reported that they spent studying outside of class. The mean estimate of study time per week was $6\frac{1}{2}$ hours for junior high students, $7\frac{1}{2}$ hours for senior high students, and 11 hours for college students. Finian (1988) found a similar estimate reported by gifted students in grades 5 through 9—$6\frac{1}{2}$ hours per week.

Delucchi and her colleagues (1987) found no correlation between reported study time and two measures of academic achievement—course grade and final test score. They concluded that students' academic success depends not on total time spent studying but on effective time management, along with other self-management skills.

In our study skills workshops, many teachers say that teaching students time management skills is one of their top priorities. Below we describe seven essential skills for managing time.

STUDY SKILL 3
Organizing a Schedule

In working with schools on study skills instruction, we have found that "procrastinating instead of studying" is most commonly identified as a top concern, by both students and teachers recalling their own experience as students.

Solomon and Rothblum (1984) define procrastination as "the act of needlessly delaying tasks to the point of experiencing subjective discomfort" (p. 503). In a study of academic procrastination among college students, the authors found that 46 percent of students reported that they always or nearly always procrastinated in writing a term paper, 28 percent procrastinated in studying for exams, and 30 percent procrastinated in reading weekly assignments. Although course grade was not significantly related to reported level of procrastination, a majority of the students said they wanted to reduce their procrastination on such tasks.

To overcome study procrastination, students should maintain a written schedule of specific times for doing their homework and other essential activities. They may also want to keep a "To-Do" list of important activities and cross off each item as it is accomplished (Lakein 1973).

The value of this type of record keeping was demonstrated in a study by Broden, Hall, and Mitts (1974). They found that training an eighth grade student to self-record her own study behavior in class helped raise the amount of time spent attending to the lesson. Using a written schedule and a To-Do list operates as a self-record of study behavior outside of class.

STUDY SKILL 4
Setting Reasonable Goals and Timelines

As students progress through school, study tasks tend to become more complex and require more time to complete. It is up to students to determine the amount of time and effort they spend on each task and the standard of quality for which they will strive. If they set their goals too high, they may procrastinate out of fear of failure, or they may actually fail because the goals are too difficult to achieve, given their level of ability and the time available. If they set their goals too low, however, tasks becomes routine and unstimulating, and students never achieve their full potential.

Students may need help from teachers in order to set reasonable goals and plan time to achieve them. Encouraging students to set minimal goals and standards for their *initial* efforts on an assignment ensures that students achieve success early and gives many students the momentum to keep working toward higher goals. It also gives students a natural "break" for reviewing their work and rewarding themselves before going back to a task with new, slightly higher goals.

STUDY SKILL 5
Setting Priorities

To set priorities, students need to identify activities, such as watching TV, that they find rewarding but that interfere with studying. They then need to consider the priority of such activities in relation to their goals. Eventually most students learn that studying is a high priority, even though they don't find it as enjoyable as other activities, and they learn how to use other activities as rewards for studying, as discussed in Study Skill 7 below.

Students also need to rank their study tasks. Assignments due the next day are obviously high priority, but so are many tasks that do not need to be done immediately. Long-term projects, reading, or reviewing for a test are high-priority tasks because of their overall importance to students' grades.

STUDY SKILL 6
Breaking Big Tasks into Subtasks and Scheduling Each Subtask

Large tasks that seem overwhelming and cannot be accomplished quickly are the very tasks that students tend to put off, either in favor of doing more immediate, short assignments, or in favor of some nonacademic activity. For example, Wittrock (1988) reported on a study of army recruits being taught to improve their reading skills:

> We originally gave them a lengthy booklet of passages to read in two weeks, one hour per day. Many of them took one look at the booklet, put it down, and gave up. We quickly learned that attention to details, such as handing out reading material no more than one page long, was critical for motivation. Any material longer than that seemed beyond some of them (p. 293).

Learning to break a large task into small tasks will help students develop good time management strategies and, as Wittrock's study shows, will help them sustain their motivation.

STUDY SKILL 7
Rewarding Yourself After Studying

Zimmerman and Pons (1986) found that high-achieving high school students reported using rewards or punishment as a consequence for success or failure significantly more than did low-achievers. This strategy was exemplified by statements such as "If I do well on a test, I treat myself to a movie."

In selecting rewards, students should consider what they would like to do instead of studying. The key is not to eliminate these activities, but to use them as a reward for studying. In other words, instead of "do something fun now, study later," students can remind themselves to "study now, do something fun later."

STUDY SKILL 8
Arriving on Time

Getting to class on time promotes efficiency and prepares students for the world of work, where people who consistently arrive late are likely to lose their jobs. Late students are usually punished with demerits or other negative incentives, but they also miss parts of lessons and upset teachers by disrupting class. Teachers are unlikely to fail students who come to class regularly and turn in their assignments, and they will be more inclined to help them when they encounter difficulty in learning.

STUDY SKILL 9
Completing Assignments on Time

An important aspect of time management is simply keeping track of assignments and their due dates. Students should write down assignments and due dates in their class notes or on a special assignment sheet.

Solomon and Rothblum (1984) found that the amount of time students reported spending to catch up on old assignments was negatively related to achievement at all three grade levels (junior high, senior high, and college), which suggests that once students start handing in assignments late or failing to complete them, they are unlikely to catch up.

Skills for Managing Stress

There are four main aspects of stress management strategies for successful studying: (1) mental alertness, (2) anxiety control, (3) physical fitness, and (4) positive self-concept. Study skills relating to each aspect are discussed below.

Mental Alertness

To carry out the varied intellectual tasks that teachers assign, students need to think clearly and exert mental effort. Just as a student's physical stamina varies, the mind's level of alertness is not constant over time and benefits from alternate periods of intense activity and rest. Students need skills to monitor and maximize their mental alertness.

STUDY SKILL 10
Scheduling Study Time to Fit Your Natural Energy Cycle

Schools cannot adjust their class and activity schedules to accommodate individual differences, but students can adjust their home schedules.

Students should become aware of their own fluctuations of high and low energy and schedule study and other activities based on that awareness. When their energy is high, for example, they can review notes for a difficult test; when their energy is low, they can do more routine work, such as filing papers or reading material that's easy to understand.

STUDY SKILL 11
Getting Enough Sleep

Some students never seem to be alert. Before teachers conclude that this is a motivation problem, they should ask students whether they are getting enough sleep. Like energy patterns, "enough" sleep is not the same for all students, but successful students know how much sleep they need and get that amount most of the time. And when their energy flags, they take short breaks to recharge their batteries.

STUDY SKILL 12
Focusing on the Task at Hand

Students are expected to attend to each task as it is presented in the classroom. Focusing is especially important when the teacher is talking or making a presentation. Students who actively listen focus their ears, eyes, and thoughts on the task at hand and learn to screen out all other perceptions, such as the attractive new student sitting next to them or the sounds of the school band outside the classroom window.

Anxiety Control

Many students experience anxiety while studying. For some students, the anxiety is specific to a particular subject. It is important for students to realize that anxiety probably cannot be completely eliminated. For example, virtually everyone—even professional speakers—experiences some anxiety before giving a speech. Students need to learn how to control anxiety, rather than trying to ignore it or drown it out completely through escape-avoidance mechanisms. Below are two general skills for controlling anxiety related to studying. Both skills have the goal of relaxing the body and calming the mind, but they approach this goal in a different manner.

STUDY SKILL 13
Using Meditation Techniques

According to Knutsen (1978), "the most basic form of meditation is giving your full attention to whatever you are doing. . . ." (p. 254). Knutsen asserts that four simple conditions achieve the positive effects of meditation: a constant mental stimulus, a passive attitude, decreased muscle tonus, and a quiet environment. Under these conditions, researchers have found that heartbeat, blood pressure, and lactase levels in the blood drop, and skin resistance rises, indicating a state of relaxation. "Long-term effects seem to include faster reaction time, increased perceptual ability, more effective interaction with the environment, superior perceptual-motor performance, and reduced use of prescribed and nonprescribed drugs" (p. 255).

STUDY SKILL 14
Using Progressive Muscle Relaxation

Progressive muscle relaxation involves alternately tensing and relaxing each muscle group on direction from a teacher or tape-recorded guide (Morris and Kratochwill 1983). Once trained in progressive muscle relaxation, students can initiate this procedure independently whenever they experience study-related anxiety. Use of progressive muscle relaxation, along with controlled breathing, promotes alertness, controls anxiety, and keeps the body healthy (Reed 1984; Matthews 1986).

Physical Fitness

While not all students can be star athletes, all can work to be physically fit individuals. Physical exercise enhances appearance and thus self-concept, and it also directly reduces stress. Pauk (1989) describes a study of college students who swam or jogged regularly. Swimmers and joggers reported decreases in tension, anxiety, depression, anger, and confusion, which presumably aided their study efforts.

STUDY SKILL 15
Getting Enough Exercise

Exercise helps strengthen the body, alleviates mental stress, and can be an enjoyable break from study tasks.

STUDY SKILL 16
Eating Nutritious Meals

What we eat and how much we eat are important to physical and mental functioning. Students need to eat appropriately to sustain their physical and mental energy. Students who start the day with a nutritious breakfast feel better and achieve more than those who skip breakfast. Eating too much, however, diverts energy needed for study to the demands of digesting the extra food. Even a moderate meal should not be eaten too soon before a study session or test because it slows down mental processes.

STUDY SKILL 17
Avoiding Harmful Substances

Researchers have found that middle and high school students who use drugs (i.e., alcohol, cigarettes, narcotics, etc.) have lower school grades than nonusers (Fors and Rojek 1983). Students who are dependent on drugs have reduced control over their emotional state and mental alertness and are not motivated to learn positive stress management skills. Continued abuse can lead to physical addiction and permanent mental deterioration.

Increasing evidence indicates that even nicotine, caffeine, and sugar, while providing temporary stress relief, may be addictive and physically damaging.

Positive Self-Concept

Solomon and Rothblum (1984) found that students who reported a tendency to procrastinate were also likely to report a fear of failure and an aversion to the tasks on which they procrastinated. This finding led them to recommend that students be taught not only time management skills, but also skills for dealing with fear of failure and perceived aversion to tasks. Such skills are treated here as aspects of developing a positive self-concept. Positive self-concept involves a sense that you have coped successfully with life's problems in the past, and confidence in your ability to cope with problems in the future.

STUDY SKILL 18
Accurate Self-Assessment

Students need to learn how to accurately assess their strengths and weaknesses and then develop ways to cope that capitalize on the strengths and minimize the weaknesses. They also need to be able to distinguish between evaluations of their performance and their basic worth as a human being. When students with a positive self-concept do more poorly on a school task than they expected or receive negative comments, they understand that these are isolated measures of their performance on certain tasks. They don't let these judgments interfere with their basic self-esteem, which remains relatively high and endures over time.

STUDY SKILL 19
Taking Responsibility for Your Learning

Researchers have found that students vary in their willingness to take responsibility for their own learning (Schmeck 1988). They also have found that students who perceive themselves as being in control of their own destiny, and responsible for their own learning, are more motivated to continue learning new skills (McCombs 1988). Self-responsibility is not simply a matter of willpower, however. It involves taking specific, goal-directed action. In their study of self-regulated learning strategies, Zimmerman and Pons (1986) found that low achievers made significantly more "reactive" and "willpower" statements than high achievers. Reactive statements indicated a lack of personal initiative. For example, when asked how he prepared for a test, a student responded, "I just do what the teacher tells me." Willpower statements were simple statements of resolve, such as "If I am having difficulty motivating myself to complete my homework, I just work harder." Despite probing, students who gave willpower statements identified no other specific strategies for learning, but "proposed to mobilize unspecified psychic forces to 'try harder.' "

Students who have developed self-responsibility refuse to accept that they are "victims" of circumstances such as their upbringing, prejudice, or inadequate teaching. Instead, they concentrate on taking action to change the conditions under their control. For example, if they are having difficulty in a class, they examine their options. Perhaps they can transfer to another class, seek help from a tutor or classmate, or devote more time to studying for the class. To become independent learners, students must learn to risk making decisions and live with the consequences of their own decisions (Slade 1986).

STUDY SKILL 20
Positive Thinking

Good problem solvers, while aware of their own shortcomings and the unpleasant aspects of school, focus on the positive aspects. For example, they choose to view a stressful encounter with another student as a challenge rather than a threat (Manzi 1986; Krantz 1983).

STUDY SKILL 21
Developing a Spiritual-Moral Viewpoint

One of the foundations of a positive self-concept appears to be a fairly well-developed spiritual, moral, or philosophical view of your own life and life in general. The particular viewpoint isn't important, only that it be sincere, carefully thought through, and actually used as a reference point for making decisions. A sense of humor, which allows students not to take life, or themselves, too seriously, appears to be an important element of a healthy life view (Cousins 1979).

Getting Help

Zimmerman and Pons (1986) found that high-achieving students seek help significantly more often than low-achieving students. The two groups' performance differed most when seeking help from teachers, but high achievers also sought assistance from other adults and from peers significantly more often.

Nelson-Le Gall and Glor-Scheib (1985) conducted an observation study of help seeking in elementary classrooms. They made a distinction between executive help seeking, in which the child's intention is to have someone else solve a problem or attain a goal for the child, and instrumental help seeking, in which the help requested is limited to whatever the child needs to solve a problem or attain a goal independently. Overall, children more frequently attempted to seek help from their classmates than from the teacher. Although most such peer exchanges were observed to be genuinely task focused, they were nonetheless discouraged by teachers. Also, peers were increasingly chosen as helpers with increasing grade level, despite teachers' discouragement of unauthorized peer interactions. Nelson-Le Gall and Glor-Scheib recommend that teachers examine whether classroom social norms of working alone, not disturbing others, and not talking to classmates are appropriate. In many instances, teachers might do better by encouraging students to seek instrumental help from each other during classroom learning activities.

One side benefit of seeking help is that it encourages students to communicate about their problems and feelings rather than suppressing or ignoring them. The high incidence of teenage suicide in our country suggests that teaching students to reach out for help with their problems, whether academic or personal in nature, is very important.

STUDY SKILL 22
Assessing the Need for Help

Some students ask for help too quickly and too often, showing dependency rather than a willingness to use their own resources effectively. Training in independence and self-responsibility is important for adolescents, particularly those who have learning disabilities (Schumaker, Deshler, and Ellis 1986).

Students need to learn how to first search for resources within themselves. If they find that they can't meet the challenge alone, however, they should be able to assess what help is available and request appropriate assistance.

STUDY SKILL 23
Identifying Sources of Help

Sources of help for students' problems are practically unlimited, but most students turn to people, books, or special courses.

Suppose a student's problem involves consistently handing in assignments late. Perhaps the student can talk to her parents to learn how they schedule their time to meet work deadlines. She could also read a self-help book on time management. Or she might take a study skills course that teaches time management skills.

Guidance counselors, teachers, relatives, and friends can often give students the help they need, or they can direct students to other sources of help. Students first need to feel comfortable about admitting that they need help. Then they can assess the kind of help they need, identify an appropriate source of help, and make a specific request.

STUDY SKILL 24
Initiating Requests for Help

The students who most need help are often the least willing to ask for it, perhaps because of embarrassment or a feeling that they "should" know what to do and that asking for help will reveal their inadequacy. Other students believe the guidance available is of little use to them. Benson (1989) conducted a survey of 8,000 students in grades 5 through 9 who are affiliated with one of a dozen religious denominations and found that

> one of the things the kids tell us is that the church becomes silent on some of the issues that they are really dealing with. What the kids are telling us is that they really want the church to help give them a perspective on the tough issues, the value issues, about chemicals and sex and friendship, questions about who I am. . . . Increasingly, we find kids telling us they get canned answers to those things, or very traditional answers that don't wash anymore (p. 33).

The findings of this study suggest that if educators want students to seek help for their problems, they must be prepared to work with them in ways that students perceive as helpful.

Methods for Teaching Self-Management Skills

Teachers spend considerable time attempting to motivate students—for example, by providing sanctions for nonperformance and rewards to recognize achievement. If they taught students self-management skills, however, students would be better able to develop and sustain their own motivation when facing difficult or seemingly boring study tasks. Thus, the remainder of this chapter provides suggestions for teaching the self-management skills we have described. These teaching methods are listed in Figure 4.2.

Organizing Study Materials and Space

Make use of a three-ring binder a schoolwide requirement. Because the binder system is simple to set up, it can be introduced at an early grade level and used with students of widely different abilities. The *Study for Success Teacher's Manual* (Gall and Gall 1988b) contains a set of lesson plans that teachers can use to teach this system to their students.

Teach students how to organize their desk. Slade (1986) found that giving learning-disabled students lessons in organizing their desk and classroom supplies enabled them to learn more complex organizational skills. He recommends that teachers actively question students for ideas about how to organize their desk so that paper, pencils, and other supplies are always close at hand.

Teachers can make organization a game, setting aside five minutes before recess for students to practice retrieving specified items or recording the amount of time it takes students to place certain items in their desks. They can follow up the activity with a question such as "How can we improve our time?" This lesson can be followed by lessons on organizing books, computer disks, and other materials in the classroom. Scheduling "clean-up" time at the end of each classroom activity is another way to encourage organizational skills.

Teach students to organize a home study space. Once students have learned how to organize materials at school, teachers should help them transfer this skill to their home study space, emphasizing that a study space improves concentration and provides a set place to store study materials. Some students may not have a regular study space, so teachers might begin the lesson by asking where students study at home. A good activity for younger students is to ask them to draw a picture of where they study at home.

Teachers can ask students to brainstorm a list of the necessary equipment for a study space (desk or table, lamp, bookcase, etc.) They can give students a time limit for setting up a study space at home and ask them to bring a drawing, photograph, or written description of the space when it has been set up. A subsequent lesson might deal with the materials that are kept in a study space—for example, paper and pencils, typewriter, dictionary. For older students, the teacher can present a lesson about filing materials for later reference.

Figure 4.2

Methods for Teaching Self-Management Skills

ORGANIZING STUDY MATERIALS AND SPACE

1. Make use of a three-ring binder a schoolwide requirement.
2. Teach students how to organize their desk.
3. Teach students how to organize a home study space.
4. Provide incentives.
5. Encourage parent involvement.

MANAGING TIME

1. Teach students how to use an assignment sheet.
2. Teach students how to schedule time.
3. Teach students how to break a large task into small tasks.
4. Show students the connection between their goals and their study efforts.
5. Provide incentives.
6. Encourage parent involvement.

MANAGING STRESS

General Procedures

1. Provide study periods.
2. Provide a school lunch program.
3. Provide opportunities for recess and physical education.
4. Provide opportunities for extracurricular activities.
5. Provide opportunities for counseling.
6. Provide a pleasant physical environment.
7. Provide a nonstressful school climate.

Teaching Activities

1. Promote good health habits.
2. Teach relaxation, meditation, and breathing techniques.
3. Offer instruction in positive thinking, personal problem solving, and self-esteem.
4. Use focusing exercises.
5. Provide incentives.
6. Encourage parent involvement.

GETTING HELP

Teaching Activities

1. Provide information about school services.
2. Use cooperative learning methods.
3. Teach a process for seeking help.
4. Encourage students to form study groups.

Teachers should discuss the problems of sharing study space or materials with other family members and the importance of keeping distractions (TV, noise, clutter) to a minimum. Students should learn that materials need to be organized and the space cleaned regularly. A diagram showing a cluttered study space and the same space after organization might be handed out. Teachers can also point out that high-achieving students regularly use "environmental restructuring" techniques such as these as a study strategy (Zimmerman and Pons 1986).

Provide incentives. Teachers can do spot checks of students' desks and binders or develop a checklist that students can use to evaluate their own, or other students', desk and binder organization. Points, praise, or a tangible reward can be given to students who have well-organized binders and desks. The entire class can be given a reward for keeping classroom files neat and orderly.

Encourage parent involvement. To gain parental support, teachers need to make specific requests of parents through newsletters, workshops, or other communications. Several researchers describe ways to help parents provide a home study space for their children (Duckett 1983; Quarg 1982; and Gall and Gall 1985). Some of their methods address the problem of a small living space or a shared study area. The teacher might request that parents do a room-by-room home survey, perhaps with the student, to rate their organization and consider specific ways that it might be improved. Even if the parents themselves do not do study-type work, they can provide a positive model by neatly storing such things as food, clothing, and tools in their home.

Good organization requires regular attention: throwing out unneeded materials, returning materials to their designated storage location, and so forth. Teachers can ask parents to help their children learn to clean their study space and sort study materials regularly.

Time Management

Teaching Activities

Teach students to use an assignment sheet. An assignment sheet is a standard form on which students write their assignments on a continuing basis, either using one sheet for each class or writing assignments for all classes on a single sheet. When each assignment has been completed and handed in, the student checks it off on the assignment sheet. Teachers can check that students have recorded their homework assignments on the sheet, and parents can ask to see the sheet when their children return home. The teacher can also ask parents to initial the assignment sheet to indicate that they have seen the completed assignment.

For teaching students time management skills, emphasis should be placed on recording the date each assignment is given and the date it is due. For tests, teachers should emphasize that students be aware of the amount of time between when the test is announced and when it will be given. As the time passes between these two dates, the teacher can periodically announce in class the time remaining before the test. The teacher should ask questions to determine whether students have scheduled time for working on an assignment or reviewing for a test. Teachers might even distribute a blank schedule form as part of each assignment and work with students in class to help them establish a schedule for carrying out the assignment.

Teach students to schedule time. Teachers can devote a lesson or series of lessons to teaching students how to schedule study time. A weekly schedule can be filled out in class at the beginning of the term as a general model. Teachers might then periodically ask students whether they are keeping to their schedule and what problems they are having with the schedule. Students can be given help in revising their schedule as needed.

Teach students to break a large task into small tasks. Teachers can assist students in breaking the large task (project completion) into small, manageable tasks and setting a schedule for completing each one. For example, for the task of writing a research report, one of the authors guided a class of eighth graders in defining each subtask (read three sources, take source notes, make an outline, draft the report, get feedback, revise). Then, working back from the due date, students were asked to set their own schedule for completing each subtask.

As work on the project proceeds, teachers should ask students how well they are keeping to their schedule. They should also demonstrate replanning, that is, how to change a schedule when tasks take less or more time than expected.

Show students the connection between their goals and their study efforts. Students need help in seeing the relationship between school success, effort, and their own long-term goals. Having students develop a budget for living on their own once they leave school often shows them just how important their education can be. Generally, students find that they need two to three times what they could earn in an entry-level job to support the lifestyle they expect to have. If they propose getting higher-paying blue-collar jobs (e.g., in forestry, mining, etc.), teachers can provide statistics about layoff, injury, and disability rates in such jobs. If students propose entering the military, teachers can provide information showing the increased level of education that the military now expects of recruits. These lessons help students develop a realistic picture of how important their efforts in school are to achieving their long-term goals.

Provide incentives. Rewards are far more effective than negative incentives in shaping students' behavior. For example, students who are in class on time can have points added to their grade or receive a tangible reward (stickers, certificates, or coupons for the school store).

Encourage parent involvement. Teachers should send letters or newsletters to parents asking them to help their children develop time management skills. The following are examples of ways that parents can help:

a. *Providing study time.* Duckett (1983) recommends that parents provide a scheduled time for home study, with a definite beginning and end, and ensure that distractions and noise are kept to a minimum during that time. Quarg (1982) suggests that parents have children put aside one to two hours each night for studying. Parents should keep demands for home chores and family activities reasonable.

b. *Monitoring study.* Parents can make sure students complete assignments and, if necessary, help them schedule time for working on assignments.

c. *Modeling time management.* Parents can demonstrate and model techniques they use for managing their own time—for example, their system for keeping track of appointments (Gall and Gall 1985).

d. *Providing tools for time management.* Parents should consider buying their children a daily schedule book, a "To-Do" pad, or an assignment book, or perhaps helping children construct their own. They should also make sure that each child has an accurate watch and, if necessary, an alarm clock.

e. *Rewarding good time management.* Parents can praise or reward students for completing assignments and getting to class on time.

Managing Stress

General Procedures

Provide study periods. Giving students free time during the school day to handle study tasks is a positive stress-reduction technique. A study period provides extra time to prepare an assignment or review for a test and reduces stress by helping students engage in constructive study behavior. As long as students don't disturb others, they may benefit as much from using the study period to rest and "recharge their batteries" during the school day.

Provide a school lunch program. A good lunch helps students stay alert and learn more in their classes. The federal school lunch program in the United States currently feeds over 24 million students each day. An attempt has been made to reduce the proportion of fat, salt, and sugar in the meal and to sample from all four food groups (dairy, meat/protein, breads, and fruits/vegetables), while still appealing to students' palates.

Provide opportunities for recess and physical education. Play or recess periods are common in elementary school. In middle and high school, however, organized phys-ed classes usually replace recess as a time for vigorous activity, sports, fun, and socializing. Even if strategies for managing stress are not explicitly discussed in class, phys ed can reduce stress by helping students maintain fitness, alertness, and a positive self-concept.

Provide opportunities for extracurricular activities. School clubs, sports programs, and creative activities such as art and music can reduce stress by providing diversions from academic subjects and opportunities for exercise and creative expression. Such programs may be a source of stress, however, if they create excessive pressure to excel or take too much time away from schoolwork. Students need guidance in setting appropriate limits to their participation in extracurricular activities.

Provide opportunities for counseling. Most schools have counselors, social workers, or nurses whose duties include counseling students who have severe academic, health, or personal problems. Counselors can help students express pent-up feelings and teach them effective techniques for managing stress, such as those described by Lazarro and Stevic (1978), Jones and Nelson (1985), and Forman and O'Malley (1984).

Provide a pleasant physical environment. Conners (1983) observes that a school's physical environment can affect students' stress level and offers suggestions for designing the school's (and the individual classroom's) environment to minimize stress—for example, using screens between classroom activity areas to reduce visual distractions. Dunn and Dunn (1978) describe ways to arrange alternative classroom environments using stimuli such as food, heat, lighting, furnishings, and teaching materials in order to accommodate students' different learning styles.

Provide a nonstressful school climate. Sylwester (1983) suggests that schools can function as an effective stress-reduction agency by providing students with information and skills they may need to solve threatening problems later in life and by creating an environment that allows staff members to believe they are helping students. Teaching students study techniques that enable them to succeed in school and later in adult life will enable a school to meet both of these conditions.

Teaching Activities

Promote good health habits. A wealth of curriculum materials is available for teaching students about nutrition, weight control, and non-abuse of harmful substances. Such topics are commonly covered in health classes or in special programs taught by school nurses or public health professionals. Phys-ed teachers can contribute to students' health by teaching about lifelong exercise and physical fitness, as well as team sports.

Teach relaxation, meditation, and breathing techniques. Matthews (1986) has developed a K–12 stress management model designed to increase students' self-confidence, poise, worth, and wellness, while reducing anxiety and timidity and developing the ability to shape aggressiveness to positive ends. He also offers suggestions for involving parents in the program. *The Relaxation and Stress Reduction Workbook* (Davis et al. 1982) provides guidelines for using various strategies to reduce stress. Other relaxation programs are described in Chapter 8 of this book in relation to reducing test anxiety.

Offer instruction in positive thinking, personal problem solving, and self-esteem. Anderson (1981) has developed a comprehensive instructional program to raise children's self-esteem called "Thinking, Changing, Rearranging." Although it was originally designed for special student populations, it is effective with average students as well.

Why Can't Anyone Hear Me?, the text for the Self-Esteem/Teen Issues Program (Elchoness 1986), includes stories and metaphors designed to help teens and preteens substitute hope, positive actions, and the expression of feelings for frustration, anger, and blame. It is accompanied by the *Guide to Adolescent Enrichment*, which provides self-esteem, reading, writing, and relating exercises. Schools can offer instruction on solving personal problems common to many students. Handling job stress, for example, would be an appropriate topic in a vocational education or career education course.

Use focusing exercises. Exercises for keeping thoughts and visual attention on a task are fairly easy to devise. We suggest that teachers start with three simple exercises. First, students can learn to "bracket," which involves mentally drawing a screen between an object they're focusing on and intruding thoughts. Second, they can focus intensely on an interesting object in order to visualize and recall its details. And third, students can play the game "Pet Rocks," which involves remembering the characteristics of a rock and distinguishing it later from other, similar rocks. Such exercises help students learn to focus their attention on one thing while ignoring distractions.

Provide incentives. Teachers can recognize students for various behaviors that demonstrate good health habits, positive thinking, personal problem solving, and focused attention. Teachers also can reward personal qualities that contribute to a stress-free school climate. For example, a student who shows a positive attitude toward others can be given a certificate or acknowledged in some other way. Many school report cards have space for noting or rating students' personal qualities.

Encourage parent involvement. When asking parents to help children learn stress management strategies, teachers should first define the components of stress management and their value for students. Then it is possible to make a variety of specific suggestions, perhaps in a newsletter sent to parents:

• Parents could be encouraged to set and monitor a bedtime for each child, based on age guidelines for typical sleep requirements.

• Parents could be encouraged to prepare bag lunches and home meals that meet specific nutritional standards and to schedule meals so that students do not study with an overfull stomach.

• Parents could be encouraged to share with their children the strategies they use to control tension. They can also be reminded of the importance of modeling the kinds of behavior they expect from their children, and the value of frequent family talks about school. Teachers can suggest possible topics.

If schools expect parents to help children with their studying, they should give specific recommendations about the help parents can provide. Parents can *enrich* students' learning by providing outside-school experiences that build on what is being learned in school; *monitor* students' learning so that they know when students need help and what type of help they need; and *coach* students by providing additional instruction on what they are studying in school (Gall and Gall 1985).

Parent-Aided Homework (Harris 1983) is a behavior modification program designed to encourage parents' involvement in their child's homework. The program emphasizes parents' providing positive reinforcement to their children for successfully completed homework assignments. Parents enforce the agreed-on time limits and provide extra learning experiences and rewards.

Home-based contingency management systems require teachers to record special education students' behavior during the school day and send a report home with each child so that parents can give appropriate reinforcement (Schumaker, Hovell and Sherman 1977).

Getting Help

Teaching Activities

Provide information about school services. Many schools pass out written information about the school during the first week of classes. This information should include a description of the special services provided by counselors, the school nurse, and other helping professionals. It also can include a summary of suggested steps to take when students have school-related concerns, namely: identify the concern, assess your ability to handle it, determine possible sources of help, and make a request for help.

Use cooperative learning methods. Slavin (1982) describes six instructional methods that require students of all levels of performance to work in small groups toward a common goal. These methods encourage students to give help to their team members or ask for help from them as learning proceeds. Slavin maintains that cooperative learning produces academic as well as social benefits for students.

Teach a process for seeking help. One way to introduce instruction on getting help is to have students identify their concerns about school. Teachers might use a survey form (as discussed in Gall and Gall 1988b) on which students can check their most frequent concerns about school and schoolwork from a list provided. A survey develops students' awareness that they *do* have concerns about school and that such concerns are not unique to them. This awareness helps students accept their problems and their need for help. Following this step, the teacher can ask students how they can solve particular problems on their own. The problems can be actual or hypothetical. Class discussions can be held to generate solutions and assess their effectiveness.

To help students learn where to find help, teachers might develop a lesson where students are asked to select one of their concerns, identify a source of help, and make a request for help within a given time. Or teachers might ask students to keep a record of their study problems and how they solve them (Gall and Gall 1988b).

Students also must be taught how to use direct communication and specific requests to get help. Gorney-Krupshaw, Atwater, Powell, and Morris (1981) trained learning-disabled students in "recruiting attention for help" by using description, modeling, rehearsal, and feedback procedures. Following training, students showed substantial improvements in their ability to seek help when needed. Van Reusen (1985) reported success with a similar training program designed to encourage learning-disabled adolescents to use self-advocacy procedures in various situations, including the conference to develop an Individual Education Plan.

Encourage students to form study groups. While schools emphasize competition, study groups foster cooperation and getting and giving help so that all may achieve academic success. Teachers should help students organize after-school study groups.

Encourage parent involvement. Staff members can use parent workshops and newsletters to show parents how they can assist their children in learning help-getting skills. Students often turn to their parents when they have a school-related problem, and parents can be encouraged to be available when this happens. In this way, parents can reinforce the appropriateness of asking for help when needed. Besides being available for routine help like assistance with selecting a paper topic or reviewing for a test, parents should be ready to help in more critical situations, too, whether by handling the problem themselves or by helping their child obtain outside help. The school can send home a list of helping sources available in the school and community and ask that parents discuss these sources with their children either right away or when a problem arises.

Parents can demonstrate that they themselves also need and seek help on occasion. They can discuss some of their own help-getting strategies with their children, from hiring an accountant to prepare tax forms to going to a physical therapist or reading a self-help book before starting a diet or exercise program.

References

Anderson, J. (1981). *Thinking, Changing, Rearranging.* Eugene, Oreg.: Timberline Press.

Benson, P. (1989). *The Quicksilver Years.* New York: Harper and Row, Cited in Castelli, J., "Children Have Big Questions." Guam, U.S.A: *Pacific Daily News*, February 21, 1987, p. 33.

Broden, M., R. V. Hall, and B. Mitts. (1974). "The Effect of Self-Recording on the Classroom Behavior of Two Eighth-Grade Students." In *Self-Control: Power to the Person*, edited by M. J. Mahoney and C. E. Thoresen. Monterey, Calif.: Brooks/Cole.

Conners, D. A. (Winter 1983). "The School Environment: A Link to Understanding Stress." *Theory into Practice* 22, 1: 15–20.

Cousins, N. (1979). *Anatomy of an Illness as Perceived by the Patient: Reflections on Healing and Regeneration.* New York: Norton.

Davis, M., E. R. Eshelman, and M. McKay. (1982). *The Relaxation and Stress Reduction Workbook.* 2nd ed. Oakland, Calif.: New Harbinger.

Delucchi, J.J., W. D. Rohwer, Jr., and J. W. Thomas. (1987). "Study Time Allocation as a Function of Grade Level and Course Characteristics." *Contemporary Educational Psychology* 12: 365–380.

Duckett, J. C. (1983). "Helping Children Develop Good Study Habits: A Parents' Guide." ERIC Document Reproduction Service No. ED 24 00 61.

Dunn, R, and K. Dunn. (1978). *Teaching Students Through Their Individual Learning Styles.* Reston, Va.: Reston Publishing.

Elchoness, M. (1986). *Why Can't Anyone Hear Me? A Guide for Surviving Adolescence.* 2nd ed. Sepulveda, Calif.: Monroe Press.

Finian, M. (1988). "Predictors of Classroom Stress and Burnout Experienced by Gifted and Talented Students." *Psychology in the Schools* 25, 4: 392–405.

Forman, S. G., and P. L. O'Malley. (Winter 1984). "School Stress and Anxiety Interventions." *School Psychology Review* 13, 2: 162–170.

Fors, S. W., and D. G. Rojek. (1983). "The Social and Demographic Correlates of Adolescent Drug Use Patterns." *Journal of Drug Education* 13, 3: 205–222.

Gall, J. P., and M. D. Gall. (1985). *Help Your Son or Daughter Study For Success.* Eugene Oreg.: M. Damien.

Gall, M. D., and J. P. Gall. (1988a). *Making the Grade.* Rocklin, Calif.: Prima.

Gall, M. D., and J. P. Gall. (1988b). *Study for Success Teacher's Manual.* 3rd ed. Eugene, Oreg.: M. Damien.

Gorney-Krupshaw, B., J. Atwater, L. Powell, and E. K. Morris. (1981). "Improving Social Interactions Between Learning Disabled Adolescents and Teacher: A Child Effects Approach." Research Report No. 45. Lawrence, Kans.: University of Kansas, Institute for Research in Learning Disabilities.

Harris, J. R. (1983). "Parent-Aided Homework: A Working Model for School Personnel." *School Counselor* 31, 2: 171–176.

Johnston, L. D., and P. M. O'Malley. (1986). "Why Do the Nation's Students Use Drugs and Alcohol? Self-Reported Reasons from Nine National Surveys." *Journal of Drug Issues* 16, 1: 29–66.

Jones, C. J., and B. Nelson. (1985). "Helping Students with Problems: What Physical Educators Can Do." *Journal of Physical Education, Recreation & Dance* 56, 2: 50–51.

Karoly, P., and F. H. Kanfer. (1982). *Self Management and Behavior Change: From Theory to Practice.* New York: Pergamon Press.

Knutsen, E. S. (1978). "The Meaning of Meditation." In *The Holistic Health Handbook,* edited by E. Bauman, A. Brint, L. Piper, and P. Wright. Berkeley, Calif.: And/Or Press.

Krantz, S. E. (1983). "Cognitive Appraisals and Problem Directed Coping: A Prospective Study of Stress." *Journal of Personality and Social Psychology* 44: 638–643.

Lakein, A. (1973). *How to Get Control of Your Time and Your Life.* New York: Wyden.

Lazzaro, E., and R. Stevic. (Fall 1978). "Counselor Initiated Counseling: Can It Be of Benefit to Clients?" *Journal of Counseling Services* 2, 3: 6–13.

Manzi, P. A. (1986). "Cognitive Appraisal, Stress and Coping in Teenage Employment." *Vocational Guidance Quarterly* 34: 160–170.

Matthews, D. B. (February 22–26, 1986). "Stress Management Model for the Elementary/Middle/High School." Paper presented at the Annual Meeting of the Association of Teacher Educators. Atlanta, Ga. ERIC Document Reproduction Service No. ED 26 70 26.

McCombs, B. L. (1988). "Motivational Skills Training: Combining Metacognitive, Cognitive, and Affective Learning Strategies." In *Learning and Study Strategies,* edited by C. E. Weinstein, E. T. Goetz, and P. A. Alexander. San Diego, Calif.: Academic Press.

Morris, R. J., and T. R. Kratochwill. (1983). *Treating Children's Fears and Phobias.* New York: Pergamon.

Nelson-Le Gall, S., and S. Glor-Scheib. (1985). "Help Seeking in Elementary Classrooms: An Observational Study." *Contemporary Educational Psychology* 10: 58–71.

Patton, J. E., T. A. Stinard, and D. K. Routh. (1983). "Where Do Children Study?" *Journal of Educational Research* 76, 5: 280–286.

Pauk, W. (1989). *How to Study in College.* 4th ed. Boston: Houghton Mifflin.

Planned Parenthood Federation of America. (1986). "National Campaign to Reduce Teen Pregnancy." *Donor Dateline.*

Quarg, P., comp. (1982). "To Read or Not to Read: A Parent's Guide." Phoenix: Affiliation of Arizona Indian Centers, Inc. ERIC Document Reproduction Service No. ED 220 233.

Reed, S. (1984). "Stress: What Makes Kids Vulnerable?" *Instructor* 93, 9: 28–32.

Schmeck, R. R. (1988). "Individual Differences and Learning Strategies." In *Learning and Study Strategies,* edited by C. E. Weinstein, E. T. Goetz, and P. A. Alexander. San Diego, Calif.: Academic Press.

Schumaker, J. B., D. D. Deshler, and E. S. Ellis. (1986). "Intervention Issues Related to the Education of Learning Disabled Adolescents." In *Psychological and Educational Perspectives on Learning Disabilities*. San Diego, Calif.: Academic Press.

Schumaker, J. B., M. Hovell, M., and J. Sherman. (1977). "An Analysis of Daily Report Cards and Parent Managed Privileges in the Improvement of Adolescents' Classroom Performance." *Journal of Applied Behavior Analysis* 10: 449–464.

Slade, D. L. (1986). "Developing Foundations for Organizational Skills." *Academic Therapy* 21, 3: 261–266.

Slavin, R. E. (1982). "Cooperative Learning: Student Teams. What Research Says to the Teacher." Washington, D.C.: National Education Association.

Solomon, L. J., and E. D. Rothblum. (1984). "Academic Procrastination: Frequency and Cognitive-Behavioral Correlates." *Journal of Counseling Psychology* 31, 4: 503–509.

Sylwester, R. (1983). "The School as a Stress Reduction Agency." *Theory into Practice* 22, 1: 3–6.

Toufexis, A. (January 26, 1987). "Getting an F for Flabby." *Time* 4: 36–37.

Van Reusen, A. K. (1985). "A Study of the Effects of Training Learning Disabled Adolescents in Self Advocacy Procedures for Use in the IEP Conference." Doctoral diss., University of Kansas, Lawrence. 46/10, p. 3000-A; *Dissertation Abstracts* order #852969.

Wittrock, M. C. (1988). "A Constructive Review of Research on Learning Strategies." In *Learning and Study Strategies*, edited by C. E. Weinstein, E. T. Goetz, E.T., and P. A. Alexander. San Deigo, Calif.: Academic Press.

Zimmerman, B. J., and M. M. Pons. (1986). "Development of a Structured Interview for Assessing Student Use of Self-Regulated Learning Strategies." *American Educational Research Journal* 23, 4: 614–628.

5

Listening, Participating, and Taking Notes in Class

It's easy to assume that students know how to listen, take notes, and participate in class. Teachers simply may not see the need to "teach" listening, a skill that children seem to develop naturally before they enter school. And they may figure that as students learn how to write they also learn how to take notes, or naturally recognize how to participate effectively in learning activities. Unfortunately, this is not the case.

Listening, note taking, and class participation are some of the most neglected of all the skills taught in school, despite research that shows they are among the most important basic study skills. Conaway (1982) found listening comprehension to be a primary factor in college students' achievement and retention: "Among students who fail, deficient listening skills were a stronger factor than reading skills or academic aptitude." In their study of college students, Palmatier and Bennett (1974) found that 75 percent of students who failed courses had never before taken notes. In contrast, they found that 99 percent of the high-performing students took lecture notes; surprisingly, only 17 percent of them had received any instruction in note taking. Palmatier and Bennett concluded, "literally no one teaches note-taking skills" (1974, p. 217).

In this chapter we discuss the study skills involved in listening, taking notes, and participating in class, and how they can be improved. We analyze why these skills are important for students and identify the specific skills that students need. Finally, we present methods and strategies that teachers can use to teach these skills.

Listening

Almost everyone, young and old, spends more time listening than reading, speaking, or writing (Devine 1978). It should be welcome news, then, that awareness of the importance of listening is greater than ever before in American society. At the national level, the current focus on basic skills education has heightened interest in listening instruction. In 1978, the

Primary-Secondary Education Act (Public Law 95-561) was amended to include listening among the basic competencies for which elementary and secondary schools are responsible. In 1983, two national task forces—the National Commission on Excellence in Education and the Task Force on Education for Economic Growth—emphasized the need for instruction in listening (Swanson 1984). Mortimer Adler, in *The Paideia Proposal* (1982), included listening as one of the skills that everyone needs in order to learn. The College Board also identified listening as one of six basic competencies that students need to be successful in college (Steil 1984). The United States is not alone in recognizing the importance of listening. In 1979, educators from more than a dozen nations formed the International Listening Association to promote the worldwide study and development of effective listening.

Effective listening involves more than just hearing words. It includes active processing, such as making efforts to appreciate, comprehend, and evaluate the speaker's message (Wolvin and Coakley 1979). In school and in most work settings, we are usually listening to comprehend spoken messages. In fact, children's success in school depends directly on their ability to listen, because listening is the main channel of classroom instruction. Wolvin (1984) found that, on average, listening is the main task expected of students during 58 percent of class time in elementary school, 46 percent of class time in high school, and 42 percent of class time in college. In some high school and college classes, students may spend as much as 90 percent of their time listening to lectures and discussions (Barker 1971).

The importance of listening is described dramatically by Friedmann:

> When students enter a classroom for the first time, they look to the teacher and wait for the messages that will tell them what to expect. Simultaneously, the teacher is sizing them up. Each is alert, attentive, listening. From that moment on, they will spend most of their time together trying to gain and hold each other's attention, striving to understand and be understood, determining where they stand with each other, silently judging and evaluating—in short, they will be concerned with listening (1986, p. 6).

Teachers use class time to conduct a variety of learning activities that require students to listen. We group these activities into two categories: (1) listening and taking notes and (2) participating in class.

Listening and Taking Notes

The teacher's primary task in the classroom is to impart information and provide instructions to students by talking to them. Students, in turn, are to listen so that they will comprehend and remember what they hear (Swanson 1984; Friedmann 1986).

Even if students listen well, however, they can't rely on memory alone to remember information presented orally in class. Forgetting begins immediately. Students typically remember less than half of a lecture at the end of a 55-minute class; one week later, their recall of the lecture drops to just 17 percent (McLeish 1976). Taking notes helps students retrieve and reorganize information in long-term memory for use in criterion tasks, such as taking tests.

Over the years, Hartley and Davies (1978), Kiewra (1985), Ladas (1980), and Jacobsen (1989) have reviewed experiments that compared taking notes in class with just listening to the teacher. They generally concluded that taking notes is more effective than just listening to the teacher. Jacobsen (1989) found a strong positive correlation between the number of critical lecture points that high school students recorded in their notes and their scores on a subsequent achievement test on the lecture. Several of the reviewers observed that students who took notes usually did not receive training in note-taking skills. Had they received training, taking notes probably would have been found to be even more effective.

There are four teacher activities that require students to listen and take notes:

1. *Explaining important concepts in assigned readings.* Teachers usually have a sense of the problems students will encounter in reading assignments and try to help by talking about certain concepts in simpler or different terms than are used in the text. The teacher may lecture, show a TV or film documentary, or invite a guest speaker to talk to the class. In these situations, students need to concentrate on the meaning of the message, not the speaker or the language being used, so that comprehension is as complete as possible. Much of the educational process involves this kind of listening (Wolvin and Coakley 1979). In addition, students must decide whether they should take notes, either because their teacher requires it or because their understanding of the material is not good.

2. *Presenting information not included in the textbook.* Teachers often present information that is not found in students' textbooks. The text may not cover a particular topic adequately, so the teacher supplements it with additional information, or the text may be out of date, so the teacher presents more recent information. Or the teacher may wish to stimulate interest by adding marginally important but colorful information to a topic that is treated blandly in the textbook.

In each of these situations, teachers present information for what they believe are sound educational reasons, not simply to pile on work (Gage and Berliner 1988). Often this information is presented in a conversational manner; students must not only listen carefully to comprehend the information, they must also determine whether they will be held responsible for it later and should take notes.

3. *Conducting demonstrations.* Teachers conduct demonstrations in virtually all subject areas to illustrate or clarify concepts and principles or to discover concepts and principles. We normally associate demonstrations with the natural sciences (e.g., a science teacher demonstrating the concept of density by suspending a variety of objects of equal size but different mass in water), but demonstrations are found in other subject areas as well. A social science teacher may have a guest speaker talk about a foreign culture and demonstrate artifacts from it, or a language arts teacher may give a speech demonstrating the effects of emotionally loaded vocabulary. Again, students need to listen to grasp the significance of the demonstration and, if necessary, take notes.

4. *Explaining assignments.* Teachers make assignments virtually every day of the week. They are the principal means by which teachers evaluate student learning. In view of their importance, students need to pay special attention when the teacher announces an assignment and explains the procedures for completing it.

Students should develop an awareness of the way their teachers typically make assignments. For example, some teachers like to make assignments at the beginning of class when students are fresh and alert; other teachers prefer to wait until the end of class. In the latter case, students need to remain especially alert in case the teacher runs out of time to make an adequate explanation. Some teachers supply explicit, perhaps even written, instructions with their assignments. The fortunate students of these teachers probably will not need to take any additional notes. But many busy teachers rely on spoken instructions that can leave students unsure about what they are expected to do unless they listen carefully and take notes (Evertson and Emmer 1982).

Participating in Class

Many of the activities that teachers conduct in class require students to participate actively in their learning by rehearsing and applying information they have acquired from lectures and readings. In these situations, students must listen carefully and respond appropriately either as individuals or as members of a group. Typically, teachers expect students to participate in five kinds of activities.

1. *Answering teachers' questions.* In most classrooms, a great deal of time is spent in question-and-answer activity (recitation). Teachers ask questions to find out how much students know and to give them an

opportunity to rehearse, interpret, and apply what they do know. Research shows that teacher questioning has a positive effect on student achievement (Gall 1984). Students participate either by answering questions or by listening to other students' answers.

Good teachers employ questioning strategies that require students to demonstrate different levels of knowledge. For example, teachers ask literal questions to determine students' factual knowledge, interpretive questions to determine students' ability to integrate this information and make inferences from it, and applied questions to determine their ability to use this information to express opinions and form new ideas. To participate successfully in recitation, students must respond with an answer of the appropriate cognitive level (Dillon 1982). If students respond incorrectly or are unable to respond at all, they must realize that they need to take action to clear up their confusion. One way to do this might be to ask questions of the teacher or of other students.

2. *Seatwork.* Teachers assign seatwork to give students practice in using and applying new information and skills (Rosenshine 1980) and to improve their understanding and retention of new information. Typically, students complete a written exercise of some kind, such as a handout, a section in a workbook, problems in a math text, or questions at the end of a chapter. This additional exposure and practice usually helps students learn more because it requires them to actively participate in their learning (Fisher et al. 1980).

Students need to learn to make efficient use of seatwork time and process information appropriately. They must learn how to monitor their understanding of information and get immediate help from the teacher if they do not understand something. Many teachers allow students to start their "homework" during seatwork, so teachers also need to learn that the more they get done in class, the less homework they will have to do later.

3. *Inquiry.* Teachers use inquiry methods to help students build higher-order thinking skills. Although the inquiry method is often associated with science, it lends itself readily to other subjects (Joyce and Weil 1986). A language arts teacher may have students examine newspaper headlines and then make generalizations about propaganda and persuasive techniques. An art class may examine magazine advertisements and make generalizations about the artistic principles being used. Literature teachers use inquiry techniques to draw conclusions about character or themes in poems and other works. In all of these cases, the teacher's purpose is not to present information but to develop students' thinking processes. Students must determine a meaningful pattern in an array of objects or information.

To profit from inquiry instruction, students must learn how to observe objects or events, detect patterns, and make inferences from them. In fact, students are frequently evaluated on their use of the process rather than on their conclusions (Orlich et al. 1990). They also must learn the value of persistent seeking and questioning. Because inferences must be supported by evidence, not wild guessing, students need to learn how to use their own observations to support their conclusions.

4. *Small-group discussions.* Teachers use small-group discussions in their classrooms to motivate students, improve their cooperative work skills, and increase their learning. Small-group discussions usually involve four to eight students, each of whom has a responsibility to participate in the discussion in an appropriate manner. For example, discussion groups might analyze the theme of a short story, identify the potential consequences of a change in the environment, speculate on the reasons for a political decision, or explore the possible uses of a new discovery in science. Discussions of this kind involve a high degree of verbal interaction among students, individual responsibility, and independent learning.

To profit from discussion, students must learn how to think and express themselves, exchange ideas, and strive to maintain a cooperative atmosphere conducive to discussion (Gall and Gall 1976). Students also must be aware of instructions and rules that apply to discussion groups.

5. *Student presentations.* In-class presentations help students improve their thinking, speaking, and cooperative work skills, and presentations often require them to use higher-order cognitive skills. An oral report, for example, may require the student to synthesize large amounts of information into an overview that the audience can comprehend easily. Presentations involve the highest degree of student participation possible in the classroom. For a few minutes, the individual student commands center stage and completely dominates the learning process. Students are judged on what they say as well as how they say it. Inevitably, presentations cause anxiety, which students need to learn how to control. They also must be aware of what the teacher expects in a presentation and be receptive to the help the teacher is willing to provide to make the presentation successful.

Skills for Listening, Participating, and Taking Notes

The 20 skills described here, and listed in Figure 5.1, are specific study skills that students must master in order to learn effectively from classroom instruction. They are applicable across a variety of modes of instruction: lecture, demonstration, recitation, inquiry, or seatwork. The first eight study skills relate to listening and participating in class, and the remaining study skills relate to taking notes.

Figure 5.1

Study Skills for Listening and Participating in Class

LISTENING AND PARTICIPATION SKILLS
1. Maintaining regular class attendance
2. Maintaining a positive attitude toward the teacher and the class
3. Reading assignments before class
4. Staying alert in class
5. Following the rules of good listening etiquette
6. Attempting to answer every teacher question
7. Asking questions when unsure about something
8. Using class time allotted for seatwork

NOTE-TAKING SKILLS
9. Taking notes when it is important to remember what the teacher is saying
10. Using teacher cues to guide note taking
11. Taking notes on definitions and examples
12. Taking notes on assignments and test dates
13. Taking paraphrase notes
14. Using abbreviations and symbols
15. Writing legible notes
16. Maintaining alertness at the end of class
17. Storing notes in a three-ring binder
18. Labeling and dating notes
19. Revising notes after class
20. Periodically reviewing notes

Listening and Participation Skills

STUDY SKILL 1
Maintaining Regular Class Attendance

Researchers have found that absenteeism is strongly related to poor school grades (DeJung and Duckworth 1985; McDill, Natriello, and Pallas 1985) and to dropping out of school (Quay and Allen 1982). Successful students attend class regularly and take advantage of the learning opportunities the classroom provides. The following are the most important reasons for attending class:

To comply with school rules. Students are required to attend class at every grade level. In fact, many teachers include attendance in students' grades. Thus, students must develop positive motivation toward school and effective self-management skills so that they attend their classes on a regular basis.

To meet learning expectations. Students who attend class regularly know what is expected of them at all times. They avoid the anxiety that results from not knowing what or how to do something that was explained in a class they missed, and they are able to plan ahead and exercise some control over their lives.

To get information the first time. Successful students go to class to hear what teachers have to say the first time they say it. They know that teachers usually explain things thoroughly the first time in class and less thoroughly thereafter because they are busy or unsympathetic to students who have missed class.

To get information firsthand. Successful students know that it is better to attend class and take their own notes than to borrow notes from another student. Borrowed notes reflect another person's thoughts and may contain errors or omissions.

To establish a regular routine for getting things done. Successful students know that they acquire skills and knowledge by accomplishing a little each day. Learning is deliberately broken down into parts that teachers present to students in segments that can be readily absorbed on a daily basis. Students who think they are getting out of work by cutting class deceive themselves because they have to make up the missed work, which means that they'll have more work to complete in less time. Moreover, in subjects such as math and foreign languages, learning is sequential, meaning that students must learn the missed material before they can move on to new material. Regular class attendance enables students to develop momentum and accomplish large tasks more easily.

To impress the teacher. Successful students know that good attendance impresses their teachers and helps to establish good relations with them. Teachers are more likely to make an extra effort to help students who attend class regularly.

STUDY SKILL 2
Maintaining a Positive Attitude Toward the Teacher and the Class

The first requirement of good listening is a good mental attitude toward the teacher and the subject being taught (Steil, Barker, and Watson 1983). Successful students know that teachers are there to make learning easier, not more difficult.

Nichols (1960) identified several behaviors that indicate a negative attitude toward instruction: calling a subject boring, criticizing the speaker's delivery, yielding to distractions, and faking attention. Each of these negative behaviors has a counterpart that indicates a positive attitude toward instruction. For example, instead of calling a subject boring, students can try to think of reasons why the subject, or certain aspects of the subject, might be interesting. Instead of criticizing the speaker's delivery, students can focus on the content of what is being said; and instead of yielding to distractions and faking attention, students can strive to maintain mental alertness.

STUDY SKILL 3
Reading Assignments Before Class

Completing reading assignments before class prepares students to take maximum advantage of classroom learning opportunities. Classroom activities and required readings are usually related. In some learning activities, such as question-answer sessions and discussion, students cannot participate successfully unless they first complete the reading assignment. In other learning activities, such as lectures and demonstrations, students may be able to get by without doing the reading first, but they make their learning harder.

Reading assignments before class gives students prior knowledge about the topic. This background knowledge, or schema, enables students to understand what the teacher is saying and increases their knowledge of the topic (Rumelhart 1980). Students who are already familiar with technical terms and concepts relevant to the topic find it easier to recognize important points and decide whether to record them in their notes. And their notes will be better organized and more accurate because they already have a general sense of how the topic is organized.

Finally, students who complete the readings before class relieve themselves of unnecessary worry about getting their work done on time.

STUDY SKILL 4
Staying Alert in Class

Successful students are alert to what goes on around them. They are aware that numerous stimuli compete for their attention at any given moment. Many of these stimuli are external, such as a dropped pencil, the teacher's voice, or street noises, while others are internal, such as daydreams, worries about grades, or plans for after school. Good listeners know how to focus on selected stimuli to the exclusion of everything else. In the classroom, this means attending to the teacher's verbal messages and making an appropriate response, such as taking notes, answering a question, or asking a question (Steil, Barker, and Watson 1983).

Attending requires effort. It is an active, rather than passive, process (Pearson and Fielding 1983). Swanson (1984) observed that the eyes, face, body, and mouth all contribute to the process of listening. The listener's eyes, alert for nonverbal cues, focus on the speaker. Facial expressions, such as thoughtfulness, puzzlement, or delight, indicate the listener's response to the speaker's message and show that the listener is following along with the speaker. And sitting upright while leaning slightly forward helps listeners move and respond to the speaker.

STUDY SKILL 5
Following the Rules of Good Listening Etiquette

Successful students practice good listening etiquette. McKibben (1982) recommends several listening behaviors that please teachers and build a solid basis for effective listening. Some of these listening behaviors are similar to other study skills in this section, but they are repeated here to emphasize their contribution to good etiquette:

1. Be on time for class and appointments.
2. Be ready to begin when class begins.
3. Be prepared to participate.
4. Be visible.
5. Turn in assignments on time.
6. Make an appointment to ask questions about personal matters.
7. Do not expect extra help if you have cut class.
8. Do not try to be the class clown.
9. Do not start getting ready to leave until the teacher is finished.
10. Do not ask questions that annoy teachers.

STUDY SKILL 6
Attempting to Answer Every Teacher Question

Answering teachers' questions enables students to check whether they understand the content they are supposed to be learning. It also provides valuable practice in rehearsing answers to questions that are likely to appear on tests.

Successful students attempt to answer questions that are addressed to other students as well as to themselves. Unfortunately, many students fail to take advantage of this opportunity to check their understanding and practice forming answers to questions. Some students are so shy or unsure of themselves that they say they don't know the answer even when they do know it. Or, if the teacher calls on another student, they breathe a sigh of relief and start thinking about something else. Silently answering someone else's question requires willpower and careful listening, but it pays off by filling gaps in knowledge.

STUDY SKILL 7
Asking Questions When Unsure About Something

Good students recognize that they need to ask questions when they do not understand something or cannot complete an assignment or answer a question in class. For example, students may lack the background knowledge needed to answer a question. Or they may have adequate knowledge, but fail to understand the question as phrased. In either case, students need to be able to ask the teacher for information or clarification.

STUDY SKILL 8
Using Class Time Allotted for Seatwork

Using class time allotted for seatwork enables students to monitor their understanding of information and to get immediate help from the teacher if they do not understand something. It may also reduce the amount of homework they'll have to do later.

Note-Taking Skills

STUDY SKILL 9
Taking Notes at Appropriate Times

Students do not need to take notes on everything that is said in class. The key decision students need to make is whether information will be needed later—for an upcoming test or class project or for personal interest. There is a twofold judgment involved here: (1) students must be able to distinguish between important and unimportant information and (2) they must decide whether they already know the information or whether it is new to them.

Students should always be prepared to take notes on formal discussions. Although some class discussions may seem aimless and hard to follow, most are planned learning activities, and good discussion leaders usually have in mind a number of points that they want to raise and explore with the class. Discussion notes may be especially helpful when students are assigned tasks that require critical thinking—for example, writing a paper that expresses and defends an opinion.

There are also less obvious instructional situations in which taking notes may be desirable, such as informal discussions that arise when someone asks a question. A question that is troubling one student may be troubling others, and the ensuing discussion will provide valuable clarification that can be noted.

Study Skill 10
Using Teacher Cues to Guide Note Taking

Students should be alert for signals and cues that teachers provide to help them listen and take notes. Some teachers are aware that many students, especially younger ones, are not proficient at taking notes, and they try to present their remarks in a manner that is easy to follow. Sometimes they speak from prepared notes to ensure that the lesson doesn't wander. They also use a variety of verbal and nonverbal signals to guide students through the lecture (Wolvin and Coakley 1985). Examples of such signals are emphasis words (e.g., "the chief cause was ..."), transitions (e.g., "now let's look at ..."), enumerations (e.g., "there are five characteristics of..."), repetitions ("let me remind you that ..."), as well as nonverbal movements and gestures. Teachers also use the blackboard, overhead transparencies, and handouts to emphasize and help organize topics that were covered orally. Students who are alert to these signals of importance find it much easier to detect the pattern in teachers' remarks and to organize their notes accordingly.

Study Skill 11
Taking Notes on Definitions and Examples

Students should pay particular attention to the specialized vocabulary used in their courses and take notes on any terms that are defined or illustrated by their teachers. These terms represent the important concepts in their courses and are the language teachers use when talking about their subjects. In introductory courses, teachers often spend considerable time defining and illustrating terms because they are critical to understanding the subject. Students should record teachers' definitions and examples in order to develop expertise in the subject as early as possible.

Study Skill 12
Taking Notes on Assignments and Test Dates

Assignments and test dates that are announced in class should be recorded along with other important information. Students can put a large "A" for "assignment" and a large "T" for "test" in the margin to draw attention to this information. If students wish, they can transfer this information later to an assignment/test log.

STUDY SKILL 13
Taking Paraphrase Notes

Students shouldn't try to make a verbatim record of everything said in class. Teachers usually speak at a rate of 125–150 words per minute (Wolvin and Coakley 1985), which makes it virtually impossible to record a teacher's exact words. Some students decide to make the effort anyway and usually find themselves with voluminous notes that are difficult to maintain and review.

Study skills experts recommend that students capture teachers' ideas and information in their own words as succinctly as possible. Researchers (e.g., Fisher and Harris 1973; Locke 1977; Bretzing and Kulhavy 1979; Kiewra 1984) have found that paraphrase notes are effective if they stress the main ideas of teachers' lectures rather than specific details. Vivid or striking words and phrases that teachers use should be recorded, if possible, because these will help students reconstruct lessons later (Rickards and Friedman 1978).

STUDY SKILL 14
Using Abbreviations and Symbols

To gain more time for listening and writing, students need to develop skill in using abbreviations and symbols for common words and recurring terms. They should avoid using so many symbols that they become confused when reviewing their notes. If necessary, students can put a key or glossary at the top of the first page of notes as a reminder of what the symbols mean.

STUDY SKILL 15
Writing Legible Notes

Deciphering illegible notes diverts valuable time and energy from other study tasks. Notes should be clear enough to make sense days or weeks later. Students whose cursive writing is hopelessly inefficient should consider adopting the modified printing method recommended by Pauk (1989). Simply using a ballpoint pen instead of a pencil can also make notes easier to read and more permanent, as can taking notes on only one side of a sheet of paper. Notes written on both sides often show through on the opposite side, making both sides difficult to read. Taking notes on only one side enables students to spread out notes from related class sessions and see the progression of ideas and information.

STUDY SKILL 16
Maintaining Alertness at the End of Class

In many courses, the last few minutes of class are more important than any other time. Teachers wrap up ideas and make last-minute assignments, sometimes forcing a lot of information into a little bit of time. Unfortunately, many students are not alert at this time. Ladas (1980) has found that concentration and quality of notes decline rapidly after the first half hour of class.

During the last few minutes of class, students should make an extra effort to remain alert and attentive to what the teacher is saying. They should take notes as rapidly as they can, and remain after class a few extra minutes, if possible, in order to record as much information as they can remember.

STUDY SKILL 17
Storing Notes in a Three-Ring Binder

Of the study skills reviewed in this chapter, this is the one most often taught in elementary and secondary schools. Students can keep a supply of punched paper in the binder, take sheets out as needed, and then place them back in the binder in the desired location. They can also keep their notes and related teacher handouts in sequence, making it easier to find and review material for class sessions over a period of time. Thus, if students know that an upcoming test will cover class material over the preceding two weeks, they can review their notes in sequence for that period of time.

STUDY SKILL 18
Labeling and Dating Notes

A simple, but nonetheless important, study skill is to record the course name and date at the top of the page prior to the start of class, which helps students focus and begin concentrating on the upcoming class session. After class, they can file the notes easily in the proper place in their binder.

STUDY SKILL 19
Revising Notes After Class

During class, students shouldn't worry about organizing their notes since there usually isn't enough time in class to organize notes into a neat pattern. The organization adopted in class can be changed later, when there is more time to reflect on the ideas in the notes.

For most students, the best way to record notes initially is in paragraph form. Lines can be skipped to separate one major idea from another. Facts and examples can be indented and enumerated under the major ideas.

The Cornell method for revising notes is widely recommended by study skills experts (e.g., Pauk 1989). Students will need loose-leaf note-paper that has an extra-wide left margin ("legal ruled" or "summary ruled" paper). The right column of the notepaper is used in class to take notes and the left column is used for reviewing the notes. Jacobsen (1989) found that this method is effective in improving the academic performance of high school students, especially those of low ability.

The first step in using the Cornell method is for students to read over and revise their right-column notes as soon as possible after class, while memory of the lecture is still fresh. They can rewrite illegible words, correct spelling, insert punctuation, add or delete words, and improve the organization of the notes, if necessary, by numbering or labeling them to show the relationship between main points and supporting details, as well as the relationship among main points. They can conclude their revision by writing a brief summary of the lesson.

After revising the notes, students should use the wide margin on the left side of the page to write key words, short phrases, questions, or symbols that summarize the main idea and pull together important facts from the right side of the page. The left column should contain cues that help students recall the information in the right column (see Gall and Gall 1988 for an example of a completed set of lecture notes that contain many such cues).

In generating left-column cues, students should reread and reflect on the information in the right column so that they can create cues that will help them recall the information later (Craik and Lockhart 1972; Pauk 1989).

STUDY SKILL 20
Periodically Reviewing Notes

Researchers have conducted many experiments to determine the effectiveness of periodically reviewing notes. Hartley and Davies (1978), Kiewra (1985), and Jacobsen (1989) examined the results of these experiments and concluded that students who review their notes perform significantly better on achievement tests than students who do not review their notes. The Cornell method of taking notes allows students to test themselves by covering the right column, reading a left column cue, and then trying to remember the information recorded in the right column.

Of course, reviewing notes helps students learn only when they have recorded critical lecture points in their notes. Notes are the only record of what was discussed during class. Unless the teacher distributed a handout summarizing the lecture, students have to rely on their own or others' notes to review that information. The quality of the review process depends on students' ability to use all of the other note-taking skills described earlier.

Teaching Listening, Participation, and Note-Taking Skills

In this section, we describe methods that can be used to teach students the study skills involved in classroom listening, participation, and note taking. The methods are listed in Figure 5.2

Figure 5.2

Methods for Teaching Listening, Participation, and Note-Taking Skills

LISTENING AND PARTICIPATION SKILLS

1. Develop a schoolwide listening program.
2. Promote listening across the curriculum.
3. Model listening skills in the classroom.
4. Provide training in listening skills.
5. Provide training in participation skills.

NOTE-TAKING SKILLS

6. Provide support for the note-taking process.
7. Model the note-taking process.
8. Provide training in note-taking skills.

Methods for Teaching Listening

Develop a schoolwide listening program. Schools can improve listening skills by providing support for a schoolwide listening program. Lundsteen (1984) recommends that, before investing in an expensive program, school districts do a needs assessment to find out what is already being done in the schools to improve listening skills. The results can be used to involve administrators in the listening program and to plan related inservice activities.

Creating public awareness is an important aspect of a schoolwide listening program. Schools, even entire districts, can advance listening awareness by making a public commitment to listen by, for instance, adopting a motto or slogan, as private businesses and corporations some-times do, to indicate to the public that they value what it has to say (Steil 1984). A motto as simple as "We Listen" can effectively model the value of listening and inspire confidence in students, parents, and the public that educators are responsive to their concerns.

Schools also can coordinate their listening education program with those of larger organizations that advocate effective listening. In Oregon, for example, many schools and colleges plan listening activities for the state's official Listening Awareness Day, held every March.

Promote listening across the curriculum. The establishment of listening instruction across the curriculum is central to a schoolwide listen-ing program. If listening is treated as an isolated language arts skill, it risks being subordinated to other important skills, such as reading and writing. However, much of the responsibility for implementing listening education can be carried out by English and language arts teachers, for whom listening skills are a special concern. They can exchange teaching methods, training experiences, and materials with other content area teachers.

A particularly effective method for teaching listening across the cur-riculum is to integrate listening instruction with the process approach to teaching writing, which involves using writing response groups. The suc-cess of these groups depends on good small-group communications, for which listening skills are essential.

Model listening skills in the classroom. One of the best ways for teachers to help students learn listening skills is to model their use by listening carefully to what students say in the classroom. To be an effective model of listening, however, teachers themselves are likely to need training in listening skills, as Steil (1977) found in his survey of secondary educators.

Some of the groundwork for training teachers in listening skills can begin with preservice programs. Lundgren and Shavelson (1974) found that systematic instruction in listening significantly improved the listening skills of preservice teachers.

Once teachers have gained some experience in the classroom, they can enhance their listening skills through inservice training in the use of indirect teaching strategies (McCaleb 1980). Many beginning teachers, lacking the confidence and listening skills to use these methods effectively, rely on direct methods of instruction, such as lecturing, which emphasize teacher presentation behaviors while limiting interaction with learners. Indirect methods of instruction, such as discussion and inquiry, provide an opportu-nity for students to express themselves while the teacher listens.

Provide training in listening skills. Rubin (1985) recommends that all elementary and secondary students be required to take a course in oral communication that covers interpersonal communication skills, such as

---

small-group decision making, and communication functions, such as imagining, describing, and expressing emotions. Relevant listening skills should be taught in the context of each of these skills and functions.

Another way to teach effective listening directly is by using oral communication exercises recommended by listening specialists. Wolvin and Coakley (1979) describe 38 exercises that develop students' listening awareness and skills. A typical exercise is the one called "If I Had a Million Dollars." It lets students at all grade levels practice attentive listening by recalling items in a sequence. Students sit in a circle. The first student begins by saying, "If I had a million dollars, I'd buy . . ." (whatever the student desires). The second student repeats what the first student said and adds another item. Succeeding students continue to add items after first repeating the previous students' items. The exercise stops when someone forgets an item and breaks the chain.

Following the breakdown of the chain, the teacher should discuss with the class how many repetitions were made before the chain broke down, whose item was forgotten, and how difficult it was to concentrate.

Wolvin and Coakley also include exercises to help students become aware of the types of nonverbal messages they communicate, determine word meanings by means of contextual clues, appreciate oral interpretation of literature, and understand the importance of good listening in their planned vocations.

The *Study for Success Teacher's Manual* (Gall and Gall 1988b) includes a lesson that teachers can use to help students develop "active listening" skills. Students use a survey form to rate their use of listening skills. Examples of questions on the form are: Do you come to class prepared? Do you ask questions in class? Do you answer the teacher's questions silently? and Do you follow the teacher's instructions? The form promotes students' awareness of listening skills and can be used by teachers to determine the need for listening skills instruction and to chart students' progress in developing these skills.

The February 1984 issue of *Curriculum Review* is devoted to listening skills instruction. It includes reviews (pages 24–38) of many print materials, multimedia kits, films, and tests that could be used in listening skills instruction.

Provide training in participation skills. One of the major ways students participate in the classroom is by answering questions about what they have read. Teachers can help students with this task by teaching them the characteristics of an effective answer to a question. Gall (1970) identifies seven such characteristics:

1. *Accuracy*. Information stated in the answer is correct.

2. *Complexity*. The answer demonstrates awareness that there is more than one way of looking at the problem stated in the question.

3. *Support*. Opinions are accompanied by reasons, facts, or explicit assumptions.

4. *Plausibility*. Predictions, solutions, and explanations stated in the answer are reasonable.

5. *Originality*. The student states ideas that are not commonplace.

6. *Clarity*. The student answers in understandable language and without mumbling.

7. *Appropriateness*. The student answers the question that was asked.

Particular characteristics may or may not be appropriate, depending on the cognitive level of the teacher's question. Showing students a question and examples of answers that do or do not contain a particular characteristic is an effective way to teach these characteristics.

It also should be useful to teach students the sources of information needed to answer questions. Pearson and Johnson (1978) differentiate three types of questions based on the information needed to answer them: (1) text-explicit questions, for which the answer is stated explicitly in the text; (2) text-implicit questions, for which the answer is available in the text, but students must integrate the necessary information across sentences or paragraphs; and (3) script-implicit questions, for which the answer must be supplied from students' background knowledge. Researchers (Raphael and Pearson 1985; Raphael and Wonnacott 1985) have found that training elementary students in the information demands of these three types of questions significantly improves their academic performance. Although the researchers' training focused on answering workbook questions, it seems likely that their procedures would also help students give good oral responses to teachers' recitation questions.

Classroom discussions are more demanding of students' participation skills than are recitations. For this reason, many teachers do not use the discussion method, even though it is a valuable tool for promoting learning, especially higher cognitive learning (Gall and Gall 1976).

Bridges (1979) classifies the participation skills involved in discussion into three types: (1) intellectual rules of discourse, such as showing concern for reasons and evidence in remarks; (2) procedural rules and conventions concerning such matters as who speaks, when, in what order, and for how long; and (3) social conventions, such as whether the norm is to be abrasive or mild in criticizing another participant's ideas. Gall and Gillett (1981) identify more specific discussion skills that correspond to these three types. Examples of these skills include inviting silent students to speak, avoiding monopolization of talk time, acknowledging and paraphrasing what other participants have said, and asking others to clarify or elaborate on their remarks.

Little is known about whether students' participation skills in discussions improve naturally with experience. It seems reasonable, however, that some improvement would occur as a result of practice. Rather than relying on experience alone, however, teachers should consider providing systematic training, which has been demonstrated to improve students' ability to participate in brainstorming groups (Osborn 1979), issues oriented groups (Lai et al. 1972; Oliver and Shaver 1966), and cooperative learning groups (Johnson and Johnson 1988).

Methods for Teaching Note-Taking Skills

Thomas and Rohwer (1986) found that only half of junior high school students report taking notes often or always when a teacher emphasizes a point in class. In high school, the figure increases to 70 percent, but this still means that many students are not taking notes to enhance their learning. There are methods that teachers at all levels can use to train and encourage students to take notes and use them effectively.

Provide support for the note-taking process. Kiewra (1984), an expert on the note-taking process, characterizes students as "notoriously poor note-takers" (p. 300). Even college students are able to record only about half of the critical ideas in a lecture (Locke 1977; Robin et al. 1977; Kiewra 1984, 1985). Until students achieve independence in note taking, teachers will need to provide instruction and support for the note-taking process.

Teachers of young children can provide initial instruction in note-taking skills by having them copy information they have written on the blackboard. This instills in young students the awareness that note taking is an essential study skill that they will use throughout their schooling. Also, they can be told that the information that a teacher writes on the board usually is important and should be recorded in their notes. Once students have copied their notes, the teacher can show students how to label and date them and place them in sequence in a three-ring binder. The concept of sequence is an important readiness skill for effective note taking and note reviewing, so it should be taught to children as soon as possible so that they can practice it extensively.

Teachers can help structure the note-taking process by distributing handouts that include "skeletal" notes containing the main ideas of a lecture, organized into headings and subheadings. They provide a framework that enables students to determine the lecture's organizational pattern. Blank spaces should be left between headings so that students can record additional notes during the lecture.

Skeletal notes can be used effectively at all grade levels and in all content areas. They are especially helpful to low-performing students, who tend to have poor listening and note-taking skills. Kiewra (1985) found that students who review a combination of skeletal notes plus their own notes have better academic performance than students who review without skeletal notes.

Another way teachers can help is to provide students with a variety of cues, as discussed under Study Skill 10 (Using Teacher Cues to Guide Note Taking).

Model the note-taking process. Using an overhead projector, teachers can take notes on a live or videotaped lecture while students listen and watch the screen. Students observe the actual note-taking process, which includes such activities as taking selective notes, using abbreviations, and organizing the notes. Afterwards, teachers can discuss the process. If a videotaped lecture was used, they can replay the tape to clarify and justify particular note-taking practices.

Provide training in note-taking skills. Training can take place as early as the upper elementary grades, or when students have developed satisfactory cursive writing skills. It can be carried out in individual classrooms or in a self-contained study skills course. Training in note taking, as in all the study skills, should take place across the curriculum to maximize its effectiveness.

Jacobsen (1989) has developed an effective training program to improve the note-taking and note-reviewing skills of at-risk high school students. Training is organized into six hour-long sessions. In the first two sessions, the teacher discusses and demonstrates many of the same note-taking skills described in this chapter: using a three-ring binder to organize and store notes; labeling and dating notes; using abbreviations and symbols; writing legibly; reading assignments before class; writing selective, organized, paraphrased notes; using teacher cues; recording definitions and examples; and paying careful attention at the end of class. In the third session, students practice these skills by taking notes on a 30-minute videotaped lecture that includes numerous illustrations and references to maps and diagrams.

Model notes on this lecture are distributed to students during the fourth session and the students are directed to compare their notes with the model notes and identify major differences. The teacher then answers students' questions and replays portions of the lecture to explain why particular information was included or not included in the model notes. The students then revise their notes to approximate the content and quality of the model notes.

The fifth session is used to train students in the Cornell method of reviewing notes. Students are supplied paper with an extra-wide left margin, shown examples of appropriate left-column cues, and then given time to generate their own cues for the notes they took on the videotaped lecture. These completed notes are handed in as an assignment for the teacher to review. In the sixth session, the teacher returns the notes to the students, along with individual recommendations for improving the quality of the review column. Students who had difficulty generating review cues are coached by the teacher on the thinking processes involved in cue generation.

The needs of their students or available instructional time may require teachers to offer more or less training than this program provides. They should give special consideration to having students hand in their notes as a graded assignment. This encourages students to take careful notes, because they know someone else will be looking at them. And, they will benefit from receiving feedback on their notes. An alternative procedure is to have students share their notes with each other and receive peer feedback.

References

Adler, M. J. (1982). *The Paideia Proposal*. New York: Macmillan.

Barker, L. L. (1971). *Listening Behavior*. Englewood Cliffs, N.J.: Prentice-Hall.

Bretzing, B. B., and R. W. Kulhavy. (1979). "Note Taking and Depth of Processing. *Contemporary Educational Psychology* 4: 145–153.

Bridges, D. (1979). *Education, Democracy and Discussion*.Windsor, England: National Foundation for Educational Research.

Conaway, M. S. (1982). "Listening: Learning Tool and Retention Agent." In *Improving Reading and Study Skills*, edited by A. S. Algier and K. W. Algier. San Francisco: Jossey-Bass.

Craik, F. I. M., and R. S. Lockhart. (1972). "Levels of Processing: A Framework for Memory Research." *Journal of Verbal Learning and Verbal Behavior* 11: 671–684.

DeJung, J. E., and K. E. Duckworth. (1985). "Absenteeism in the High School." *R & D Perspectives*. Eugene: Center for Educational Policy and Management, University of Oregon.

Devine, T. G. (1978). Listening: What Do We Know After FiftyYears of Research and Theorizing? *Journal of Reading* 21: 296–304.

Dillon, J. T. (1982). "Cognitive Correspondence Between Question/Statement and Response." *American Educational Research Journal* 19: 540–551.

Evertson, C. M., and E. T. Emmer. (1982). "Effective Management at the Beginning of the School Year in Junior High Classes. *Journal of Educational Research* 74: 485–498.

Fisher, C. W., D. C. Berliner, N. N. Filby, R. Marliave, L. S. Cahen, and M. M. Dishaw. (1980). "Teaching Behaviors, Academic Learning Time, and Student Achievement: An Overview." In *Time to Learn*, edited by C. Denham and A. Lieberman. Washington, D.C.: National Institute of Education.

Fisher, J. L., and M. B. Harris. (1973). "Effect of Note-taking and Review on Recall." *Journal of Educational Psychology* 65: 301–304.

Friedmann, P. G. (1986). *Listening Processes: Attention, Understanding, Evaluation*. Washington, D.C.: National Education Association.

Gage, N. L., and D. C. Berliner. (1988). *Educational Psychology*. 4th ed. Boston: Houghton Mifflin.

Gall, M. D. (1984). "Synthesis of Research on Teachers' Questioning." *Educational Leadership* 2: 40–47.

Gall, M. D. (1970). "The Use of Questions in Teaching." *Review of Educational Research* 40: 707–721.

Gall, M. D., and J. P. Gall. (1988a). *Making the Grade*. Rocklin, Calif.: Prima.

Gall, M. D., and J. P. Gall. (1988b). *Study for Success Teacher's Manual*. 3rd ed. Eugene, Oreg.: M. Damien.

Gall, M. D., and J. P. Gall. (1976). "The Discussion Method." In *The Psychology of Teaching Methods: Seventy-fifth Yearbook of the National Society for the Study of Education*, edited by N. L. Gage. Chicago: University of Chicago Press.

Gall, M. D., and M. Gillett. (1981). "The Discussion Method in Classroom Teaching." *Theory Into Practice* 19: 98–103.

Hartley, J., and I. K. Davies. (1978). "Note-taking: A Critical Review." *Programmed Learning and Educational Technology* 15: 207–224.

Jacobsen, D. R. (1989). "The Effects of Taking Class Notes Using the Cornell Method on Students' Test Performance and Note-taking Quality." Doctoral diss., University of Oregon.

Johnson, D. W., and R. T. Johnson. (1988). *Cooperation and Competition*. Hillsdale, N.J.: Erlbaum.

Joyce, and M. Weil. (1986). *Models of Teaching*. 3rd ed. Englewood Cliffs, N.J.: Prentice-Hall.

Kiewra, K. A. (1985). "Investigating Notetaking and Review: A Depth of Processing Alternative. *Educational Psychologist* 20: 23–32.

Kiewra, K.A. (1984). "Acquiring Effective Notetaking Skills: An Alternative to Professional Notetaking." *Journal of Reading* 27: 299–302.

Ladas, H. (1980). "Summarizing Research: A Case Study." *Review of Educational Research* 50: 597–624.

Lai, M. K., M. D. Gall, R. Elder, and R. Weathersby. (April 1972). "Evaluation of *Discussing Controversial Issues*." Paper presented at the annual meeting of the American Educational Research Association, Chicago.

Locke, E. A. (1977). "An Empirical Study of Lecture Note Taking Among College Students." *Journal of Educational Research* 71: 93–99.

Lundgren, R. E., and R. J. Shavelson. (1974). Effects of Listening Training on Teacher Listening and Discussion Skills." *California Journal of Educational Research* 25: 205–218.

Lundsteen, S. W. (1984). "How to Assess Your Listening Needs." *Curriculum Review* 23: 22–23.

McCaleb, J. L. (1980). "Indirect Teaching and Listening." *Education* 102: 159–164.

McDill, E. L., G. Natriello, and A. M. Pallas. (1985). "Raising Standards and Retaining Students: The Impact of Reform Recommendations on Potential Dropouts." Johns Hopkins University Report 358. Baltimore: Center for the Social Organization of Schools.

McKibben, M. L. (1982). *Listening, Study Skills, and Reading: Measuring and Meeting College Freshman Needs in the 1980's*. Paper presented at the annual meeting of the International Listening Association, Washington, D.C.

McLeish, J. (1976). "The Lecture Method." In *The Psychology of Teaching Methods: Seventy-fifth Yearbook of the National Society for the Study of Education*, edited by N. L. Gage. Chicago: University of Chicago Press.

Nichols, R. G. (1960). *The Supervisor's Notebook*. Glenview, Ill.: Scott, Foresman.

Oliver, D. W., and J. P. Shaver. (1986). *Teaching Public Issues in the High School*. Boston: Houghton-Mifflin.

Orlich, D. C., R. J. Harder, R. C. Callahan, D. P. Kauchak, R. A. Pendergrass, A. J. Keogh, and H. Gibson. (1990). 3rd ed. *Teaching Strategies, A Guide to Better Instruction.* Lexington, Mass.: D.C. Heath.

Osborn, A. F. (1979). *Applied Imagination.* 3rd ed. New York: Scribners.

Palmatier, R. A., and J. M. Bennett. (1974). "Notetaking Habits of College Students." *Journal of Reading* 18: 215–218.

Pauk, W. (1989). *How to Study in College.* Boston: Houghton Mifflin.

Pearson, P. D., and D. D. Johnson. (1978). *Teaching Reading Comprehension.* New York: Holt, Rinehart and Winston.

Pearson, P. D., and L. Fielding. (1983). *Instructional Implications of Listening Comprehension Research.* Reading Education Report No. 39. Urbana: University of Illinois, Center for the Study of Reading.

Quay, H. C., and L. B. Allen. (1982). "Truants and Dropouts." In *Encyclopedia of Educational Research*, vol. 5, 5th edition, edited by H. E. Mitzel. New York: The Free Press.

Raphael, T. E., and P. D. Pearson. (1985). "Increasing Students' Awareness of Sources of Information for Answering Questions." *American Educational Research Journal* 22: 217–236.

Raphael, T. E., and C. A. Wonnacott. (1985). "Heightening Fourth-grade Students' Sensitivity to Sources of Information for Answering Comprehension Questions." *Reading Research Quarterly* 20: 282–296.

Rickards, J. P., and F. Friedman. (1978). "The Encoding versus the External Storage Hypothesis in Note Taking." *Contemporary Educational Psychology* 3: 136–143.

Robin, A., R. M. Foxx, J. Martello, and C. Archable. (1977). "Teaching Note-taking Skills to Underachieving College Students." *Journal of Educational Research* 71: 81–85.

Rosenshine, B. V. (1980). "How Time is Spent in Elementary Classrooms." In *Time to Learn*, edited by C. Denham and A. Liebermans. Washington, D.C.: National Institute of Education.

Rubin, D. L. (1985). "Instruction in Speaking and Listening: Battles and Options." *Educational Leadership* 42: 31–36.

Rumelhart, D. E. (1980). "Schemata: The Building Blocks of Cognition." In *Theoretical Issues in Reading Comprehension*, edited by R. J. Spiro, B. C. Bruce, and W. F. Brewer. Hillsdale, N.J.: Erlbaum.

Steil, L. K. (1984). "Listen and Learn: Improving Listening Across the Curriculum." *Curriculum Review* 23: 13–16.

Steil, L. K. (1977). "Longitudinal Analysis of Listening Pedagogy in Minnesota Secondary Public School." Doctoral diss., Wayne State University.

Steil, L. K., L. L. Barker, and K. W. Watson. (1983). *Effective Listening.* New York: Random House.

Swanson, C. H. (1984). Monitoring Student Listening Techniques: An Approach to Teaching the Foundations of a Skill. Paper presented at the annual meeting of the Eastern Communication Association, Philadelphia.

Thomas, J. W., and W. D. Rohwer, Jr. (1986). "Academic Studying: The Role of Learning Strategies." *Educational Psychologist* 21: 19–41.

Wolvin, A. D. (1984). "Teaching Teachers to Listen." *Curriculum Review* 23: 17–19.

Wolvin, A. D., and C. G. Coakley. (1979). *Listening Instruction.* Urbana, Ill.: ERIC Clearinghouse on Reading and Communication Skills.

Wolvin, A. D., and C. G. Coakley. (1985). *Listening.* Dubuque, Iowa: William C. Brown.

6

Completing Reading Assignments

Learning to Read

The main purpose of reading assignments in the primary grades is to teach children how to read. In practice, this means teaching decoding skills and skills for comprehending the literal meaning of simple text by having children read aloud, read silently, respond orally to questions, and complete worksheets.

A variety of study skills or study attitudes are involved in the process of learning to read: classroom participation skills, especially those involved in speaking, listening, and following directions; writing skills; self-management skills, especially the skill of focusing and maintaining attention; and motivation. Although these skills and attitudes traditionally have not been considered part of beginning reading instruction, we believe they strongly affect students' ability to learn. Teachers should introduce these study skills and attitudes as early as kindergarten.

Focusing and maintaining attention is particularly important in the early stages of learning to read:

> For the beginning reader, decoding the text is a difficult task. Consequently, the combined demands of decoding and comprehension may exceed the limited attention capacity of the student. When combined demands from these two essential tasks exceed the student's attentional capacity, the tasks cannot be performed simultaneously. In order to overcome this apparent impasse, the beginning reader uses a simple strategy, namely, that of attention switching. First, attention is used for decoding. After decoding is done, attention is switched to the comprehension task. . . . Attention switching is time consuming, puts a heavy demand on short-term memory, and tends to interfere with recall (Samuels and Kamil 1984, pp. 197–198).

It seems likely that training in attentional skills (see Chapter 4) would help beginning readers switch attention more easily.

Although most students know how to read after a year or two of elementary reading instruction, a significant number do not master basic decoding and comprehension skills and need continued instruction in these skills at higher grade levels. Systematic study skills instruction, with particular emphasis on classroom participation, attentional skills, and motivational skills, can supplement remedial reading instruction.

Reading to Learn

Once students have learned how to read—usually by the third or fourth grade—their next challenge is to learn how to acquire knowledge from textbooks. (We use the term "textbook" to refer to all forms of required school reading—texts, magazines, reference books, training manuals, poetry, etc.) By the time students reach middle school, most of their teachers' instruction and most of their study activities will be centered around textbooks (Cole and Sticht 1981; Goodlad 1976).

A major task that confronts young students is figuring out the distinctive organization of each of their textbooks and determining how to use it to facilitate their learning. The difficulty of the task is increased by the different styles of textbooks in different content areas. The structure and organizational features of a math text, for example, are quite different from those in a social studies text. And fiction takes many varied forms that challenge students' comprehension skills.

As students progress through school, reading tasks become more complex and difficult. In the lower grades, literal comprehension is typically all that is required. This means reading the text and identifying basic facts (e.g., names, dates, places, events) in it. In the upper grades, students are expected to become more sophisticated readers. They read in order to acquire skills (e.g., computational skills, foreign language skills, scientific inquiry skills), make inferences (e.g., to infer characters' motives or the author's point of view), or take stands on issues (e.g., to agree or disagree with decisions made by government leaders). Students also are expected to remember more and more textbook content for tests and to write more papers that make use of information in their textbooks and library reference materials.

In the upper grades, reading assignments become longer and teachers assign more reading as homework, while offering less assistance for completing assignments. From high school to college, this shift in assistance is particularly dramatic. High school teachers may occasionally help students by conducting in-class prereading, reading, and postreading activities on parts of the text, but college professors rarely offer this type of assistance. Professors expect all textbook assignments to be completed as homework, and class time is often spent on content that is related to, but not the same as, the content covered in the textbook.

The Status of Textbook Reading Instruction

Unfortunately, most students receive very little instruction in study skills for reading. Initial reading instruction is dominated by the use of basal readers rather than textbooks (Paris, Wixson, and Palincsar 1986), which teach reading skills in isolation from meaningful academic content. Students may learn *how to read*, but they do not learn *how to read to learn* academic content.

The situation does not improve when students are regularly assigned textbook readings. Teachers spend virtually no class time teaching students how to comprehend their textbooks. This phenomenon has been documented at both the elementary level (Durkin 1978–79; Hare and Borchardt 1984) and the secondary level (Slinger 1981; Bullock, Laine, and Slinger in press).

Given this lack of instruction, it is not surprising that many students are unable to learn from textbooks and that so many citizens are functionally illiterate. Louis Harris and Associates (see DeCrow 1972) found, for example, that over 13 million adults in the United States were unable to read typical forms and documents distributed by government agencies and businesses. And Duffy (1976) found that 18 percent of Navy recruits read below the eighth grade level.

One approach that teachers have taken to deal with this problem is to assign textbooks with a readability level that corresponds to the reading skills students have acquired through trial-and-error and incidental instruction. In fact, publishers have lowered the readability of most school textbooks dramatically in recent years (Chall, Conrad, and Harris 1987). This is at best a short-term solution, because students must be able to read more sophisticated textbooks if they wish to attend college or acquire training for technologically sophisticated occupations. A far better solution is to provide students with systematic instruction in textbook reading skills.

Initial reading instruction is important to students' success in school. Although the tasks involved in this type of instruction require study skills, these skills are different from those involved in reading textbooks. They primarily involve classroom participation and self-management. Educators who are planning a study skills program for primary students should see chapters 4 and 5 for appropriate study skills. The skills we review in this chapter, however, can be useful for planning ways to help young readers make the transition from "learning to read" to "reading to learn."

Study Skills for Reading Assignments

Reading straight through, sentence by sentence, paragraph by paragraph, is a simple method of reading. Perhaps you can recall using this method. If the assignment were to read pages 122 to 156 in a textbook, for example, you would turn to page 122 and then to page 156 to get a sense of how much reading was required. Then you would begin reading, and every now and then you would check to see how much you had to read before reaching page 156. Upon reading the last sentence, you would feel that you had now "studied" the text.

This approach is common because it does not require much time or effort. It is a weak approach, however, because it does not include strategies for deep processing—moving new information from short-term memory into long-term memory. Researchers and study skills experts have identified study skills and strategies that effectively engage students in deep processing of text. Figure 6.1 lists these skills and strategies.

Figure 6.1

**Study Skills and Strategies
for Doing Reading Assignments**

PREREADING STUDY SKILLS
1. Allocating time for deep processing
2. Analyzing the structure of the text
3. Determining the nature of the criterion task

NOTE TAKING AND UNDERLINING
4. Underlining important information
5. Taking paraphrase notes
6. Making an outline or graphic organizer
7. Summarizing a reading passage

COMPREHENSION MONITORING AND ENHANCING
8. Monitoring comprehension while reading
9. Generating and answering questions about the text
10. Reading at an appropriate speed

READING STRATEGIES
11. Using the SQ3R reading strategy
12. Using the Reciprocal Teaching reading strategy.

All the skills and strategies in Figure 6.1 involve making the text personally meaningful to the student. It seems likely that a student who has a greater repertoire of such skills and strategies can make various types of text more meaningful than a student who has a limited repertoire:

> A repertoire of [study strategies] helps students to perform a wide spectrum of tasks. A carpenter often has one or two favorite hammers that she uses for most tasks, but her tool box will contain more than a dozen different hammers for special jobs. Similarly, a good repertoire contains many different types of strategies for the student to choose from, providing both fluency and flexibility. If a high school student is having difficulty making sense of what he is reading in his American history textbook, he could take a break; but this might not be sufficient to solve the problem. A student with a more flexible repertoire might also try taking a break, but if this did not work, she could then try different methods: re-reading, calling a friend in the same class, reading other related material in the library, speaking to the teacher, asking a parent, or looking over class notes (Weinstein et al. 1988/1989, p. 18).

The kind of repertoire recommended by Weinstein and her colleagues is reflected in the following discussion of study skills and strategies. All the skills and strategies may not be effective for every kind of reading, but each can be used for specific kinds of reading.

Most of the research on study skills that we review here concerns textbooks or textbook-like reading passages, but the study skills also apply, with some adaptation, to various forms of literature.

STUDY SKILL 1
Allocating Time for Deep Processing

Deep processing requires more time than superficial processing. In a recent study, Wandersee (1988) found evidence suggesting that this extra time leads to increased academic achievement. The study involved 133 college students, all majoring in teacher education, who answered a study habits questionnaire. One of the data analyses tallied the typical number of "passes" students reported making in the average reading assignment:

> "I just read it once" was coded as a 1-pass approach. "Taking notes while reading and then studying my notes before the test" was categorized as a 2-pass approach while "Read it through once, go through it again and highlight the important things, then study those points" was categorized as a 3-pass approach (Wandersee 1988, p. 73).

In this context, repeated "passes" over the text reflect a deep-processing approach to reading.

Wandersee found that approximately 25 percent of the college students made only one pass through a textbook assignment. Approximately 60 percent made two passes, and only 12 percent made three passes or more. Significantly, the number of passes made correlated positively (r = .27) with students' grade point average.

Wandersee did not determine whether students who make more passes require more time to complete reading assignments, but this is probably so. Their reward for their time, however, is a probable increase in their academic achievement. Using the time management skills discussed in Chapter 3, students can make sure that they have time to do this kind of reading.

STUDY SKILL 2
Analyzing the Structure of the Text

School textbooks, unlike most other reading materials, are written to be studied in depth. Textbook authors structure their material to facilitate the study process, and students who understand the concept of "structure" and how to analyze it are likely to learn more than students who lack this understanding.

Textbooks contain many structural elements to guide students' reading. Most obvious is their division into separate chapters, each with its own title. Chapter titles cue students about what to expect, giving them a general mental set, or schema, about what each chapter includes. Students need to learn how to use this schema to help assimilate the information in each chapter.

Center headings, side headings, and paragraph headings within chapters perform a similar function by helping students organize their reading into useful blocks. In a well-organized book, each heading introduces a clearly defined body of content that can be read quickly. While holding each "chunk" of content in short-term memory, students can use deep-processing techniques to store that chunk in long-term memory. Without headings every half-page or so, students might read so much content that when they do stop for deep processing, they no longer remember what they have read.

Structural elements in textbooks vary, depending on the subject being taught. In math textbooks, for example, students need to realize that worked-out examples of algorithms can help them understand and complete the problem sets that are to be done as seatwork and homework. History textbooks generally do not have this feature, but instead are likely to use comments and questions at the start of the chapter and in the side margins to guide the reader through the chapter. Students need to develop skill in understanding structural elements and using them to improve their reading comprehension.

Narrative texts (e.g., short stories, novels, folktales) have a different structural organization than textbooks. Researchers have found that most narrative texts share a common structure, or what they call a "story grammar":

> The first rule simply defines a story as consisting of a setting, theme, plot and a resolution, which usually occur in that sequence. The second rule is that the setting consists of the characters and usually the location and time of a story. The third rule is that the theme of a story consists of the main goal and main character. . . . The plot consists of a series of episodes, which are designed to help the main character reach his goal. Each episode consists of a subgoal, and a resolution of the attempt. After several episodes, an outcome occurs which matches the goal of the main character, ushering in a final resolution. These rules apply to many stories, folktales and dramas, and give us a common framework for understanding them (Guthrie 1977, p. 575).

The results of several research studies show that teaching students the nature of story grammar improves their comprehension of narrative text (Singer and Donlan 1982; Short and Ryan 1984; Carnine and Kinder 1985; Idol 1987).

STUDY SKILL 3
Determining the Nature of the Criterion Task

The ability to determine which information is important and how well it should be learned is an essential study skill for effective reading. In reading for their own purposes, students can decide for themselves which information is most important. In school, however, the importance of text information is a function of the criterion task specified by the teacher—usually a written test. The test, then, defines which information is more or less important, and how it needs to be processed. For example, suppose students encounter the name of the longest river in the United States while reading their text. If they can anticipate that the test may include a question about this fact, they can focus attention on it while reading the text. They can also store the fact in long-term memory in a way that makes later recall easy for them.

Anderson and Armbruster (1984) formulated the principle that "when the criterion task is made explicit to the students before they read the text, students will learn more from studying than when the criterion task remains vague" (p. 658). For example, researchers have found that students do better on tests when they know the questions that will be on the test or when they know the instructional objectives that will be tested.

Teachers are not as likely to be as explicit about the nature of the criterion task as researchers are in their laboratory studies. Therefore, students need to develop skill in determining the form and content of the test by searching for cues in the teacher's behavior (this skill is discussed further in Chapter 8). Examples of such cues are the structure of the teacher's previous tests, the content of test review sessions, and teacher comments like, "Pay special attention to. . . ."

Similar principles apply to other criterion tasks as well. For example, students who are doing research to write a paper can work more effectively if they are able to analyze the paper's specific requirements and then focus on relevant information in their reading.

STUDY SKILL 4
Underlining

Underlining or highlighting important parts of the text while reading stimulates active reading because it requires students to search the text for important content. The underlined or highlighted text is a cue that facilitates later review of the text.

Armbruster and Anderson (1984) reviewed research findings on the effectiveness of underlining and highlighting. Several studies showed the technique to be neither more nor less effective than other reading techniques, while other studies showed it to be more effective. In research involving high school students, Schnell and Rocchio (1975) found that the students who underlined their text earned higher scores on a subsequent test than did students who had just read the text or who read text that had already been underlined for them.

The results of a study by Fowler and Barker (1974) suggest why underlining and highlighting are effective, at least under certain circumstances. The study revealed that students were more likely to answer a test question correctly if they had highlighted the relevant information in their text. It appears, then, that the critical step in highlighting is not the act of highlighting (or underlining), but rather the act of deciding which information in the text is important enough to merit highlighting. Highlighting probably does not help if students choose information that is irrelevant to the criterion task.

STUDY SKILL 5
Taking Paraphrase Notes

Taking notes, whether paraphrase or verbatim, requires more effort than either rereading the text or underlining it. It requires rereading and composing. Students need to learn when this extra effort might improve their learning. Young students who have little manual dexterity will derive little or no benefit from taking notes on reading assignments. Their effort is better spent rereading the text or underlining it. Students who have good writing skills but whose attention easily strays should consider taking notes on most, if not all, reading assignments. Peper and Mayer (1978) theorize that taking notes after reading each paragraph or other unit of text enhances attention and thus improves reading comprehension.

Students who read with good attention are more selective about when to take notes. Taking notes is justified (1) when information needs to be stored in long-term memory and (2) when information can be made more meaningful by reorganizing it. For example, suppose the text consists primarily of facts, terms, and easily comprehended information. Underlining or highlighting this information in the text itself is probably just as effective as copying it into notes. Suppose, however, that the text provides a complex explanation or description. Students can improve their understanding by mentally organizing this information and then writing notes to represent this organization. The notes are not a verbatim copy of the text, but a paraphrase that represents students' mental organization of it.

The importance of mentally organizing text material is most apparent in the case of taking notes on fiction, essays, philosophical treatises, and artistic criticism. The important information in this material might be difficult to cue just by highlighting. Instead, students need to read the assignment and then reflect on its characters, setting, plot, themes, symbols, reasoning, and so on. Reflection may extend to making comparisons within the text or with other texts that students have read. Taking notes would help students in these situations if it involved recording their thoughts on the text.

Mentally organizing information in the form of notes enhances learning by making the text more meaningful and by helping students transfer information from short-term memory to long-term memory. Notes also help by guiding review of information so that it is easily retrieved from long-term memory.

Anderson and Armbruster (1984) reviewed the research on taking notes on text and concluded that studies have produced "mixed results, with most studies showing that note taking is no more effective than other methods" (p. 666). They observe, however, that much of this research did not examine the appropriateness of note taking for the particular situation being studied.

One research study reviewed by Anderson and Armbruster investigated the effectiveness of taking notes under what we believe to be appropriate circumstances. The researchers (Bretzing and Kulhavy 1979) worked with high school students, who generally can be assumed to have the skills for sustained note taking. The test given the students involved constructed response items requiring integration of information. We would expect paraphrase notes to be effective in this situation because they allow meaningful organization of bits of information. In fact, the students who took notes on the reading assignment *did* do better on the test than did students who only read the text or underlined it. A subsequent study, this time involving college students, yielded similar results (Bretzing and Kulhavy 1981).

STUDY SKILL 6
Making an Outline or a Graphic Organizer

Our discussion of the two preceding study skills—underlining and taking paraphrase notes—focused on their role in learning small units of information in the text. There are several study techniques that can help students understand how these units of information relate to one another.

A written outline is the traditional technique. Research on its effectiveness extends back to at least the 1930s (Barton 1930; Salisbury 1935). In outlining, students use roman numerals for main concepts, letters for subordinate concepts or details that support the main concepts, and arabic numerals for concepts or details that support the subordinate concepts. More complex outlining systems may be necessary to represent some types of information.

Anderson and Armbruster (1984) concluded from their review of research that outlining is effective, but only if students receive extensive training in its use. A study that was published subsequent to their review yielded similar findings (Bianco and McCormick 1989). The researchers trained a small group of learning-disabled secondary students in outlining skills. The students' ability to outline improved dramatically, but the improvement required ten days of instruction for 30 minutes each day. Effects of outlining on reading comprehension were not assessed in the study.

Because outlining is time-consuming and requires a particular writing style, it probably should not be taught until students are in the upper grade levels. Even then, they are not likely to use outlining unless they wish to learn the content of a complex reading assignment to a high level of mastery.

A simpler and more generally applicable method for organizing information is to use graphic organizers. Suppose, for example, that students were reading a unit on the American system of constitutional government. They might be expected to understand that the Constitution calls for three branches of government (legislative, executive, judicial) and governing bodies under each branch. The information units and their relationships can be depicted graphically as shown on the next page.

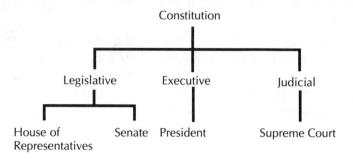

For most students, this graphic organizer would be easier to construct than a written outline of the same information. And the relationship between concepts probably would be easier to comprehend and remember.

Researchers have investigated the theoretical basis of graphic organizers and their effectiveness in enhancing reading comprehension. Their versions of graphic organizers are similar, but called by different names: networks (Dansereau 1979), maps (Armbruster and Anderson 1980, Anderson 1979), concept maps (Moreira 1979; Stewart, Vankirk, and Rowell 1979), and structured overviews (Walker 1979). There is some evidence that using graphing techniques to represent the organization of text improves learning (Moore 1987; Van Patten, Chao, and Reigeluth 1986).

Students should be familiar with a range of graphic organizers so that they can illustrate concepts, and relationships between concepts, that are distinctive to various disciplines. Jones, Pierce, and Hunter (1988/1989) provide a useful compilation of graphic organizers and the types of concepts and relationships that each can be used to represent. Their discussion includes the spider map, series of events chain, continuum scale, compare/contrast matrix, problem/solution outline, network tree, fishbone map, human interaction outline, and cycle.

STUDY SKILL 7
Summarizing a Reading Passage

The major cognitive processes involved in summarizing text are: (1) judging the importance of each piece of information in the text and including only important information in the summary; (2) identifying high-level, general concepts to substitute for low-level, detailed ideas in the text; and (3) writing the summary (Hidi and Anderson 1986).

The complexity of these processes helps to explain why students develop summarization skills very slowly (Brown and Day 1983; Garner 1982; Garner and McCaleb 1985; Hare and Borchardt 1984; Ricciardi 1984). Even many college students cannot summarize text accurately and efficiently. Some research has shown that using this study technique facilitates learning from texts (Doctorow, Marks, and Wittrock 1978; Taylor and

Berkowitz 1980; Murrell and Surber 1987), whereas other research (reviewed by Anderson and Armbruster 1984) has found that it has no more effect than other study techniques. Writing text summaries may be effective, but only for students who can do so with proficiency.

To become proficient, students need to learn summarization skills at an early age and practice them often. Teachers should not, however, expect students to use this technique for independent study until they become proficient readers and writers. Many students won't reach this stage until the later high school years. Until then, they can make simple paraphrase notes and graphic organizers, or underline and highlight the text if they are allowed to do so. Also, students should be told that summaries, by their nature, focus less on details and more on main ideas; therefore, students should not rely on summarizing as their sole study strategy if they expect to learn and remember a substantial amount of detailed information in the text.

STUDY SKILL 8
Monitoring Comprehension While Reading

Monitoring comprehension during reading is one of the most important reading study skills. Beginning with the pioneering work of Flavell (1978), researchers have used the term "metacognition" to refer to this monitoring process. The term also refers to students' awareness of how their minds work while reading.

In reviewing research, Baker and Brown (1984) found consistent evidence that good readers have better comprehension monitoring skills than poor readers. For example, Clay (1973) found that higher-achieving beginning readers, when asked to read orally, spontaneously corrected 33 percent of their errors, while lower-achieving beginning readers corrected only 5 percent of their errors. Kavale and Schreiner (1979) obtained similar findings in a study of average and above-average sixth grade readers.

It seems that effective comprehension monitoring involves two separate study skills. The first is the ability to recognize, while reading, that one's comprehension has failed. The second is the ability to select and use an appropriate strategy for correcting the failure.

A good reader proceeds smoothly and quickly as long as his understanding of the material is complete. But as soon as he senses that he has missed an idea, that the track has been lost, he brings smooth progress to a grinding halt. Advancing more slowly, he seeks clarification in the subsequent material, examining it for the light it can throw on the earlier trouble spot. If still dissatisfied with his grasp, he returns to the point where the difficulty began and rereads the section more carefully. He probes and analyzes phrases and sentences for their exact meaning; he tries to visualize abstruse descriptions; and through a series of approximations, deductions, and corrections he translates scientific and technical terms into concrete examples (Whimbey 1975, p. 91).

This description of comprehension monitoring highlights several techniques for correcting comprehension failures: reading ahead, rereading when comprehension fails, and finding and visualizing concrete referents for abstract concepts. Several other techniques may be helpful as well. For example, students can relate the content to knowledge that they already have, a technique that researchers have found good readers regularly use (Anderson 1977; Brown, Smiley, Day, Townsend, and Lawton 1977). If readers lack an adequate knowledge base, they can build one by reading other sources on the same topic.

Some comprehension failures occur simply because readers don't understand a word in the text. Students can use several techniques to deal with this problem: (1) sound out the word by doing a phonetic analysis, (2) do a structural analysis to determine whether any parts of the word are meaningful, (3) do a contextual analysis to determine the meaning of the word by the way it is used in a sentence or passage, and (4) look up the meaning of the word in a dictionary. There is indirect evidence (reviewed by Gough 1984; Johnson and Baumann 1984) suggesting that these techniques are effective for this purpose.

Study Skill 9
Generating and Answering Questions About the Text

Study Skill 8 involves comprehension monitoring *during* the act of reading the text. Students should also check their comprehension *after* reading the text by asking themselves questions about what they have just read.

Anderson and Biddle (1975) found that answering textbook questions generally helps to improve adults' learning, but other researchers (Levin and Pressley 1981; Pressley and Forrest-Pressley 1985) found that this technique is not nearly as effective for young students, perhaps because they don't often look back to the text for answers to questions they can't answer (Garner, Macready, and Wagoner 1984). Several studies have found that this problem can be corrected by training children in particular look-back techniques (Garner, Hare, Alexander, Haynes, and Winograd 1984; Raphael and Pearson 1985).

Many texts do not provide questions for checking comprehension, so students need to be able to generate their own questions and then answer them. Wong (1985) reviewed 27 studies of question generating and found positive effects on student reading comprehension in the majority of them. Studies that failed to find positive effects usually provided inadequate training in how to generate questions or allowed insufficient time for students to both read and form questions.

Several studies found that good readers, even without special training, are likely to ask questions to help themselves understand what they are reading (Garner and Alexander 1982; Smith 1967). This suggests that training in how to generate questions may be more important for low-performing students than for other students. Wong and Jones (1982) found that such training improved the achievement of learning-disabled students, but not that of regular students.

STUDY SKILL 10
Reading at an Appropriate Speed

It seems reasonable that as students speed up their reading, they will process the content less deeply and thus perform less well on a test of their reading comprehension. In one study, college students who were induced to read text selections at a moderate pace did better on a test than did students who were induced to read them at a fast pace (McConkie, Rayner, and Wilson 1973).

Using a reading rate that is appropriate to the reading difficulty of the text is suggested by the findings of several studies. Fullmer (1980) found that when students read at approximately 700 words per minute, their comprehension was no better than chance. Most students probably need to read at a much lower rate. Carver's (1973a, 1973b) several studies showed that a rate of approximately 300 words per minute was optimal for college students. And Taylor (1964) found that, on average, college students read at a rate of 280 words per minute—near Carver's optimum rate. Taylor also found that average reading rates increase with each grade level: 138 words per minute in third grade, 185 in sixth grade, 214 in ninth grade, and 250 in twelfth grade.

Students may need to read slower than these normative reading rates, depending on their reading comprehension level and the nature of the criterion task. The skill, then, is not to be able to read at a specified reading rate, but to vary the rate to fit the assignment.

STUDY SKILL 11
Using the SQ3R Reading Strategy

SQ3R is an acronym for the five steps that comprise a comprehensive reading strategy developed by Robinson (1941) nearly half a century ago:

1. *Survey* the text headings quickly to acquire a conceptual map of the material to be read. (This step corresponds to Study Skill 2 in Figure 6.1.)

2. Ask *questions* about the text by turning each heading into a question. (This step corresponds to Study Skill 9 in Figure 6.1.)

3. *Read* the text purposively to answer the question.

4. *Recite* by making brief notes about the text or using self-recitation or both. (See Study Skills 5, 6, and 7 in Figure 6.1).

5. *Review* by rereading notes and by generating and answering questions. (See Study Skill 9 in Figure 6.1.)

The strategy is generally consistent with the principles of effective reading that have emerged from the research investigations reviewed above. Perhaps for this reason, the SQ3R strategy is still widely advocated.

Various adaptations of SQ3R have been developed to suit the needs of different student populations and reading contexts (see Adams, Carnine, and Gersten 1982; Gall and Gall 1988; Kahn 1978; Thomas 1978) .

Adams and her colleagues (1982) reviewed six studies on the effectiveness of SQ3R with junior high school, high school, and college students. They concluded that the results were "mixed" (p. 31). One explanation is that some researchers may have provided insufficient training, thus preventing students from mastering the strategy. Adams and her colleagues addressed this problem by providing systematic instruction in a variation of the SQ3R strategy for a group of average fifth grade students. (Their variation, called SCORER, is discussed further in Chapter 8.) Students who were instructed individually for four days, 30 to 40 minutes daily, outperformed a group of untrained students on a measure of reading comprehension administered the day following training and again two weeks later.

The five steps of SQ3R require a substantial amount of time and effort. Because it is much simpler just to read the text, or to read and underline it, students need to be convinced that the time and effort required to apply SQ3R will improve their reading comprehension and test performance. And they need to schedule enough study time to apply each step of the strategy.

Although taking notes is not a major feature of SQ3R, students may do so in Step 4 (Recite). The 1-2-3 Reading Method combines SQ3R and the Cornell note-taking method (Gall and Gall 1988). Students write each text heading in the left column of a sheet of notepaper. They then summarize the text under that heading by writing a brief note in the right column. Notes on important details in the text take the form of a cue word or phrase in the left column and a corresponding note in the right column (e.g., "Project Blue Book" in the left column and "Air Force project to identify UFOs" in the right column). Students then review their comprehension by trying to recall the information in the right column from the cues and headings written in the left column.

SQ3R is useful for the first reading of text and also for review prior to a test. This latter use of SQ3R, as well as some of the individual study skills listed in Figure 6.1, is discussed in Chapter 8.

STUDY SKILL 12

Using the Reciprocal Teaching Reading Strategy

Palincsar and Brown (1984) have developed a text reading strategy that synthesizes the methods used by successful readers into four activities: (1) generating questions about the content of the text, (2) summarizing the content, (3) clarifying information in the text, and (4) predicting upcoming content from cues in the text or from prior knowledge of the topic. Students are expected to engage in all four of these activities after reading each segment of the text. The segments can be small or large depending on students' reading ability.

Palincsar and Brown's method for teaching this reading strategy, called *reciprocal teaching*, is described later in this chapter. They do not give the corresponding reading strategy a separate label; for our purposes, we choose to label it the *reciprocal teaching reading strategy*.

Several research studies (summarized in Palincsar, Ransom, and Derber 1988/1989) investigated the effectiveness of this reading strategy for students in elementary through middle grades. The studies consistently showed that students trained in reciprocal reading dramatically improved their comprehension scores.

Reciprocal teaching and SQ3R both emphasize actively engaging students with the text, and they incorporate similar engagement activities: generating questions about the text, making a summary of the text, and monitoring comprehension. Reciprocal teaching may be more appropriate than SQ3R for young or low-performing students, however, because it can be modeled and practiced effectively in reading groups. SQ3R seems more appropriate for older or high-performing students because it is essentially an independent reading strategy. Also, it may require note-taking skills in order to be used effectively.

Methods of Teaching Study Skills for Reading Assignments

General Methods

Increasing students' reading skills repertoire should be one of the primary goals of K–12 study skills instruction. Researchers have found that most college students know only a few ways to study textbook material and usually rely on a single method (Simpson 1984; Wandersee 1988). In a study involving 90 college students, Ryan (1984) reported that students used "relatively unsophisticated" strategies to monitor their comprehension of textbooks. Their primary strategies were attempts to recall information in the text by responding to study guide questions or by a process of mental review. Only six students tried to integrate different parts of the text into a common framework, to devise examples of principles and concepts, or to determine the relationship between each text section and its heading. Not one student reported using a graphic organizer to monitor comprehension. The reading strategies of K–12 students are no doubt even less sophisticated. Teachers need to teach students a variety of skills and strategies for doing their reading assignments because no one skill or strategy is suitable for all purposes.

There are several general models for teaching the study skills listed in Figure 6.1 (see Brown, Campione, and Day 1981; Pearson and Dole 1987; Winograd and Paris 1988/1989). We consider here Pearson and Dole's five-step model (summarized in Figure 6.2) because it is consistent with the other models, although more detailed:

1. *Modeling and explanation.* The teacher can model how the particular study skill is to be used by thinking aloud while reading a sample of text to or with the class. For example, if the skill being taught is how to underline important statements in the text, the teacher and students can read each sentence together, and the teacher can make comments like "In this sentence, the author defines the concept of culture, so I'd double-underline 'culture' to remind me that this is a key term and that it's defined here." All the skills listed in Figure 6.1 can be modeled by thinking aloud in this manner.

Modeling should be supplemented by an explanation of how the skill improves reading comprehension and where it is appropriately used. Duffy, Roehler, Meloth, and Vavrus (1986) list guidelines for providing instructional explanations while teaching reading comprehension skills.

2. *Guided practice.* Students should practice the skill and "think aloud" for the teacher, so that the teacher can determine whether they are using an appropriate cognitive process. The teacher should offer suggestions and encouragement and, if necessary, reteach the skill using modeling and explanation.

3. *Further explanation.* Teachers should help students consolidate their learning to this point by again explaining why the skill is helpful and when it should be used.

4. *Independent practice.* The teacher should provide independent practice exercises and should also repeat the preceding steps for students who have difficulty completing them.

5. *Application.* Pearson and Dole emphasize that this final step is critical. The teacher asks students to move from practice exercises to actual textbook assignments. According to Pearson and Dole, it is at this step that "students realize true 'ownership' of their strategies" (p. 159).

Figure 6.2

**Methods of Teaching Study Skills
for Reading Assignments**

GENERAL METHODS

1. Modeling and explanation
2. Guided practice
3. Further explanation
4. Independent practice
5. Application

SPECIFIC METHODS

1. Teaching the SQ3R reading strategy
2. Teaching students how to analyze text structure
3. Teaching students how to make graphic organizers
4. Teaching students summarizing skills
5. Teaching question-generating and question-answering skills
6. Improving students' comprehension monitoring

Instruction in applying reading skills is an ongoing activity because students will encounter different textbook challenges from one subject to the next, and from one grade level to the next. Ideally, each teacher will assess students' reading skills, review the skills needed for success in that class, and teach students how the skills apply to the textbook assignments for that class. This means that content teachers must also be study skills teachers. Study skills specialists can teach general skills for studying textbooks, but they probably will not be able to teach students how to use the particular structure of each textbook to prepare for the criterion tasks set by the teacher using that textbook.

Pearson and Dole's model is appropriate for teaching any of the skills listed in Figure 6.1. Because each skill involves a complex thinking process, however, we recommend teaching only one or two skills at a time. Once the five-step sequence is completed, another skill or two can be introduced into students' repertoire.

Specific Methods

Reading specialists have developed a variety of specific methods for teaching study skills needed for reading assignments. The methods are listed in Figure 6.2 and discussed below.

Teaching the SQ3R Reading Strategy

We recommend that teachers first introduce students to a general reading strategy, such as SQ3R, and then teach specific study skills for reading. SQ3R gives students a feeling for the total process of doing a textbook reading assignment. Once they understand that process, they are better able to see the relevance of the individual study skills.

Two methods are especially helpful in teaching SQ3R. The first involves using a sample of text and an overhead projector to model the five steps of SQ3R. The teacher and students together examine the same chapter from a textbook used in class. The teacher starts by showing students how she surveys the chapter by looking for center, side, and paragraph headings. Next, she puts a blank transparency (lined to look like notebook paper with a wide left column) on the overhead projector.

The teacher then thinks aloud to demonstrate to the class how she examines the first heading and turns it into a question, which she writes in the left column of the transparency. The next step is for the teacher and students to read the text that follows the heading. Then the teacher explains her thought process in answering the question suggested by the heading, and writes the answer in the right column of the transparency. She can make additional notes on the transparency to record significant details in the text.

The teacher repeats this process for several headings until it is clear that students understand the process. Then she shows the class how the notes recorded on the transparency can be used to review the text when preparing for a test, writing assignment, or other task.

This lets students see and hear each step of SQ3R and enables most students to begin practicing the strategy under teacher guidance. The class can be asked to read the same section of text and take SQ3R-type notes on it. The teacher can check the notes for accuracy and completeness, and students can check one another's notes and comment on them.

SQ3R is typically used for textbook assignments, but it can also be used to study novels, stories, or other forms of fiction. For example, suppose students are reading a novel that has chapter titles. In this case, each chapter title is a "heading" that can be turned into a question. The teacher can model for students the process of reading the chapter and then making a note of the answer (again, use a transparency and overhead projector).

It also is helpful for teachers to give students a set of cue words to guide their reading of fictional works. Typical cue words are *plot, characters, setting,* and *theme.* The teacher can show students how to write each cue word in the left column of the notesheet after reading a chapter in the novel. She can then model the process of using the cue words to take notes about important points in the chapter, such as a twist in the plot, the introduction of a new character, a revelation about the personality of a character who had been introduced previously, or a theme that became apparent to the reader.

This same process can even be applied to poetry. The teacher can show students how to turn a poem's title into a question, and how to use cue words (e.g., metaphor, simile, rhyme, symbol) to guide their reading, appreciation, and review of the poem.

Another useful technique to help students master SQ3R is to give them a worksheet that cues their use of each step of the strategy. An example of this type of worksheet is shown in Figure 6.3, which shows actual student notes on a textbook assignment.

Teaching Students How to Analyze Text Structure

Teachers can explain general ways of structuring text, such as using chapters, chapter sections, and subheads. And they can discuss other features that help guide the reader—the table of contents, index, glossary, chapter summary, and chapter questions. Modeling the proper use of these structural indicators and providing practice opportunities is the best way to ensure that students learn how to use text structure to improve their study.

Teachers can also explain the special structural features of different kinds of text. First, they need to analyze the text to determine how it is organized and what students should learn from it. For example, teachers may find that each chapter of a history textbook is structured to present a series of major events and a theme that ties them together. They may then decide that they want students to determine the causes and consequences of each event, and how each event reflects the chapter's theme. Keeping this analysis in mind, teachers can show students how history chapters are organized and then model how to read the chapter to identify significant events, their causes and consequences, and the ways in which they reflect the chapter's theme. Finally, teachers can give students opportunities for practice and feedback so they can study the textbook effectively.

Larkin and Reif (1976) followed this procedure to help college students in a physics course learn how to read their assigned textbook. Their analysis revealed that the physics textbook, and science textbooks in general, emphasized relations between quantities that are usually expressed by equations (e.g., distance can be defined as speed multiplied by time, $d = st$).

Figure 6.3

Example of a Completed SQ3R Worksheet

Name **Jackie Jefferson**

Course **Social Sciences I**

Date **October 15, 1989**

Textbook **The Metropolitan Community**

Chapter **3**   Pages **47-61**

I. SURVEY the chapter (take about 5 to 10 minutes). As you survey the chapter, answer the following questions.

A. What is the title of the chapter? **The World and the U.S.**

B. Is there a chapter summary at the beginning or end of the chapter? **YES**
On what page(s) is this summary located? **47** Be sure to read any summary information.

C. What are the main subheadings in this chapter? Please list them below:

1. **Globes and maps show places on the earth**
2. **Directions and the poles**
3. **The equator and the hemispheres**
4. **Map symbols**
5. **Countries in North America**
6. **Learning More About Maps: What scale means/measures**
7. **How maps show distance**
8. _____

D. Please describe one or two illustrations, graphs, charts, pictures, or cartoons that stood out as you surveyed the chapter.

Page 58 shows an actual size drawing of an ice cream cone and a scale drawing of it

E. Are there study questions listed at the end of the chapter? **YES**
If so, be sure to read them.

F. Are there key vocabulary words listed at the end of the chapter? **NO**
If so, be sure to read them.

(continued)

G. Can you describe in one or two brief sentences what this chapter will be about?

It will tell me how maps are used to show what the world and different countries look like.

II. QUESTION yourself about the chapter by turning the major subheadings that you listed in part I-C into questions. Use who, what, where, when, why, and how when developing your questions.

1. How do globes and maps show places on the earth?
2. What do directions and poles show us?
3. What are equators and hemispheres?
4. What is the purpose of map symbols?
5. What are the countries in North America?
6. What are scales, and what are they used for?
7. How do maps show distance?
8. _____

III. READ one major subheading area of the chapter at a time and then RECITE the answer(s) to the question(s) you asked for each major subheading in section II.

A. Answer question 1 from section II, using one or two sentences.

Globes and maps help us learn geography and how to find places on our planet. They do this by: categorizing land and water separately and labeling each country and each body of water.

B. Answer question 2 from section II, using one or two sentences.

Directions and poles are north, south, east, west, NE, SW, etc. They help us locate places on a map or globe.

(continued)

C. Answer question 3 from section II, using one or two sentences.

Equators and hemispheres divide the earth in half. The equator is an imaginary line around the middle of the earth, and the north and south hemispheres are what make up each half.

On the back of this page, answer the rest of your subheading questions.

IV. REVIEW the entire chapter by going back through the chapter and outlining the main points. Your main points come from the headings, main ideas, and key words.

A. *Globes and maps*
  1. *globes are three-dimensional*
  2. *maps are two-dimensional*
  3. *help us locate bodies of water, countries, cities, and land forms*

B. *Directions and poles*
  1. *N, S, E, W*
  2. *in between directions: NE, SW, etc.*
  3. *north and south poles*

C. *Equator and hemispheres*
  1. *equator splits earth in half*
  2. *north and south hemispheres*
  3. *Make it easier to locate places on map or globe*

Therefore, they focused their study skills instruction on helping students to selectively attend to text descriptions of these relations; to discriminate between the quantities in each relation; to discriminate between similar relations presented in the text; and to apply the relations by reading sample problem solutions and then solving other problems on their own.

Larkin and Reif modeled and explained this reading strategy for a group of students and then gave them opportunities for practice and feedback. They found that the group receiving instruction demonstrated significantly better learning from their textbook than an untrained group.

In a similar type of study, Samuels and his colleagues (1988) looked at scientific journal articles that college students in educational psychology classes are asked to read. Their analysis of the structure of these articles revealed that they typically consist of four main sections: problem, method, results, and conclusions. Each main section is further organized into sub-sections. Students trained to analyze the text structure of scientific journal articles were able to read and recall significantly more of the information in them than were untrained students.

Other researchers have been concerned with training young students to recognize and use the text structure (also called "story grammar") of narrative text to guide their study behavior. In the study by Idol (1987), learning-disabled and low-achieving students in grades 3 and 4 were taught a "story mapping" procedure:

> Story mapping brings the reader's attention to important and interrelated parts of a narrative story. These story parts can be thought of as a type of story schemata for organizing and categorizing important story components (p. 197).

Students learned the story mapping procedure by answering ten questions about the structure of each story they were assigned to read. The ten questions are:

1. Where did this story take place?
2. When did this story take place?
3. Who were the main characters in the story?
4. Were there any other important characters in the story? Who?
5. What was the problem in the story?
6. How did _____ try to solve the problem?
7. Was it hard to solve the problem? Explain.
8. Was the problem solved? Explain.
9. What did you learn from reading this story? Explain.
10. Can you think of a different ending (p. 197)?

Idol's training method is similar to the five-step training method described earlier. She found that learning-disabled and low-achieving students were able to learn how to use story mapping independently, and that their comprehension of narrative text improved significantly.

Short and Ryan (1984) used a similar training method that significantly improved the reading comprehension of a group of low-achieving fourth grade boys. Instead of the ten story-mapping questions in Idol's method, however, they taught students to use a list of just five story-grammar questions:

1. Who is the main character?
2. Where and when did the story take place?
3. What did the main character do?
4. How did the story end?
5. How did the main character feel (p. 228)?

Teaching Students How to Make Graphic Organizers

In our discussion of Study Skill 6 (making a written outline or graphic organizer), we noted that Jones, Pierce, and Hunter (1988/1989) identify nine types of graphic organizers: spider maps, series of events chains, continuum scales, compare/contrast matrices, problem/solution outlines, network trees, fishbone maps, human interaction outlines, and cycles. They comment that students need to survey the text and decide which type of graphic organizer is most appropriate to represent it. For example, if the text describes nuclear and extended families and the characteristics of each, a compare/contrast matrix probably would be most appropriate for representing this information. If the text describes how a nuclear family forms and changes over time, however, a series-of-events chain would be the most appropriate graphic organizer.

Constructing a graphic organizer is not a simple matter. Once the appropriate type of organizer is selected, students need to construct it in stages by actively reading the text. This skill needs to be systematically taught to students. Jones and her colleagues describe a five-step training procedure for this purpose:

1. Present at least one good example of a completed graphic organizer.
2. Model how to construct either the same graphic or the one to be introduced.
3. Provide procedural knowledge about when students should use the graphic and why, and what their responsibility is in the learning process.
4. Coach the students as a whole class and then in small groups.
5. Give the students opportunities to practice making graphics individually and independently, and then give them feedback (p. 24).

This training procedure is similar to the general process for teaching text-study skills described earlier.

Teaching Students Summarizing Skills

Graphic organizers (Study Skill 6) and verbal summaries (Study Skill 7) are similar in that both enable students to check their understanding of the main ideas in a text. Because the two skills have similar purposes, teachers should consider teaching them at the same time. They can inform students that both skills promote reading comprehension by representing a large amount of text in an abbreviated, easily grasped format. Some students may benefit more from the visual format of graphic organizers, whereas other students may benefit more from the verbal format of summaries.

Anderson and Hidi (1988/1989) developed four recommendations for teaching summarization skills:

1. Choose simple text for students who are just beginning to develop these skills. Narratives are generally easier for students to summarize than are expository texts. Using short excerpts that deal with familiar concepts and ideas simplifies the task of summarization.

2. Let students see the text while summarizing it. "To remember a text and summarize it at the same time may be too much to ask of a beginner" (p. 27).

3. Focus students' attention on summarizing *important* information in the text and clarify the concept of importance. Anderson and Hidi recommend that students' summaries stress information that they believe the author thinks is important. Teachers should discuss the various ways that authors signal importance: introductory statements, topic sentences, summary statements, underlining, italics, repetition, and phrases directly stating that a fact or idea is important (Armbruster 1984). Teachers can illustrate each of these techniques by noting their presence in different samples of text.

4. Teach students to prepare *writer-based* summaries. Anderson and Hidi distinguish between *writer-based summaries*, which students prepare to help themselves understand the text; and *reader-based summaries*, which students use to show someone else (usually the teacher) that they understand the text or to stimulate their interest in it. With this distinction in mind, they recommend that students first be taught how to prepare writer-based summaries, which are easier to do and are more generally useful to students. Once they have mastered this skill, students can be taught how to prepare reader-based summaries.

Summarization skills develop slowly. Students will need extensive instruction if they are to become expert summarizers.

Teaching Students Question-Generating and Question-Answering Skills

Study Skill 12 involves the use of the reciprocal teaching reading strategy to study text material. Palincsar and Brown, the developers of the strategy, also developed an instructional method that helps teachers guide students through the strategy, from its introduction to the ability to apply it independently without teacher supervision.

Palincsar and Brown (1989) recommend that instruction begin with a set of direct-instruction lessons over a period of five days or so. Each lesson focuses on one of four reading comprehension activities that the strategy comprises: question generating, summarizing, clarifying, and predicting. The next step is for the teacher to conduct daily lessons with students in small groups (typically four to eight students). In each lesson, the teacher engages in a "dialogue" with the students about the text they are reading:

> When the dialogues begin, the teacher assumes principal responsibility for leading and sustaining the discussion. The teacher also can model skilled use of the [activities] for understanding the text. However, even from the first day of instruction, the children are encouraged to participate in the dialogues, for example, by commenting on the teacher's summary or by suggesting additional predictions. The teacher supports each student's participation by providing specific feedback, additional modeling, explanation, and prompting (Palincsar and Brown 1989, p. 33).

As the lessons proceed, the teacher gradually shifts responsibility for initiating and sustaining the dialogues to the students (the nature of these dialogues is further discussed in Paris, Wixson, and Palincsar 1986). Instruction continues until the teacher determines that the students have internalized the reciprocal teaching reading strategy.

This strategy involves several text comprehension techniques besides question generating. Davey and McBride (1986) developed and tested a five-lesson training program that teachers can use to focus specifically on developing students' question-generating ability. In the first lesson, the teacher provides a rationale for the value of question generating in studying text materials. He also explains the difference between "think" questions and "locate" questions (i.e., questions that can be answered by locating and underlining information in the text). In the second lesson, students are taught how to construct these two types of questions.

The third lesson focuses on teaching students how to identify important information in a text passage and then generate "think" and "locate" questions that ask about this information. The fourth and fifth lessons provide an opportunity for students to practice their skills and evaluate their use of the skills using a checklist.

Davey and McBride found that use of this instructional method led to significant improvement in the text-reading skills of a sample of sixth grade students. The method was equally effective for students of all reading abilities represented in the study.

Another way to teach students how to generate questions about text passages is to have them practice by turning the assignment into a game. To start the game, students read a passage and each generates several questions about it. One student then directs a question to another student in the class. If the student answers correctly, she gets to ask the next question. An incorrect answer means that the student who asked the question gets to ask another question from her list of self-generated questions. The teacher directs the activity to ensure that all students have the opportunity to ask and answer questions. This method is effective for students at any level—from primary school through college.

Text comprehension also can be enhanced by answering questions provided in the text. Raphael and Pearson (1985) developed and tested a method for teaching students how to answer these questions effectively. Their method focuses on three types of question-answer relationships:

> A text explicit (TE) question-answer relationship is a question with words comprising both the question and answer information stated explicitly in a single sentence of the text. A text implicit (TI) question-answer relationship is a question with answer information available in the text, but requiring the reader to integrate information across sentences or paragraphs in the text. A script implicit (SI) question-answer relationship is a question for which the information appropriate as an answer is not available in the text, requiring the readers to fill in the gaps from their own knowledge bases (Raphael and Pearson 1985, p. 220).

Students work through a series of instructional booklets that teach these question-answer relationships in four daily lessons. The teacher also explains and models each relationship and guides students' use of the booklets. Raphael and Pearson found that a sample of sixth grade students trained in this method made significant gains in their ability to answer questions in text materials, and in their ability to identify the question-answer relationship represented by each question. The method had the most effect on students of average and low reading ability.

Garner and her colleagues (1984) developed and tested a similar instructional method, but with emphasis on training students in a "look-back" strategy, which helps them determine when and where they should look back in their text for answers to content questions. The method significantly improved performance in the question-answering and look-back behavior of a group of remedial readers at the upper elementary and middle school levels.

Improving Students' Comprehension Monitoring

There is evidence that students across all grade levels fail to adequately monitor their comprehension (Pressley, Goodchild, Fleet, Zajchowski, and Evans 1989). This problem can be corrected by systematic instruction in comprehension monitoring skills (see Study Skill 8).

One of these skills, as we mentioned previously, is the ability to recognize that your comprehension has failed or is weak. Researchers are not sure, however, about how this skill should be taught. A possible approach is to teach it while teaching the study skills and strategies shown in Figure 6.1. For example, suppose students are being taught how to make a summary of a reading passage. The teacher can cue students to monitor how much difficulty they experience in writing the summary, and whether they believe their summary accurately represents the text. If students report difficulty or are uncertain about their summary, the teacher can help students label this phenomenon as an instance of comprehension failure or weakness. He also can emphasize that such methods as summarizing, question generating, and constructing graphic organizers are useful, in part, because they help students monitor their comprehension.

The other aspect of comprehension monitoring that we identified in our discussion of Study Skill 8 is the ability to select and use an appropriate method for correcting comprehension failures. Haller, Child, and Walberg (1988) identify several of these methods in their review of research on metacognition training: trying to understand the text by relating it to what you already know, rereading the section of the text that is confusing or rereading preceding sections of text, reading ahead in the text, and relating details to main ideas. To their list we would add the methods of reading other sources on the topic, seeking help, and determining the meaning of unfamiliar vocabulary. Haller and her colleagues concluded from their review of research that instruction in these methods to detect and correct comprehension failures substantially and consistently improved students' reading comprehension. Metacognition instruction was found to be particularly effective for students at the middle-school level.

* * *

Jones (1988) recently summarized several extensive reviews of the research literature on instruction in text-reading strategies of the type listed in Figure 6.1:

> The more explicit the level of strategy instruction, the greater the effects; this was true not only of studies involving training of average and above average students but also of studies involving the training of low-achieving students (p. 239).

Less explicit instruction, by Jones' definition, involves the teacher's merely making requests for students to use a particular reading strategy or giving simple guidelines on its use. More explicit instruction involves explanation of text features involved in use of the strategy and instruction in applying the strategy.

References

Adams, A., D. Carnine, and R. Gersten. (1982). "Instructional Strategies for Studying Content Area Texts in the Intermediate Grades." *Reading Research Quarterly* 18: 27–54.

Anderson, R. C. (1977). "The Notion of Schemata and the Education Enterprise." In *Schooling and the Acquisition of Knowledge*, edited by R. C. Anderson, R. J. Spiro, and W. E. Montague. Hillsdale, N.J.: Erlbaum.

Anderson, R., and W. Biddle. (1975). "On Asking People Questions About What They Are Reading." In *The Psychology of Learning and Motivation*, vol. 9., edited by G. H. Bower. New York: Academic Press.

Anderson, T. H. (1979). "Study Skills and Learning Strategies." In *Cognitive and Affective Learning Strategies*, edited by H. F. O'Neil, Jr., and C. D. Spielberger. New York: Academic Press.

Anderson, T. H., and B. B. Armbruster. (1984). "Studying." In *Handbook of Reading Research*, edited by P. D. Pearson. New York: Longman.

Anderson, V., and S. Hidi. (December 1988/January 1989). "Teaching Students to Summarize." *Educational Leadership* 46, 4: 26–28.

Armbruster, B. B. (1984). "The Problem of Inconsiderate Text." In *Comprehension Instruction: Perspectives and Suggestions*, edited by G. G. Duffy, L. R. Roehler, And J. Mason. New York: Longman.

Armbruster, B. B., and T. H. Anderson. (1980). "The Effect of Mapping on the Free Recall of Expository Text." Tech. Rep. No. 160. Urbana: University of Illinois, Center for the Study of Reading. ERIC Document Reproduction Service No. ED 182 735.

Baker, L., and A. L. Brown. (1984). "Metacognitive Skills and Reading." In *Handbook of Reading Research*, edited by P. D. Pearson. New York: Longman.

Barton, W. A. (1930). *Outlining as a Study Procedure*. New York: Teachers College, Columbia University.

Bianco, L., and S. McCormick. (1989). "Analysis of Effects of a Reading Study Skill Program for High School Learning-Disabled Students." *Journal of Educational Research* 82: 282–288.

Bretzing, B. B., and R. W. Kulhavy. (1981). "Note Taking and Passage Style." *Journal of Educational Psychology* 73: 242–250.

Bretzing, B. B., and R. W. Kulhavy. (1979). "Note Taking and Depth of Processing." *Contemporary Educational Psychology* 4: 145–153.

Brown, A. L., and J. D. Day. (1983). "Macrorules for Summarizing Texts: The Development of Expertise." *Journal of Verbal Learning and Verbal Behavior* 22: 1–14.

Brown, A. L., J. C. Campione, and J. D. Day. (1981). "Learning to Learn: On Training Students to Learn from Tests." *Educational Researcher* 10: 14–21.

Brown, A. L., S. S. Smiley, J. Day, M. Townsend, and S. C. Lawton. (1977). "Intrusion of a Thematic Idea in Children's Recall of Prose." *Child Development* 48: 1454–1466.

Bullock, T., C. Laine, and E. Slinger. (In press). "Reading Instruction in Secondary English and Social Studies Classrooms." *Reading Research and Instruction*.

Carnine, D., and D. Kinder. (1985). "Teaching Low-Performing Students to Apply Generative and Schema Strategies to Narrative and Expository Material." *Remedial and Special Education* 6: 20–30.

Carver, R. P. (1973a). "Effect of Increasing the Rate of Speech Presentation upon Comprehension." *Journal of Educational Psychology* 65: 118–126.

Carver, R. P. (1973b). "Understanding Information Processing, and Learning from Prose Materials." *Journal of Educational Psychology* 64: 76–84.

Chall, J. S., S. Conrad, and S. Harris. (1987). *An Analysis of Textbooks in Relation to Declining SAT Scores*. Princeton, N.J.: College Entrance Examination Board.

Clay, M. M. (1973). *Reading: The Patterning of Complex Behavior*. Auckland, New Zealand: Heinemann.

Cole, J. Y., and T. G. Sticht. (1981). *The Textbook in American Society.* Washington, D.C.: Library of Congress.

Dansereau, D. F. (1979). "Development and Evaluation of a Learning Strategy Training Program." *Journal of Educational Psychology* 71: 64–73.

Davey, B., and S. McBride. (1986). "Effects of Question Generation Training on Reading Comprehension." *Journal of Educational Psychology* 78: 256–262.

DeCrow, R., ed. (1972). *Adult Reading Development: An Information Awareness Service.* Washington, D.C.: National Reading Center Foundation (ERIC No. ED 068 808).

Doctorow, M., C. Marks, and M. Wittrock. (1978). "Generative Processes in Reading Comprehension." *Journal of Educational Psychology* 70: 109–118.

Duffy, G. G., L. R. Roehler, M. S. Meloth, and L. G. Vavrus. (1986). "Conceptualizing Instructional Explanation." *Teaching and Teacher Education* 2: 197–214.

Duffy, T. M. (1976). "Literacy Research in the Navy." (September 1976). In *Reading and Readability Research in the Armed Services,* edited by T. G. Sticht and D. W. Zapf. HumRRO RF-WO-CA-76-4. Alexandria, Va.: Human Resources Research Organization.

Durkin, D. (1978–79). "What Classroom Observations Reveal about Reading Comprehension Instruction." *Reading Research Quarterly* 14: 481–533.

Flavell, J. H. (1978). "Metacognitive Development." In *Structural/Process Theories of Complex Human Behavior,* edited by J. M. Scandura and C. J. Brainerd. Alphen a. d. Rijn, The Netherlands: Sijthoff and Noordhoff.

Fowler, R. L., and A. S. Barker. (1974). "Effectiveness of Highlighting for Retention of Text Material." *Journal of Applied Psychology* 59: 358–364.

Fullmer, R. (1980). "Maximal Reading and Auding Rates." Doctoral diss., Harvard University.

Gall, M. D., and J. P. Gall. (1988). *Study for Success Teacher's Manual.* Eugene, Oreg.: M. Damien Publishers.

Garner, R. (1982). "Efficient Text Summarization: Costs and Benefits." *Journal of Educational Research* 75: 275–279.

Garner, R., and P. Alexander. (1982). "Strategic Processing of Text: An Investigation of the Effects on Adults' Question-Answering Performance." *Journal of Educational Research* 75: 144–148.

Garner, R., V. C. Hare, P. Alexander, J. Haynes, and P. Winograd. (1984). "Inducing Use of a Text Lookback Strategy Among Unsuccessful Readers." *American Educational Research Journal* 21: 789–798.

Garner, R., and J. D. McCaleb. (1985). "Effects of Text Manipulations on Quality of Written Summaries." *Contemporary Educational Psychology* 10: 139–149.

Garner, R., G. B. Macready, and S. Wagoner. (1984). "Readers' Acquisition of the Components of the Text-Lookback Strategy." *Journal of Educational Psychology* 76: 300–309.

Goodlad, J. I. (1976). *Facing the Future: Issues in Education and Schooling.* New York: McGraw-Hill.

Gough, P. B. (1984). "Word Recognition." In *Handbook of Reading Research,* edited by P. D. Pearson. New York: Longman.

Guthrie, J. T. (1977). "Story Comprehension." *The Reading Teacher* 30: 574–577.

Haller, E. P., D. A. Child, and H. J. Walberg. (1988). "Can Comprehension Be Taught? A Quantitative Synthesis of 'Metacognitive' Studies." *Educational Researcher* 17, 9: 5–8.

Hare, V. C., and K. M. Borchardt. (1984). "Direct Instruction of Summarization Skills." *Reading Research Quarterly* 21: 62–78.

Hidi, S., and V. Anderson. (1986). "Producing Written Summaries: Task Demands, Cognitive Operations, and Implications for Instruction." *Review of Educational Research* 56: 473–493.

Idol, L. (1987). "Group Story Mapping: A Comprehension Strategy for Both Skilled and Unskilled Readers." *Journal of Learning Disabilities* 20: 196–205.

Johnson, D. D., and J. F. Baumann. (1984). "Word Identification." In *Handbook of Reading Research,* edited by P. D. Pearson. New York: Longman.

Jones, B. F. (1988). "Text Learning Strategy Instruction: Guidelines from Theory and Practice." In *Learning and Study Strategies*, edited by C. E. Weinstein, E. T. Goetz, and P. A. Alexander. San Diego, Calif.: Academic Press.

Jones, B. F., J. Pierce, and B. Hunter. (December 1988/January 1989). "Teaching Students to Construct Graphic Representations." *Educational Leadership* 46, 4: 20–25.

Kahn, M. S. (1978). "E.S.P.: Not Just Another Expository Textbook Study Method." *College Student Journal* 12: 372–374.

Kavale, K., and R. Schreiner. (1979). "The Reading Processes of Above Average and Average Readers: A Comparison of the Use of Reasoning Strategies in Responding to Standardized Comprehension Measures." *Reading Research Quarterly* 15: 102–128.

Larkin, J. H., and F. Reif. (1976). "Analysis and Teaching of a General Skill for Studying Scientific Text." *Journal of Educational Psychology* 68: 431–440.

Levin, J. R., and M. Pressley. (1981). "Improving Children's Prose Comprehension: Selected Strategies That Seem to Succeed." In *Children's Prose Comprehension: Research and Practice*, edited by C. M. Santa and B. L. Hayes. Newark, Del.: International Reading Association.

McConkie, G. W., K. Rayner, and S. Wilson. (1973). "Experimental Manipulation of Reading Strategies." *Journal of Educational Psychology* 65: 1–8.

Moore, D. W. (1987). "Vocabulary." In *Research Within Reach: Secondary School Reading*, edited by D. E. Alvermann, D. W. Moore, and M. W. Conley. Newark, Del.: International Reading Association.

Moreira, M. (1979). "Concept Maps as Tools for Teaching." *Journal of College Science Teaching* 26: 218–230.

Murrell, P. C., Jr., and J. R. Surber. (April 1987). "The Effect of Generative Summarization on the Comprehension of Main Ideas from Lengthy Expository Text." Paper presented at the annual meeting of the American Educational Research Association, Washington, D.C.

Palincsar, A. S., and A. L. Brown. (1989). "Instruction for Self-Regulated Reading." In *Toward the Thinking Curriculum: Current Cognitive Research* (1989 Yearbook), edited by L. B. Resnick and L. E. Klopfer. Alexandria, Va.: Association for Supervision and Curriculum Development.

Palincsar, A. S., and A. L. Brown (1984). "Reciprocal Teaching of Comprehension-Fostering and Comprehension-Monitoring Activities." *Cognition and Instruction* 1: 117–175.

Palincsar, A. S., K. Ransom, and S. Derber. (December 1988/January 1989). "Collaborative Research and Development of Reciprocal Teaching." *Educational Leadership* 46, 4: 37–40.

Paris, S. G., K. K. Wixson, and A. M. Palincsar. (1986). "Instructional Approaches to Reading Comprehension." In *Review of Research in Education*, edited by E. Rothkopf. Washington, D.C.: American Educational Research Association.

Pearson, P. D., and J. A. Dole. (1987). "Explicit Comprehension Instruction: A Review of Research and a New Conceptualization of Instruction." *The Elementary School Journal* 88: 151–166.

Peper, R. J., and R. E. Mayer. (1978). "Note-Taking as a Generative Activity." *Journal of Educational Psychology* 70: 514–522.

Pressley, M., and D. Forrest-Pressley. (1985). "Questions and Children's Cognitive Processing." In *The Psychology of Questions*, edited by A. C. Graesser and J. B. Black. Hillsdale, N.J.: Lawrence Erlbaum.

Pressley, M., F. Goodchild, J. Fleet, R. Zajchowski, and E. D. Evans. (1989). "The Challenge of Classroom Strategy Instruction." *Elementary School Journal* 89: 301–342.

Raphael, T. E., and P. D. Pearson. (1985). "Increasing Students' Awareness of Sources of Information for Answering Questions." *American Educational Research Journal* 22: 217–236.

Ricciardi, P. (August 1984). "Children's Selection of the Critical Elements of Prose Passages." Paper presented at the annual meeting of the American Psychological Association, Toronto.

Robinson, F. P. (1941). *Diagnostic and Remedial Techniques for Effective Study*. New York; Harper and Brothers.

Ryan, M. P. (1984). "Monitoring Text Comprehension: Individual Differences in Epistemological Standards." *Journal of Educational Psychology* 76: 248–258.

Salisbury, R. (1935). "Some Effects of Training in Outlining." *English Journal* 24: 111–116.

Samuels, S. J., and M. L. Kamil. (1984). "Models of the Reading Process." In *Handbook of Reading Research*, edited by D. Pearson. New York: Longman.

Samuels, S. J., R. Tennyson, L. Sax, P. Mulcahy, N. Schermer, and H. Hajovy. (1988). "Adults' Use of Text Structure in the Recall of a Scientific Journal Article." *Journal of Educational Research* 81: 171–174.

Schnell, T. R., and D. Rocchio. (1975). "A Comparison of Underlining Strategies for Improving Reading Comprehension and Retention." In *Reading: Convention and Inquiry* (24th Yearbook of the National Reading Conference), edited by G. H. McNinch and W. D. Miller. Clemson, S.C.: National Reading Conference.

Short, E. J., and E. B. Ryan. (1984). "Metacognitive Differences Between Skilled and Less Skilled Readers: Remediating Deficits Through Story Grammar and Attribution Training." *Journal of Educational Psychology* 76: 225–235.

Simpson, M. L. (1984). "The Status of Study Strategy Instruction: Implications for Classroom Teachers." *Journal of Reading* 28: 136–142.

Singer, H., and D. Donlan. (1982). "Active Comprehension: Problem Solving Schema with Question Generation for Comprehension of Complex Short Stories." *Reading Research Quarterly* 19: 166–194.

Slinger, E. L. (1981). "A Systematic Observation of the Extent to Which Students in Secondary Content Area Classrooms Are Given Instruction in Reading Assigned Material." Doctoral diss., University of Oregon, Eugene.

Smith, H. K. (1967). "The Responses of Good and Poor Readers When Asked to Read for Different Purposes." *Reading Research Quarterly* 3: 56–83.

Stewart, J., J. Vankirk, and R. Rowell. (1979). "Concept Maps: A Tool for Use in Biology Teaching." *American Biology Teaching* 41: 171–175.

Taylor, B., and S. Berkowitz. (1980). "Facilitating Children's Comprehension of Context Material." In *Perspectives on Reading Research and Instruction* (29th Yearbook of the National Reading Conference), edited by M. L. Kamil and A. J. Moe. Washington, D.C.: National Reading Conference

Taylor, S. E. (1964). *Listening*. Washington, D.C.: National Education Association.

Thomas, K. (1978). "The Directed Inquiry Activity: An Instructional Procedure for Content Reading." *Reading Improvement* 15: 138–140.

Van Patten, J., C. Chao, and C. M. Reigeluth. (1986). "A Review of Strategies for Sequencing and Synthesizing Information." *Review of Educational Research* 56: 437–471.

Walker, N. M. (1979). "The Effect of Graphic Organizers on the Learning of Social Studies Content and Attitude Toward Reading." In *Research in Reading in the Content Areas: The Fourth Report*, edited by H. L. Herber and J. D. Riley. Syracuse, N.Y.: Syracuse University, Reading and Language Arts Center.

Wandersee, J. H. (1988). "Ways Students Read Texts." *Journal of Research in Science Teaching* 25: 69–84.

Weinstein, C. E., D. S. Ridley, T. Dahl, and E. S. Weber. (December 1988/January 1989). "Helping Students Develop Strategies for Effective Learning." *Educational Leadership* 46, 4: 17–19.

Whimbey, A. (1975). *Intelligence Can Be Taught*. New York: Dutton.

Winograd, P., and S. G. Paris. (December 1988/January 1989). "A Cognitive and Motivational Agenda for Reading Instruction." *Educational Leadership* 46, 4: 30–36.

Wong, B. Y. L. (1985). "Self-Questioning Instructional Research: A Review." *Review of Educational Research* 55: 227–268.

Wong, B. Y. L., and W. Jones. (1982). "Increasing Meta-Comprehension in Learning Disabled and Normally Achieving Students through Self-Questioning Training." *Learning Disabilities Quarterly* 5: 228–239.

7
Writing School Papers

The Importance of Writing Skills

People are expected to write, both in school and later in life. Students are required to write test answers, complete worksheets for various courses, and write compositions such as term papers, essays, book reports, journals, and stories. Upon entering the world of work, they will need to write resumes, letters, company newsletters, or memoranda. Indeed, a large variety of jobs involve writing, now that the economic foundation of modern society has shifted from trade and industry to information and service. For this reason, writing, among other communication skills, is increasingly important for economic success, and indeed for survival. Despite the prevalence of television and other electronic media, written communication continues to be essential to full functioning in our society.

> Writing can give you power, for we live in a complicated technological society, and those people who can collect information, order it into significant meaning, and then communicate it to others will influence the course of events within the town or nation, school or university, company or corporation. Information is power (Murray 1987, p. 4).

In Western society, most people expect persons holding prominent positions, particularly intellectual leaders, to be both skillful and prolific writers. Throughout history, the power of the written word to influence others' thoughts and actions has been tremendous.

Common Types of Writing

Students may write on their own initiative as an adjunct to other tasks—for example, taking notes on assigned reading or keeping a journal of their thoughts and ideas. Writing is usually assigned by the teacher, however, and is expected to adhere to certain standards and conventions. This chapter is concerned with the study process that students use to carry out assigned writing, particularly the process of writing a *school paper*, by which we mean any type of writing assignment that is sufficient in scope to require a systematic writing process. Typically, a paper can be defined as a piece of writing that is a page or more in length, is revised before being handed in, and takes more than one class period to complete.

The Status of Students' Writing Skills

Despite the importance of writing, many people in the United States have limited writing ability. A report of findings from the 1986 National Assessment of Educational Progress indicates that the writing skills of students in American schools are inadequate "for people who must live and work in an increasingly complex and technological society" (American School Board Journal 1987). While most students tested had basic reading and comprehension skills, only 22 percent of eleventh graders, 15 percent of eighth graders, and 4 percent of fourth graders wrote letters judged adequate or better. Furthermore, students' attitudes toward writing deteriorate steadily through the grades (Applebee, Langer, and Mullis 1986). A "substantial proportion" of eleventh graders, the NAEP concluded, will be graduated from high school without having developed the reasoning skills they need to communicate their ideas in writing (American School Board Journal 1987).

Improvement in writing ability is in part a developmental process that occurs naturally over time (Emig 1983). Yet writing is also a highly skilled process, and thus subject to the need for careful instruction and practice in order to develop fully. The prevalence of college composition courses that include remedial writing skills indicates that most college students did not learn to write well in elementary and secondary school.

Through classroom observation in two schools and a national questionnaire survey of teachers, Applebee (1981) found that most student writing involved short activities such as note taking, short-answer and multiple-choice tests, fill-in-the-blank exercises, math calculations, and the like. Even in the rare cases when students were asked to write a paragraph or more, writing was often used merely to test knowledge of specific content, with the teacher in the role of examiner. Applebee observed that such writing makes minimal demands on students' compositional ability, because the teacher already knows what should have been said and thus gives students credit simply for repeating correct information, rather than requiring them to formulate their own ideas clearly.

> Contrasted with the writing to display knowledge, [writing to communicate ideas] is also more difficult; the writer has to organize and communicate opinions to a reader who does not already know what is going to be said and who may well hold an opposing opinion (Applebee 1981, p. 105).

Applebee also found that when students were asked to write assignments of a page or more in length, prewriting activities were limited, with students typically beginning to write within three minutes after the teacher gave the assignment. In addition, the teacher was the sole or primary audience for the writing; errors in writing mechanics were the main focus of teacher feedback; and most writing was completed in one draft, with no opportunity or expectation for revision.

In Applebee's study, teachers of English (and to a lesser extent teachers of business education and foreign languages) were more likely to help students with the writing task. Teachers of science, social science, and math were more likely to be concerned with the accuracy of information and soundness of conclusions, rather than with students' writing style. Ninth graders were given somewhat more help with their writing than eleventh graders and were less likely to be held strictly accountable for the accuracy of their work.

Applebee concluded his study by observing that teachers seem to conceptualize writing as "a simple skill which a given student has or does not have." He noted that there was "little reflection in the practices we observed of recent studies of composing which suggest that writing is a process with a number of distinct stages, each with its own focus and demands" (p. 102).

Until the 1970s, very few educators wrote about the *process* involved in writing, nor was there much focus on teaching steps of the writing process to students. Students were typically assigned a paper of a required length and topic and were expected to write a finished product, turn it in for grading, and have it returned. They were seldom given feedback on their writing or the opportunity to revise their papers.

If teachers gave written feedback on papers, it focused mainly on spelling and grammatical errors, with perhaps a global comment on the paper's overall acceptability to the teacher ("good," or "needs more explanation"). If opportunities for revision were provided, students generally limited themselves to correcting spelling and minor grammatical errors. Despite research on how good writers actually write, overall the *teaching* of writing has changed very little.

Ames (1985) found that most composition textbooks prior to 1970 strongly emphasized grammar while not even mentioning the topic of revision. The authors of these books apparently believed that grammar and punctuation were essential to good writing and that they should be taught through workbook exercises rather than as part of real-life writing. In fact, as research reviewed later in this chapter shows, a focus on grammar in writing instruction is associated with lower-quality writing.

In his survey of secondary schools, Applebee (1981) found that only three percent of observed class time involved writing of at least a paragraph in length. In a subsequent survey of popular high school textbooks, Applebee (1984) found that texts in all subjects were for the most part constructed around exercises requiring only minimal writing. While literature and science texts supplemented this base of restricted activity with more extensive writing tasks, textbooks in other subjects, including grammar and composition, "offered few if any suggestions for more extended tasks."

The Nature of the Writing Process

Various authors have attempted to define the types of writing expected of students. Moffett (1979) distinguished among four definitions in common use:

1. *Handwriting* is the physical act of placing words on a page.
2. *Taking dictation and copying* is recording graphically one's own words or the words of others.
3. *Crafting* is fashioning units of discourse into meaningful patterns.
4. *Authoring* is elaborating inner speech into outer discourse for a specific purpose and a specific audience.

Consistent with Emig (1982), we consider only crafting and authoring as writing:

> Handwriting, spelling, punctuation, and matters of usage will be viewed not as autonomous and discrete skills but as support systems in a developmental sequence. Writing will be regarded as a continuous, coordinated performance and a process of immense perceptual, linguistic, and cognitive complexity (p. 2021).

In the past 20 years, some writers and educators have begun to focus on the need to teach students the writing *process* in order to ensure that they have the skills to produce an acceptable written *product*. Many models of the writing process have emerged, including the following.

Neubert and McNelis (1986) conclude from "seminal studies" of the writing process that it has three major steps:

> . . . prewriting (topic selection, audience and purpose consideration, data gathering, and organization), and drafting and revision (looking again at the draft and making appropriate changes in ideas followed by editing for the surface features of grammar, spelling, and punctuation) (p. 54).

Romano (1987) describes five stages that writers go through when producing a paper:

1. *Percolating* is the process of preparing to write. It occurs throughout the writing process, and includes not only thinking but also "anything done in relation to the piece of writing aside from producing a draft or revising one," such as brainstorming or drawing diagrams of ideas (p. 56).

2. *Drafting* involves "getting a vision down on paper, cutting loose with it, so to speak, with little regard to refinement and correctness, but much regard to making meaning" (p. 56).

3. *Revising* is when "matters of clarity, emotional payoffs, precise word selection, and fully developed, connected thinking are most often addressed" (p. 56).

4. *Editing* involves "correcting errors of spelling, punctuation, grammar, and usage," and should occur "when students believe they are finished with the shape and content of a piece of writing" (p. 73).

5. *Publishing* is "any public presentation" of writing. It is an opportunity to celebrate "the triumphs that occur quietly in writers' minds and are subsequently put on paper . . . a chance to share without criticism those struggled-over words with an audience" (p. 76).

Schumm and Radencich (1984) describe a model for teaching upper elementary or junior high school students how to write a term paper. Their model focuses less on the underlying thought processes involved in producing a piece of writing, and more on the tangible behaviors the student demonstrates as the written piece evolves over time. The 11 stages of their model are:

1. Deciding on a topic.
2. Developing a thesis statement.
3. Locating information.
4. Developing a bibliography.
5. Making a tentative outline.
6. Taking notes.
7. Completing an outline.
8. Writing a rough draft.
9. Revising the rough draft.
10. Writing the final draft.
11. Evaluating the final draft.

Most models of the writing process describe it as a series of steps, from initial idea to final draft. For instance:

1. Identify what you are supposed to do in the paper.
2. Brainstorm ideas for the paper.
3. Do library research if necessary.
4. Organize your ideas into an outline.

5. Write a first draft of the paper.
6. Get feedback on the draft, and revise it.
7. Hand in a neat copy of the final paper (Gall and Gall 1988b).

Some models emphasize the writer's thinking process, while others emphasize the writer's observable behaviors. Many models attempt to represent the recursive, or cyclical, nature of the writing process. Even the originators of those models that appear to be linear (a sequence of steps in a fixed order) acknowledge that the steps can occur in different orders and are often repeated at various stages during the process.

The criteria of writing quality are a matter of disagreement among writing educators. Some stress formal aspects of the paper (punctuation, grammar, word usage, neatness), whereas others stress creativity of ideas and expression. Samway (1987) discusses the problems of using holistic ratings for student papers, a common method of evaluation. She argues that holistic ratings are based on a deficit model rather than a best performance model, and that in her study such ratings "did not allow the raters to peek into the greatness of each child" (p. 297). Samway cites the writing samples of a Spanish-speaking student that are eloquent but nongrammatical, noting:

> Five of the seven stories that he wrote received scores that indicated that, if they had been written for the designated New York state writing test, he would have failed the test and been targeted for remedial writing instruction (Samway 1987, p. 291).

Samway argues that this student's later writing and the ideas he contributed to other students during writing conferences demonstrate "the growth that is occurring, albeit sporadically, even haphazardly." She concludes:

> Brief but regular narrative comments indicating progress, strengths, and weaknesses placed in a cumulative folder along with samples of a child's writing would certainly tell us more about individual children and their writing growth than [formal tests] simply because they do not ignore the multifaceted nature of writing when it evolves in a human environment (Samway 1987, p. 297).

Samway's comments have important implications for teaching study skills for writing school papers. In evaluating students' writing, teachers must address more than the overall quality of a paper and its discrete elements. They must also consider the students' personal and intellectual characteristics, so they can discern and encourage progress. At least through the stage of drafting, teachers need to spend more time helping students to improve the content of their writing (expression of ideas) and less time correcting grammar, spelling, and other aspects of writing form. This focus on writing content is particularly critical for disadvantaged students.

Writing Instruction for Disadvantaged Students

John-Steiner and Tatter (1985), in their encyclopedic review of the language development of the disadvantaged, note the effects of poverty on language:

> Economic conditions which severely limit the frequency and duration of verbal interactions between children and caretakers, and which restrict the elaboration of these interactions and the functions or purposes for which they are used in daily life, are likely to place children at a disadvantage in language development (p. 2887).

Our observations of the learning needs of disadvantaged children suggest that they will benefit even more from study skills instruction in the writing process than average or above-average students. Because disadvantaged students often know little about writing conventions, focusing on correct spelling and grammar before encouraging them to express their ideas can doom them to continued failure in writing. The ability to express thoughts in writing does not depend on a large vocabulary and high reading comprehension scores. Writing can build on the spoken language skills of any individual or group, whether those skills correspond to the middle-class norm or not. Thus, disadvantaged children in particular will benefit from writing instruction that encourages students to pay more attention to ideas and to the refinement of those ideas than to correct spelling and grammar.

Study Skills for Writing Papers

Regardless of the subject or course in which the writing task is assigned, students need certain basic skills to write good school papers. Our list of study skills for writing school papers, shown in Figure 7.1, is a synthesis of the models described earlier. Each skill except the last represents a step in the writing process; the last study skill involves using the computer as a word-processing tool.

STUDY SKILL 1
Defining the Writing Task

The school writing task generally consists of writing an answer to a teacher-specified question. In the earlier grades, these questions and answers tend to be simple and short. In the later grades, writing assignments become more complex, and students need to clarify the requirements of each assignment before proceeding.

To write good school papers, students must develop skill in analyzing the following aspects of the writing task:

1. *Purpose of the writing assignment.* For example, is the purpose to summarize information about a topic, or to make judgments based on the information?

2. *Audience.* Often the teacher is the only reader of the paper, so the teacher becomes the assumed audience. Teachers can define another audience, however—for example, students' peers.

3. *Form of writing.* The form of expression may vary widely depending on the teacher's assignment or the students' preferences; for example, the "paper" can be a poem, news article, report, journal entry, or short story.

4. *Length of paper.* This is often specified as a certain number of pages or as covering a certain scope of content.

5. *Sources.* A technical report will generally have many references, whereas a short story may not have any.

6. *Due date.* Many school papers must be done by a specified time, or a grade penalty is given.

STUDY SKILL 2
Specifying the Paper Topic

Students often find it difficult to choose a topic of interest and to limit it; their selections are often too narrow or too broad, or they do not meet assignment requirements (Schumm and Radencich 1984). Students need to learn how to select a topic that (1) is of interest to them, (2) meets the teacher's requirements, and (3) is of manageable breadth, neither too broad nor too narrow.

Parker (1979) observes that schools are much better at teaching students *about* things than they are at teaching them *how to do* things. Thus it is not surprising that so many students write their papers "about" the topics the teacher assigns or merely describe information obtained from a single source. For example, the student writes "about" whales, or "discusses" the Cuban missile crisis, never stating a single opinion or interpretation. Too many student papers are simply regurgitations of whatever is written in a book or encyclopedia entry on the topic.

We recommend stating the topic as an intellectual task to be solved by writing the paper. We suggest that students begin their topic sentence with a phrase like, "The purpose of this paper is to . . ." and continue with a phrase like:

1. make *comparisons* between _____ and _____.
2. show the *development* of a(n) _____.
3. *evaluate* and criticize _____.
4. *analyze* why _____ happened.
5. Explore the *consequences* of _____.

This approach helps the writer develop a focused topic and stay within its scope. Moreover, the intellectual task forces students to learn more than information; they must also learn how to think critically.

STUDY SKILL 3
Developing a Writing Plan

The most important study skill for writing papers may be the ability to form and follow a "writing plan," which is simply a list of things to do in an appropriate sequence. A writing plan requires the discipline to do what needs to be done, even when the writer prefers to do something else. For example, students who have planned adequately know when they need to go to the library to check other sources, even though they would prefer to start drafting the paper. At a later point, they might conclude that they should stop searching for sources so as to stay on schedule, even if they believe their search could be more thorough.

Organizing one's use of time is an important aspect of the writing plan.

> Because writing tempts one and, to a degree, requires one to do many things at once . . . there's a need for procedures that can order and focus the writer's energy and postpone some problems until later, all in the name of managing time and balancing constraints" (Hull and Bartholomae 1986, p. 47).

Better writers do not commit themselves to text right away, but devote time to sorting through possible approaches, ideas, and arguments (Flower and Hayes 1980).

Students must plan in order to carry out all the steps in the writing process within the available time. In doing this, they should realize that writing requires substantial time. It could easily take 36 hours to bring a 15-page paper from initial planning through a typed final copy (Gall and Gall 1988a).

Once students have decided generally how much time to devote to the paper, they need to plan a writing schedule. Planning involves self-management skills, including that of breaking a big task into small, manageable tasks (see Chapter 4). Students' goals should be to complete each small task by a certain date.

Flower and Hayes (1980) observe that the planning process, begun before writing begins, continues afterward, "as a writer refines her intentions in concert with the development of her text, true to the recursive nature of composing" (p. 47). Some expert writers spend a great deal of effort replanning, often simply by thinking about their final goal and how well they are reaching it. Replanning can result in revising the outline of the paper, getting new information, or revising parts of the paper that already have been written.

STUDY SKILL 4
Generating Ideas

Advocates of the process approach to writing instruction emphasize having students generate ideas before beginning to draft their papers. Murray (1987) suggests various strategies for generating ideas, including brainstorming, mapping, free writing, and making a concept tree.

Brainstorming. Both Schumm and Radencich (1984) and Gall and Gall (1988b) recommend brainstorming as a technique for generating ideas for a school paper. Brainstorming involves three steps: (1) define a problem; (2) think of as many ideas as possible as quickly as possible to solve the problem, suspending critical judgment and letting the ideas flow; and (3) use critical judgment to select the best idea. Brainstorming can be used to get ideas at various points in the writing process—for example, to develop points for an outline or to select better phrases when revising the paper.

Free writing. This technique for generating ideas involves writing in an uninhibited way about whatever you are thinking. Hillocks (1987) reviewed the research on the effectiveness of this technique and found that free writing by itself had little effect on writing quality. He noted, however, that free writing is often combined with prewriting, opportunities for feedback, and revising. These activities may increase its effectiveness.

Tree making. Murray (1987) recommends that students make "trees" to generate ideas and map their relationships. Students draw the tree as a set of bubbles, each containing a separate idea. Lines, like the branches and twigs of an actual tree, are drawn between bubbles to show that they are related to each other. As each idea is written and placed in a bubble, it may spark associations with other ideas that are then written and placed in bubbles. Because the ideas can be written as words and phrases, the emphasis is on idea generation rather than on text composition.

STUDY SKILL 5
Collecting Information

Teachers often specify that a particular source (e.g., a school encyclopedia entry on a given topic) must be used in writing a paper, or they require that a certain number of sources be used. Although not every assignment has these requirements, good writers generally look at one or more sources.

To do this part of the writing task well, students need to know how to (1) select library materials, including dictionaries and encyclopedias, to research a topic; (2) use the index and table of contents to find information in a book; and (3) use skimming and scanning to get a quick overview of materials (Schumm and Radencich 1984). They also need to learn the appropriate procedure for putting together a bibliography of their resource materials (Schumm and Radencich 1984; Gall and Gall 1988a).

Kobasigawa (1983) investigated the ability of fourth and eighth grade students to use information retrieval skills in conducting school research projects. He conceptualized information retrieval as a process of answering questions (called "retrieval questions") that arise in the course of writing a research paper. The process includes two subprocesses: a search process, which involves determining where the desired information is likely to be located, and an evaluation process, which involves determining the suitability and sufficiency of gathered information for answering retrieval questions. Eighty percent of the fourth graders and all of the eighth graders correctly identified the index, table of contents, or both, as places to look in a book to find out about its topics. Only 40 percent of the younger children, but all of the older children, were able to suggest topics or key words to use in finding information in a book relevant to a retrieval question.

Kobasigawa (1983) also found that fourth graders, when asked to evaluate collected information according to how well it answered specific retrieval questions, were less critical than the eighth graders. They judged the information as adequate because "everything is true" and "the spelling is correct," without noticing that the information failed to answer two of the three retrieval questions. It appeared that the younger children were evaluating the report in terms of a different criterion, namely "you'll get a better mark if you write more" rather than whether the information was adequate to answer given retrieval questions. When asked to select one of three books most appropriate for investigating the current locations of wolves in the world, only 30 percent of the fourth graders and 50 percent of the eighth graders selected the most recently published book.

Kobasigawa's findings suggest that students are not learning to retrieve and evaluate research information needed for writing reports as early and as well as teachers may assume. This conclusion is supported by a review of research by McQuade (1987), who found evidence in several studies that determining contradictions in source materials (an evaluative task) is difficult for many students.

Besides written sources, students can get information from individuals or organizations to use in their papers. They need to develop observation and interview skills in order to collect this information, but the result is likely to be a more original, thoughtful paper than is possible by simply reading information in written sources.

STUDY SKILL 6
Organizing Ideas into a Plan for the Paper

Traditionally, outlining has been the recommended procedure for organizing ideas prior to writing a paper. Murray (1987) describes the formal outline as one that "uses arabic and roman numerals and capital and small letters to break a subject down into categories and subcategories in a logical sequence" (p. 145). He comments that such an outline may be appropriate for a highly structured subject, but that the formal outline is not appropriate for every topic or for every writer, because it implies a linear, logical means of organization. A similar view is expressed by McQuade (1987):

> Children's organizing abilities are intuitive. Piagetian theory stated that the cognitive ability of the student at this age is not receptive to mechanical instruction alone, that of outlining or "first you find the topic sentence." Children at this stage can develop their own organization through numerous

conferences throughout the entire writing process. . . . Ultimately the question-and-answer periods produce a logical written structure through the student's ability to confirm in his own words what he knows about his subject of choice (p. 6).

Murray (1987) describes a variety of alternatives for bringing order to ideas, including the following:

1. *Titles*. Writing many titles before starting the paper can help students capture the direction of the story, a glimpse of its limitations and pace . . . [and] tone" (Murray 1987, p. 134).

2. *Leads*. Leads can be the first line, sentence, paragraph, or series of paragraphs to start the paper. Like the title, the lead provides direction and establishes the pace and tone of the piece.

3. *Ends*. To get a sense of direction, many good writers determine where they want to end before they begin to write.

4. *Sequences*. The writer simply lists the main points that will be made and then moves them around until each point clearly leads to the next one.

Murray also identifies a dozen different ways of "outlining," that is, organizing paper ideas in written form. For example, the writer can use boxes to dramatize the importance of certain points; brainstorm questions the reader will ask when reading the written piece and put them in the likely order the reader will ask them; use flow charts or concept trees; list each writing element on an index card and then display the cards on a cork board; and make file folders for each writing topic.

While many of the skills discussed so far also involve writing, their primary focus is on thinking, planning, and collecting information. In the remaining steps, these processes continue, but the student now puts more energy into actually constructing a written *product* consistent with the requirements of the assignment. Producing a first draft can be viewed as the "Go" decision to write, the decision to gather the fruits of one's thinking up to that point.

STUDY SKILL 7
Drafting the Paper

Some expert writers recommend a brainstorming process when writing a first draft. Murray (1987), for example, offers several recommendations, including lowering your standards, writing fast, writing without notes, and writing with your ear. Of course, this writing strategy is based on the assumption that careful planning occurred during all the preceding stages of the writing process. Another strategy is to use a conversational tone, as if speaking or writing a personal letter, so that the words will flow naturally (Gall and Gall 1988a).

The main reason many students have difficulty writing their first draft is that they view it as their *only* draft. One of the strongest aspects of the process approach to writing is its premise that writing evolves through many stages and forms, and that it can and should be changed often to reflect the author's changes in thinking, new knowledge, response to feedback, and sudden inspirations. The first draft may be viewed, then, not only as imperfect in style but also as incomplete, as only partial coverage of what the final version of the paper will provide.

Monahan (1984) did a case study of eight twelfth grade students writing compositions for two audiences: teachers and peers. Four of the writers were classified as "basic" (relatively unskilled) and four as "competent" (relatively skilled) on holistically scored pieces of writing for a teacher audience. The results indicated that the competent writers concentrated on content in producing their drafts and revisions, whereas the basic writers concentrated on the difficulties they were having with penmanship. Monahan identified strategies to help basic writers produce text more easily—for example, learning calligraphy to improve their handwriting, or using computers to produce typed text. By simplifying text production, such strategies presumably enable writers to focus more energy on composition, and thus improve the quality of their papers' content.

STUDY SKILL 8
Getting Feedback on the Draft

If teachers and students accept the importance of revision in the writing process, it follows that there must be some opportunity for students to get new ideas about what they have written and suggestions for improving it. Accordingly, advocates of the writing process (e.g., Ames 1985) place high value on conferencing and response groups. The purpose is threefold: (1) to give students a heightened experience of their own writing by reading it, or hearing it read, to other students; (2) to give students reader feedback on their writing; and (3) to take a break from writing, which allows students to get a fresh perspective on the topic and what they have to say about it. Conferencing and response groups generally provide oral feedback to students, but written feedback can also be requested or required.

Neubert and McNelis (1986) describe the Writing Response Group, a form of cooperative learning in which small groups of student writers provide feedback on the strengths and limitations of one another's writing during the revision stage of the writing process. Students are encouraged first to praise, then to question, and then to "polish," that is, give suggestions for specific improvements. Neubert and McNelis note that response groups not trained in their method tend to give polish suggestions first and to neglect the praise element.

STUDY SKILL 9
Revising the Paper

Revision, at least among professional writers, occurs continually as the author shapes the text to the form desired. It is treated here as a separate skill to highlight its importance.

Revision, in terms of its etymology and its application in the writing process, means "seeing again." As Proett and Gill (1986) observe, however, revision has been viewed by too many teachers, and hence students, as simply a process of recopying an assignment neatly in ink; correcting grammar, punctuation, and spelling; or "tidying up the writing to suit the whims of an English teacher" (p. 21).

Boiarsky (1980) analyzed the drafts of published papers written by herself and three other professional writers. She found that writers engage in 11 specific activities during the revision process:

1. *Altering form* (the genre, voice, person, tone, or style) so that it is appropriate for the content or audience.

2. *Reorganizing* ideas, sections, paragraphs, or sentences, to increase the paper's coherence and clarity.

3. *Creating transitions* to achieve a smooth flow between ideas, sections, paragraphs, sentences, or phrases.

4. *Deleting* redundant, excessive, or irrelevant details.

5. *Expanding* the paper to provide additional detail and power to ideas.

6. *Emphasizing particular ideas.*

7. *Subordinating ideas* to clarify relationships between them.

8. *Creating immediacy* by using direct quotes and the first- or second-person voice.

9. *Altering syntactic structures* to clean up awkward sentences and vary sentence patterns.

10. *Using different language* to improve specificity, accuracy, and tone.

11. *Correcting* grammar, punctuation, and spelling.

Boiarsky notes that writers do not engage in these activities in any particular order, and often one revision leads to another in a "chain reaction."

In the study by Monahan (1984) discussed above, competent twelfth grade writers made a wider range of revisions and tended to revise in extended episodes in which one revision was cued by and related to an earlier revision. Basic writers, by contrast, made isolated revisions. The "episodic" revision strategy of Monahan's competent writers seems similar to the "chain reaction" of revision described by Boiarsky (1980) as common to professional writers.

Monahan concludes that basic writers were constrained by their view of writing as a draft-redraft process with corrections made during the production of the second draft. By contrast, competent writers were aware of the possibility of revision at a variety of points in the writing process.

Research on the revision stage of writing a good school paper gives the lie to the notion that good writers just breeze through the writing process, with the words flowing easily and smoothly. Instead, effective writing "is painstakingly constructed, revision after revision, the product of an elaborate thinking process" (Gall and Gall 1988a, p. 96).

Study Skill 10
Editing the Paper and Producing a Neat Final Copy

Editing involves the correction of spelling, punctuation, and grammar. A paper that is rich in content but poorly edited is likely to be downrated by even the most forgiving reader. In fact, because teachers tend to emphasize editing over other kinds of revision, editing can be viewed as being just as important as revision in producing the final version of a school paper.

Editing need not be left to the final stage of writing. Many authors edit as they go along. Generally speaking, however, good writers include a final edit in their writing process (Calkins 1983).

Perl (1979) found that unskilled college writers orally corrected errors in their papers as they reread them without actually making the corrections on paper. Monahan (1984) observed the same phenomenon in his study of "basic" and "competent" twelfth grade writers. These results suggest an interesting gap in the cognitive processing of poor writers. Perhaps poor writers do not actually notice their own errors in spelling, punctuation, and grammar when they read their writing. Or perhaps they view written language merely as a shorthand code for spoken language, rather than as a separate communication medium with its own rules of correctness and precision.

Study Skill 11
Publishing the Paper

How the end of the writing process is defined is often important to the success of the entire effort. A typical school-oriented model, for example, ends with evaluation of the final draft (Schumm and Radencich 1984), and other models conclude with production of the final version (Gall and Gall 1988a). Romano (1987) notes, however:

> The *editing* and *publishing* stages of a writing process should arrive holding hands. To edit something that has no chance of publication wastes a writer's time; to publish something that hasn't been edited invites readers to dismiss a writer's words. Editing is necessary only when writers have said what they intended (or learned to intend) and are now ready to publish the writing in some way (p. 56).

Mayher, Lester, and Pradl (1983) define publishing as "any public presentation." And Graves and Hansen (1983) contend that if students know their writing will be published, they will think and write like authors, keeping their intended audience in mind throughout the writing process. This is important in developing writing skill.

STUDY SKILL 12
Using a Computer to Write the Paper

Some advocates of the process approach to writing argue that composing on a computer can improve students' writing. In examining the use of a computer as a writing skill, we need to consider the various ways, from simple to complex, in which a computer can aid writing:

1. It can replace the task of producing text by handwriting or typing with producing text by computer keyboarding.

2. It can simplify the tasks of correcting typing errors, moving text around in the paper, and adding and deleting text.

3. It can speed the review of spelling and word usage through software programs such as spelling checkers, dictionaries, and encyclopedias.

4. It can simplify composition by providing storage and display features and on-screen prompts that help writers consider and experiment with text options as they create and modify text.

Using the computer to produce text has definite advantages. For students who know how to type, keyboarding on a computer is faster and takes less physical energy than writing by hand or using a typewriter. Monahan (1984) notes that "basic" twelfth grade students in his study found it difficult to transcribe quickly and effortlessly, and as a result concentrated more on penmanship than on content. He suggests that using computers might "lessen the executive burden of mental tasks like writing" (p. 302).

Using the computer to correct text allows students to continuously modify their work by moving, replacing, or deleting text—from a single letter to a section of several pages or more. And students are more apt to review and correct their work when they know that they can do so quickly and easily.

The third and fourth uses of the computer are more complex. Most spelling checkers, for example, cannot correct homonym errors (e.g., "too" instead of "to"). Also, some teachers question whether students will learn to spell or use footnotes correctly if they rely on automated programs to correct their draft.

Haas and Hayes (1986) did a study to empirically test the notion that computers aid revision. They first interviewed 16 experienced computer users, who were graduate students or faculty members at a university. All mentioned advantages of using the computer to write: text generation is quicker and "freer"; the text appears on the screen in a "neat" form; a variety of formatting options are available; and the machine is "fun" to use.

Users also complained, however, that the text on the computer screen was difficult to read. Almost all these writers took time to print a hard copy for high-level revision and critical reading. The authors noted that the problem of reading text on the computer screen could be reduced to some extent by using high-resolution screens and by locating computers in properly lit rooms.

Finally, various software programs are available that purport to aid the actual composition process. As Scardamalia and Bereiter (1986) comment, however:

> Software design is currently more determined by what computers can do than by what students need. . . . Although there is much talk . . . about enhanced tools that will facilitate mental processes in writing, the prototype software that has actually appeared consists mainly of additional information-manipulating aids for the writer who already has highly sophisticated composing strategies (p. 797).

Wetzel (1985) reviewed several studies that were designed to measure improvements in students' writing through the use of writing software programs. The programs included combinations of the following: dynamic support for writing (e.g., on-screen prompts), opportunities to communicate with peers by electronic mail or newspapers, or a process approach to writing that emphasized planning, composing, and retrieving text. In six studies involving a treatment less than four months long, improvement in writing quality compared with that of a control group was not significant, but in three studies in which treatment lasted four to nine months, significant improvement in writing quality was found. In his own research, Wetzel found no significant difference in writing improvement between third, fourth, and fifth graders taught a process writing program using computers and a control group. The improvement of the fast typists in the experimental group, however, was significantly greater than that of the slow typists. Wetzel concluded that potential benefits of computer use were weakened by the short duration of the instructional program (eight weeks) and by the limited typing skills of the students (all could write faster with a pen than with the computer).

Methods of Teaching Study Skills for Writing School Papers

The act of writing a school paper is complex and requires sophisticated cognitive skills. It is little wonder that so many students have difficulty performing this task. Nothing short of systematic instruction over a long period of time will be necessary to help most students develop the necessary study skills. Many colleges have developed writing courses to help their students, especially entering freshmen, but this type of instruction is needed at much lower grade levels as well.

The methods described here can be used in a writing course or integrated into the curriculum. The methods are summarized in Figure 7.2.

Figure 7.2

Methods of Teaching Study Skills for Writing School Papers

GENERAL PROCEDURES

1. Assign homework that requires writing.
2. Integrate study skills instruction with actual writing tasks.
3. Allocate sufficient time for writing instruction.
4. Show examples of well-written school papers.

TEACHING ACTIVITIES

1. Teach students how to define the writing task meaningfully.
2. Allow students to choose their own topic.
3. Teach students how to specify the paper topic as a mental task.
4. Help student break the paper assignment into small tasks.
5. Encourage free writing, brainstorming, and invisible writing to help students generate ideas.
6. Teach students how to evaluate information needed for a school paper.
7. Present alternative methods for organizing ideas for a paper.
8. Use exercises to help students develop a first draft.
9. Use conferencing and writing response groups to provide feedback on paper drafts.
10. Teach various approaches for making revisions.
11. Provide opportunities for students to publish their writing.

Teachers may wish to become familiar with the process approach to writing instruction before teaching study skills in this area. We recommend *The Writing Process*, a staff development videotape and printed leader's guide developed by the Association for Supervision and Curriculum Development in 1981 in conjunction with the Cedar Rapids Community Schools in Iowa. In the videotape, a narrator presents five stages of the writing process: determining the purpose for writing, prewriting, drafting, revision, and publication. Teachers are shown teaching each stage to children in three actual classrooms, one each at the elementary, middle school, and high school levels. The videotape also presents the Praise-Question-Polish method of student feedback that has been studied by Neubert and McNelis (1986), to which we referred earlier.

General Procedures

Assign homework that requires writing. The most recent national assessment of Americans' writing ability (Applebee, Langer, and Mullis 1987) found a consistent, positive relationship between students' average writing achievement scores and the amount of homework they reported receiving. Also, students who reported that they had been given no writing assignments (reports or essays) during a six-week period had lower reading achievement than students who reported three or more such writing assignments during the same time period. These results suggest that assigning homework in general (some of which probably involves writing), and reports or essays in particular, helps students develop writing skills.

Integrate study skills instruction with actual writing tasks. Applebee and his colleagues found that students taught a process-oriented approach to writing wrote no better than those who reported receiving little or no process-oriented instruction. The researchers suggest a possible explanation for these negative findings:

> [If such strategies] have been incorporated into classrooms in ways divorced from actual reading and writing tasks, and without teaching students how to use them to advantage in their own reading and writing, the potential of such activities to improve student performance may have been unwittingly subverted. (Applebee, Langer, and Mullis 1987, p. 37).

The message to teachers is that students need specific, guided instruction in each of the various skills involved in the writing process and opportunities to apply them in a unified way in composing school papers.

Allocate sufficient time for writing instruction. Calkins (1983) wrote a book based on her research as a participant-observer in an elementary school, documenting in detail how teaching writing in one third grade classroom evolved from a traditional approach, focused on short exercises, with the teacher correcting writing "errors," to a writing workshop. The most important shift was in the time given to writing:

> The children's writing reflected the staccato rhythm of the classroom. Youngsters whipped off papers in quick bursts, writing without much forethought or deliberation. "Get it done" seemed to be the motto. . . . No wonder the children wrote in September on topics in which they had no investment. There was no time for investment, for sustainment. There was no time for doing one's best, then making one's best better (p. 30).

The classroom teacher extended the initial 15-minute writing slot to 20 minutes, then to 30, then 40. "By the middle of October, children spent three or four hours a week in writing workshop and then, to get even more time, they sometimes elected to write during recess" (p. 30). The children thought about their writing at home, planned their writing, and "began writing as if there was a tomorrow" when they could reread and change, if desired, what they had written (p. 31).

Show examples of well-written school papers. Models of good writing can provide information that students can use in planning their own papers. Hillocks (1987) discusses the tradition of presenting model compositions exemplifying good writing to students. The underlying assumption is that students will evaluate, and then imitate, the models, and thereby improve their own writing ability. Hillocks' review of research indicates, however, that models alone have only a small positive effect on students' writing. Hillocks suggests that more powerful effects did not occur because students were not directly taught how to produce a paper exhibiting the characteristics of the models.

By contrast, Beach (1983) found that students' writing improved when teachers gave them examples of "model" informational reports, explained why the models were good, and showed how they were constructed. For example, using the model, the teacher reviewed how notes had been made into sentences, and sentences combined in various ways to form a good paragraph. Then students received a second set of model notes and as a group generated sentences from the notes and combined them into an entire report. Beach (1983) cited positive changes in examples of students' writing from before to after instruction, and noted "that many of the students enjoyed the unit because they felt they were learning how to do an important academic task, rather than being assigned the task and then allowed to sink or swim" (p. 220).

Scardamalia and Bereiter (1986) report that students in grades three and higher were able to extract knowledge of literary features from examining model texts. They suggest, however, that explicit presentation of this information might be more effective than examination of models.

Teaching Activities

Teach students how to define the writing task meaningfully. Earlier we explained that defining the writing task includes identifying its purpose, audience, form, length, sources, and due date. Teachers tend to constrain the writing task artificially by setting arbitrary requirements on the length of the paper, number of sources to be used, and dates by which various stages (outline, rough draft, etc.) will be completed. Writing becomes more meaningful when students are asked to think about how purpose, audience, and form are related, and to keep these aspects in mind throughout the writing process. Thus, teachers could encourage better writing, including better planning of the writing task, if they spent more time showing students the importance of the paper's purpose, possible audience, and form. Students could then become more active in specifying appropriate paper length, set of sources, and dates for completion of each writing stage consistent with achieving their own writing purpose.

Lester (1982) describes how teachers can present writing activities to encourage students to have a real purpose in mind when they write, rather than writing merely to satisfy the teacher's objective. For example, she describes a writing task in which students read the first two paragraphs of a story and then are asked to guess what happens in the rest of the story or write the rest of the story, and then compare their endings with the "real" author's ending. Lester defines the teacher's objective here as "to help students understand prediction in the writing process"; for students, however, the objective is "to match wits with the author of the real story" (p. 21). Lester urges that writing be taught as a consequential composing activity, in which the writing has a real purpose because it is a means to an end rather than an end in itself.

The various genres of writing, which students are typically expected to distinguish and produce, can all be defined from a consequential point of view:

> Improved writing, which is the teacher's learning objective, is always implicit and subordinate to the explicit student purpose, which . . . ranges from getting an opinion or response published (letter to the editor), publishing a story or having a story read by others (story-writing, articles or poems for school newspapers and magazines), assembling a bike (directions writing), baking a cake (recipe-writing), building something (supply list), putting on a play (script-writing) (Lester 1982, p. 23).

By making their purpose in writing a paper a consequential activity, students develop a clearer sense of audience and of the form or genre that will best communicate the message they wish to send. Furthermore, Lester's comments make clear that the first skill in the writing process, defining the writing task, is closely intertwined with the last skill, publishing the paper.

Scardamalia, Bereiter, and Fillion's (1981) *Writing for Results: A Sourcebook of Consequential Composing Activities* contains many exercises that teachers can assign. Newman (1987) describes several similar activities that involve improvising on a word processor: inserting "forgeries" into text, analyzing a poem through free writing, and substituting synonyms for key words in a text. She discusses how such improvised activities are superior to structured software programs in encouraging students to explore and reflect on their reading and writing strategies.

Allow students to choose their own topic. Ames (1985) and McQuade (1987) concluded from their reviews of writing research that if students are allowed to write on self-chosen topics, they will probably choose to write much more. Allowing students to choose their own topic gives them interest in their writing, thus encouraging motivation and creativity. Although many language arts texts supply topics or "story starters" for students' writing activities, students should be encouraged to generate and select their own topic ideas.

Teach students how to specify the paper topic as a mental task. In Gall and Gall 1988b, we describe an activity for teaching students how to define a paper topic as an intellectual, or mental, task to be accomplished in writing the paper. Teaching students this method of defining a topic addresses the criticism that much instruction in writing, as in other areas, is based on a knowledge-telling rather than knowledge-generating model of student performance (Scardamalia and Bereiter 1986). Teachers who have received too many papers that merely summarize information from encyclopedias and other standard sources can use this method to encourage students to add their own ideas, interpretations, and problem-solving strategies to the task of writing a paper. Such papers facilitate better learning of content and its meaning, and are also much more interesting for the reader.

Help students break the paper assignment into small tasks. Gall and Gall (1988b) include a detailed lesson on breaking a task into subtasks in their study skills manual for teachers. Although it does not specifically address writing papers, a teacher could use the task of writing a paper to carry out the lesson. Having students define the tasks involved in writing a paper gives them much more ownership of the process than giving them a list of steps. We have also found that students are better able to schedule their time for completing each task if they are actively involved in defining, or at least listing, all the necessary tasks themselves.

We similarly described an activity in which a parent helps a student break a big task (writing an paper) into smaller, manageable tasks and schedule each subtask. The assignment is broken down into deciding on a topic, asking the librarian to help find sources, reading at least three sources, outlining the paper, and so on. Then the parent is advised to help the child spot any critical tasks that might have been skipped and if so, add them to the list of steps in a reasonable order.

While breaking a task into its components is important, students must also be taught to view the entire writing task as a whole. Applebee (1984) argues that the process approach to writing instruction has failed because it "has been inadequately and improperly conceptualized as a series of activities or steps in the writing process." Applebee proposes "instructional scaffolding" as an alternative concept to guide the teaching of writing as a unified whole. A "scaffold" is defined as a flexible structure that helps students accomplish writing tasks within explicit guidelines, but encourages them to use writing as a tool for learning rather than merely to display acquired knowledge.

Encourage free writing, brainstorming, and invisible writing to help students generate ideas. Free, or automatic, writing is a method for encouraging students to generate ideas while working individually. The writer is told to suspend critical judgment and "let the writing flow, seeing if language will carry you towards meaning" (Murray 1987). After a short period of free writing, the writer looks at the writing to see if certain themes or directions can be found. If so, the writer can focus on these themes or directions. If not, the writer can try other strategies, such as mapping or brainstorming, to generate ideas.

Blind writing, also called invisible writing, takes free writing a step further (Daiute 1985). Using a word processor, students are encouraged to write freely with the computer screen darkened, so that they cannot see their output. Thus students are prevented from evaluating and censoring ideas as they emerge. For students who are timid about writing, blind writing provides a stimulus to get them started.

Brainstorming has been encouraged also, often with students working in groups (McQuade 1987). Group brainstorming encourages cooperative learning and also increases the pool of available ideas that each student can consider in planning and writing a paper.

To learn brainstorming in a group, students might specify a problem, such as finding name for a new soap. By "piggybacking," or letting one idea build upon another, a small group of students would quickly generate a long list of possible solutions:

Soap – Clean – Wash – Clean Bill – Fresh Spring – Rain Clean – Pure – Skin Glow – Skin Clean – Fresh Scent – Skin Fresh – Fresh and Clean – Dirt Away – Suds – Soapy Suds – Scrub – Fresh Scrub – Rub It Off – Rub and Scrub – Soapy Scrub – Scrub 'n' Glow (Gall and Gall 1988a)

Similarly, students could use brainstorming and piggybacking to generate ideas for writing any aspect of a paper, such as the title for a short story or the name of a key character.

Free writing, brainstorming, and invisible writing can be used throughout the writing process whenever a fresh flow of ideas is needed—for example, to specify the intellectual task that writing the paper will accomplish, to select the topic, setting, or genre, to define characters, or to determine the outcome of an action sequence. Murray (1987) provides extensive guidelines for using the techniques described above in these ways.

Teach students how to evaluate information needed for a school paper. The standard approach to teaching students about collecting information needed for writing assignments is to show them the characteristics of cards in the card catalog, the classification of library books, and perhaps the use of indices such as the *Reader's Guide to Periodical Literature* (Gullette and Hatfield 1975). These are useful study skills, but students also need to learn skills for selecting sources appropriate for investigating a given topic and skills for analyzing sources to determine the relevance of information to a topic.

Hillocks (1987) taught these skills to students using the inquiry method, which he found had a stronger positive effect on writing quality than any other of the six instructional treatments he examined in his meta-analysis of methods of teaching writing. In inquiry teaching, students are engaged in observing and analyzing a phenomenon from their own perspective and are encouraged to discover information, concepts, or generalizations for themselves.

Among the activities in which Hillocks engaged students were the following:

Find and state specific details that convey personal experience vividly, examine sets of data to develop and support explanatory generalizations, or analyze situations that present ethical problems and develop arguments about those situations (Hillocks 1987).

Engaging students in inquiry about their paper topics helps them discover what they already know about the topic and identify aspects of the topic that they need to explore by examining other sources.

Present alternative methods for organizing ideas for a paper. Traditionally students have been taught to organize their ideas for a paper by first writing a formal outline. Murray (1987) argues that expert writers rarely *start* with an outline, although they may develop one once a draft is in hand in order to get an overall view of the paper's organization. Expert writers use many different ways to organize their ideas, as described earlier.

Several approaches for teaching younger, novice writers how to organize their ideas have been identified. For example, McKenzie (1979) taught students in grades three to six to graph information from different sources in a "comparison chart." This is a worksheet that lists a topic (e.g., igloos) at the top of the page and information sources along the left margin, by title and author if prose sources are used, and by descriptive information if a different kind of source (e.g., a diagram or photograph) is used. Across the top of the page students list their questions about the topic (e.g., What is an igloo? and How are igloos furnished?) Information that is relevant to answering each question is recorded in the appropriate cells of the chart. Once the chart is filled in, students can be guided in writing sentences that summarize the answers on which sources agree and sentences that elaborate on detailed information in each source or point out disagreements between sources.

McQuade (1987) and Beach (1983) propose methods similar to McKenzie's. In their methods, students are trained to ask questions about their topic and take notes on information in sources that are relevant to answering their questions. Then students group their notes and turn them into text. Many teachers require students to take source note on 3" x 5" cards, with the rationale that students can then arrange the notecards into a rough outline or draft of their paper.

Calkins (1983) suggests a different method for teaching young children to organize their ideas. It involves having students: (1) write thoughts at random (free writing) on one side of a piece of paper, (2) cut apart the text to establish piles of related material, (3) write about the information in each pile, and (4) edit and revise.

And Scardamalia and Bereiter (1986) describe an instructional method called *procedural facilitation* in which students are given cue cards to prompt reflection during their planning (for example, "An important point I haven't considered yet is. . . .").

Rather than teach one organizational approach to all students, teachers should help students discover a wide range of methods for organizing their ideas. Students should be encouraged to use the method that best suits their learning style and their writing purpose. Teachers can provide a list to remind students of various organizing methods, let them select a method, and have them hand in the results of the method they used (e.g., a concept tree or comparison chart). Teachers can give students feedback on their organization of ideas before they revise their draft.

Use exercises to help students develop a first draft. Various methods can be used to help students improve the quality of their writing. These methods are summarized here because drafting is the first study skill involving actual composition, although the same methods apply as well to the skill of revising the paper.

In a study involving persuasive writing, Glynn, Britton, Muth, and Dogan (1982) found that freeing the students from concerns about the form of their presentation simplified the writing task, allowed them to think about their arguments, and led to more effective generation of arguments.

Hillocks (1979) found that when students observed and experienced immediate stimuli with all their senses and then wrote about what they saw and felt, the quality of their compositions improved. In contrast, traditional instruction in grammar or paragraph structure did not substantially improve the quality of students' drafts (Hillocks 1987). Hillocks did find, however, that sentence combining and use of scales improved writing quality. Sentence combining involves giving students sets of simple sentences that they must combine into a more complex syntactic structure. Scales are rating criteria (e.g., elaboration, word choice, organization) that students use to judge and revise their own compositions.

Newman (1987) describes various composing activities that students can carry out by hand, but preferably using a word processor. She argues that such activities improve students' ability to reflect on, and hence revise, their writing. In one activity, students are to insert forgeries into text, matching the author's style of writing so that the additions will be undetectable by fellow students.

Use conferencing and writing response groups to provide feedback on paper drafts. Perhaps the best way for students to improve their writing is to get feedback on it and then use that feedback to revise the paper. Two instructional methods have been developed for these purposes.

One is conferencing, where the teacher or someone else provides feedback to students on their ideas for the paper, or on their draft (Scardamalia and Bereiter 1986). When teachers provide feedback, they need to exercise certain cautions. First, they should avoid focusing on the technical aspects of the paper (a common tendency) and instead focus on the ideas being expressed. Second, teachers should not automatically give students feedback on their papers. Rather, they should encourage students to develop the skill of determining for themselves when they need feedback and asking for it.

Even if teachers are trained to provide feedback that focuses on substance, the sheer numbers of students in their classes can quickly make the task of giving every student feedback on every paper unmanageable. According to a colleague of ours, the San Diego School District for several years has hired college students to serve as readers. They give students specific, written feedback on their papers.

A more helpful form of conferencing is for students to give one another feedback in groups, where they each present their paper (or ideas) while other students ask questions and give suggestions and encouragement. Graves and Hansen (1983) describe a conferencing procedure suitable for students as young as first graders. One student sits in "the author's chair" and reads his paper, and other students respond with accepting comments, then questions. The conferences give students a growing understanding of "the author concept," thereby improving their skill as writers.

Hunt (1987) points out that some types of feedback may be more helpful to writers than others. Using a popular animal story, "The Bat Poet," Hunt demonstrated that the "professional" responder is "positive, support-ive, educational, and 'kind' " but is also "condescending, judgmental, and of no use to the aspiring bat poet" (p. 230). By contrast, the "emotional" responder responds emotionally to the writing, giving the writer "more confidence in the communicative and affective power of his writing" (p. 231). Hunt's discussion demonstrates the value of encouraging students to give each other more "emotional" and less "professional" feedback.

The Praise-Question-Polish method of giving feedback to students was cited earlier. Neubert and McNelis (1986) describe it as "a form of cooper-ative learning in which small groups of student writers provide feedback on the strengths and limitations of each other's writing during the revision stage of the writing process" (pp. 54–55). Each writing response group contains student writers of like ability. They first observe a "fishbowl" demonstration in which the teacher and a small group of students role-play a feedback session. Then each group examines a student's draft, trying to answer focus questions that the teacher has provided. For example, in examining a fable, elementary students might be asked, "Are the personalities of the characters appropriate for what happens in the story?" In examining a letter to a state representative recommending changes in the legislative process, secondary social studies students might be asked, "Did the letter give at least three reasons for the stated recommendations?" and "Are the reasons logically sequenced?" Students are then asked to answer focus questions using the PQP form—Praise ("What is good about the writing?" etc.), Question ("What do you not understand?" etc.), and Polish ("What specific improve-ments can be suggested without actually making the changes for the author?"). As noted earlier, the Praise-Question-Polish method is presented in *The Writing Process*, a videotape for teachers (ASCD 1981).

Teach various approaches for making revisions. If we expect stu-dents to revise their papers, we must teach them what revision involves and give them time and incentive for making revisions. Graves and Hansen

(1983) describe how the "author's chair" conferencing approach helped students revise their papers:

> Now they reread with a view to making the part under construction consistent with the overall intention in the piece. The child discovers inconsistencies and will choose to cut and paste for reorganization, choose to organize a story by chapter in order to make it more clear, or write a complete second draft that includes "a lot more information" (pp. 181–182).

Monahan (1984) asked the teachers of student writers in his study how they taught revision. Seven of the nine teachers claimed that they taught revision by having students write second drafts using a checklist that was either taken from a grammar text or developed by the teacher. Monahan noted that "the basic writers seem to approach revision as a two draft, checklist type of operation," which would be consistent with the instruction they received (p. 301). One wonders how the competent writers learned to revise in a more thorough way, since apparently they were not being taught revision in their current classes.

Boiarsky (1980) describes a method for teaching students a "cut and paste" revision process. The method is based on a chart listing 11 types of problems that lead professional writers to revise, for example, "form inconsistent with content and/or audience," "sentences too long, windy," and "incorrect punctuation." The chart then describes 11 revision activities for addressing such problems, for example, "altering form," "improving syntactic structures," and "cleaning up." Also included are more specific examples of each revision activity.

Have students use a computer to write papers. If teachers want students to use computers to write papers, they must consider the issues of skill, availability, and appropriate software. First, students need to know how to type and use word-processing software. Both books and computer-based programs exist for teaching these skills (Daiute 1985).

Second, students must have access to computers at school or at home. Teachers should consider whether students who have home computers should be allowed to use them to write school papers, since it gives them an advantage over students who don't have computers. On the other hand, requiring a handwritten paper when students have learned to use, and may prefer, writing with a computer seems to place an undue burden on them.

Computers can foster higher-order composing abilities, but their potential has not yet been fully realized. Some software programs engage students in a writing process by inserted probes to which students respond in their own writing. The probes may present an outline of points that the paper should cover. For example, if the paper is a book report, these probes might be: "What is the theme of the book?" and "Name the main characters and briefly describe the outstanding physical and personality features of each one." When a student has responded to all the probes, they can be erased from the text and what remains is a paper written by the student. Scardamalia and Bereiter (1986) mention two such software programs, one of which "supplies sentences, leaving the user to determine events," and another that "leaves the user to make structural and stylistic decisions, the computer doing the rest of the work of producing an essay" (p. 797).

Current information about writing programs for computer use is available from several sources. The *Educational Software Preview Guide*, published annually, lists software for K–12 instruction that has been favorably reviewed by educators at participating sites (International Society for Technology in Education 1990). Software preview centers are attached to most major universities. For example, at the University of Oregon, a Software Preview Room is maintained at the Center for Advanced Technology in Education. *The Writing Notebook Journal*, published four times a year, helps educators integrate technology into their writing instruction in the humanities and literature (Creative Word Processing in the Classroom 1990).

For a nominal fee, a teacher can obtain a disc copy and supporting documentation for FrEdWriter (Free Education Writer) and then make copies for student use. FrEdWriter includes various programs for Apple computers that ask students questions about and help them organize a piece of writing. It may be purchased from CUE Softswap in Concord, California.

Provide students with neat paper rules to produce the final copy of the paper. The *Study for Success Teacher's Manual* (Gall and Gall 1988b) includes a lesson for teaching students the following "neat paper skills," which are based on the research of Anderson-Inman and her colleagues (1984):

1. Use 8½" x 11" paper in good condition.
2. Write on front side only.
3. Stay inside left and right margins.
4. Name at top, right side.
5. Title on top line, centered.
6. Skip line between sections.
7. Write so letters "sit" on line.
8. Erase completely.
9. No smudges or scribbles.
10. Number pages.

We encourage teachers to add to or modify the list and suggest that it be presented to students as a handout. We also recommend an in-class lesson of one or more sessions in which students are requested to write (or copy) a paper of at least two paragraphs, following all the rules stated in the handout.

Students who learn these skills will have less difficulty producing neatly typewritten or computer-prepared papers later in their school years.

Provide opportunities for students to publish their writing. Graves (1983) claims that publishing student papers is important because it helps students see themselves as genuine authors and encourages others to react, thus giving students a stronger sense of audience. Students undoubtedly discover writing problems that they missed during the revision process and thus become more able to develop solutions to similar writing problems when they write their next paper.

Graves recommends binding children's best papers in hard covers to better approximate the professional meaning of "publishing." He also recommends having students experience other aspects of publishing, for example:

1. Different size books (bound in cardboard).
2. Book team (children team up as author and illustrator).
3. Cumulative book (children add their papers on a given theme to an already-started book on that theme).
4. Individual books of various types.
5. Class yearbook.
6. Joint publication—teacher and children (e.g., a class magazine).
7. Joint publication—child and child.

Graves warns that publishing should not be used as a substitute for a writing program, but rather "as the end of a long process of working with children" on their writing (p. 63). He notes that "maintaining writing folders, in which all of the child's work for the year is kept, is also an important adjunct of the publishing" (p. 63).

Another common means of "publishing" students' work is to display it on a bulletin board or wall in the classroom or hallway of the school (Beach 1983). We have observed simple writing tasks take on added meaning when students were informed that all, or the best, papers would be displayed in this fashion.

According to Romano (1987), the most common kind of publication in his class is oral sharing, in which each student sits on an "author's stool" and reads aloud a finished paper. The teacher can read the work if the student is exceptionally shy.

References

Ames, N. H. (1985). "Three Differences Between Product and Process Approaches to Composition: Topic Choice, Revision, and the Writing Conference." ERIC Document Reproduction Service No. ED 261 379.

American School Board Journal. (1987). "National Assessment of Educational Progress: Students Aren't Literate Enough." *American School Board Journal* 174, 6: 14.

Anderson-Inman, L., H. M. Walker, and J. Purcell. (1984). "Promoting the Transfer of Skills Across Settings: Transenvironmental Programming for Handicapped Students in the Mainstream." In *Focus on Behavior Analysis in Education,* edited by W. L. Howard, T. E. Heron, D. S. Hill, and J. Trap-Porter. Columbus, Ohio: Charles E. Merrill.

Applebee, A. N. (1984). *Contexts for Learning to Write: Studies of Secondary School Instruction.* Norwood, N.J.: Ablex.

Applebee, A. N. (1981). *Writing in the Secondary School: English and the Content Areas.* Urbana, Ill.: National Council of Teachers of English.

Applebee, A. N., J. A. Langer, and I. V. Mullis. (1987). *Learning to Be Literate in America.* Princeton, N.J.: National Assessment of Educational Progress, Educational Testing Service.

Applebee, A. N., J. A. Langer, and I. V. Mullis. (1986). *Writing Trends Across the Decade, 1974–1984.* Princeton, N.J.: National Assessment of Educational Progress.

Association for Supervision and Curriculum Development. (1981). *The Writing Process.* Videotape and Leader's Guide. Alexandria, Va.: Association for Supervision and Curriculum Development.

Beach, J. D. (1983). "Teaching Students to Write Informational Reports." *The Elementary School Journal* 84, 2: 213–220.

Boiarsky, C. (1980). "Cut and Paste and Other Revision Activities." *English Journal* 69, 8: 44–48.

Calkins, L. M. (1983). *Lessons from a Child: On the Teaching and Learning of Writing.* Exeter, N.H.: Heinemann.

Creative Work Processing in the Classroom. (Jan./Feb. 1990). *The Writing Notebook Journal* 7, 3. Eugene, Oreg.: Creative Work Processing in the Classroom.

Daiute, C. (1985) *Writing and Computers.* Reading, Mass.: Addison-Wesley.

Emig, J. (1982). "Writing, Composition, and Rhetoric." In *Encyclopedia of Educational Research,* edited by N. E. Mitzel. New York: The Free Press.

Emig, J. (1983). *The Web of Meaning: Essays on Writing, Teaching, Learning, and Thinking.* Upper Montclair, N.J.: Boynton/Cook.

Flower, L. S., and J. R. Hayes. (1980). "The Dynamics of Composing: Making Plans and Juggling Constraints." In *Cognitive Processes in Writing,* edited by L. W. Gregg and E. R. Steinberg. Hillsdale, N.J.: Erlbaum.

Gall, J. P., and M. D. Gall. (1985). *Help Your Son or Daughter Study for Success.* Eugene, Oreg.: M. Damien.

Gall, M. D., and J. P. Gall. (1988a). *Making the Grade.* Rocklin, Calif.: Prima.

Gall, M. D., and J. P. Gall. (1988b). *Study for Success Teacher's Manual.* 3rd ed. Eugene, Oreg.: M. Damien.

Glynn, S. M., B. K. Britton, K. D. Muth, and N. Dogan. (1982). "Writing and Revising Persuasive Documents: Cognitive Demands." *Journal of Educational Psychology* 74: 557–567.

Graves, D. H. (1987). *Balance the Basics: Let Them Write.* New York: Ford Foundation.

Graves, D. H. (1983). *Writing: Teachers and Children at Work.* Portsmouth, N.H.: Heinemann.

Graves, D. H., and J. Hansen. (1983). "The Author's Chair." *Language Arts* 80: 176–183.

Gullette, I., and F. Hatfield. (1975). *Test of Library Study Skills.* Marietta, Ga.: Larlin.

Haas, C., and J. R. Hayes. (1986). "What Did I Just Say? Reading Problems in Writing with the Machine." *Research in the Teaching of English* 20, 1: 22–35.

Hillocks, G., Jr. (1979). "The Effects of Observational Activities on Student Writing." *Research in the Teaching of English* 13: 23–35.

Hillocks, G., Jr. (May 1987). "Synthesis of Research on Teaching Writing." *Educational Leadership* 44, 8: 71–82.

Hull, G., and D. Bartholomae. (April 1986). "Teaching Writing as Learning and Process." *Educational Leadership* 43, 7: 44–53.

Hunt, R. A. (1987). "'Could You Put in Lots of Holes?' Modes of Response to Writing." *Language Arts* 64, 2: 229–232.

International Society for Technology in Education. (1990). *Educational Software Preview Guide.* Eugene, Oreg: ISTE.

John-Steiner, V., and P. Tatter. (1985). "Language Development of the Disadvantaged." In *International Encyclopedia of Education*, edited by T. Husen and T. N. Postlethwaite. Oxford: Pergamon Press.

Kobasigawa, A. (1983). "Children's Retrieval Skills for School Learning." *Alberta Journal of Educational Research* 29, 4: 259–271.

Lester, N. B. (1982). "Whose Purpose Is It Anyway?" *Arizona English Bulletin* 24, 2: 18–23.

Mayher, J. S., N. Lester, and G. M. Pradl. (1983). *Learning to Write/Writing to Learn.* Upper Montclair, N.J.: Boynton/Cook.

McKenzie, G. R. (1979). "Data Charts: A Crutch for Helping Pupils Organize Reports." *Language Arts* 56: 784–788.

McQuade, M. T. (1987). "Implications for Teaching Report Writing Using the Informal Process." ERIC Document Reproduction Service No. ED 274 976.

Moffett, J. (1979). "Integrity in the Teaching of Writing." *Phi Delta Kappan* 61: 276–279.

Monahan, B. D. (1984). "Revision Strategies of Basic and Competent Writers as They Write for Different Audiences." *Research in the Teaching of English* 18(3): 288–304.

Murray, D. M. (1987). *Write to Learn.* 2nd ed. New York: Holt, Rinehart, and Winston.

Neubert, G. A., and S. J. McNelis. (April 1986). "Improving Writing in the Disciplines." *Educational Leadership* 43, 7: 54–58.

Newman, J. M. (1987). "Online: Improvising with a Word Processor." *Language Arts* 64, 1: 110–115.

Parker, R. P., Jr. (1979). "From Sputnik to Datrmount: Trends in the Teaching of Composition." *English Journal* 68, 6: 32–37.

Perl, S. (1979). "How Teachers Teach the Writing Process: Final Report." ERIC Document Reproduction Service No. ED 255 920.

Proett, J., and K. Gill. (1986). *The Writing Process in Action: A Handbook for Teachers.* Urbana, Ill.: National Council of Teachers of English.

Romano, T. (1987). *Clearing the Way: Working with Teenage Writers.* Portsmouth, N.H.: Heinemann.

Ryan, G. (1979). "How Well Do Our Children Write." *PTA Today* 12, 3: 27.

Samway, K. (1987). "Formal Evaluation of Children's Writing: An Incomplete Story." *Language Arts* 64, 3: 269–298.

Scardamalia, M., and C. Bereiter. (1986). "Research on Written Composition." In *Handbook of Research on Teaching.* 3rd ed. Edited by M. C. Wittrock. New York: Macmillan.

Scardamalia, M., C. Bereiter, and B. Fillion. (1981). *Writing for Results: A Sourcebook of Consequential Composing Activities.* La Salle, Ill.: Open Court.

Schumm, J. S., and M. C. Radencich. (1984). "Readers'/Writers' Workshops: An Antidote to Term Paper Terror." *Journal of Reading* 28, 1: 84.

U.S. Bureau of the Census. (1987). *Statistical Abstract of the United States: 1988.* Washington, D.C.

Wetzel, K. (1985). "The Effect of Using the Computer in a Process Writing Program on the Writing Quality of Third, Fourth, and Fifth Grade Pupils." Doctoral diss., University of Oregon, Eugene.

8
Taking Tests

Characteristics of Tests

Tests are typically used to assess students' prior learning in a course, and students' academic success is based on test performance more than on any other single factor. Test preparation and test taking are also important learning processes themselves. For both these reasons, test-taking skills should be a major focus of study skills instruction. We use the term "test" to include all assessments of student knowledge or ability, regardless of how much material they cover or when they occur in the course of study. Because of their versatility and convenience, *written* tests are the primary method for evaluating student learning. *Performance* tests are also popular; for example, to pass the fitness component of a physical education class, students must demonstrate skills (e.g., push-ups) or participate in activities (e.g., the 100-meter dash) while being evaluated for the quality and quantity of their effort.

Teachers generally grade students individually, but some schools are experimenting with cooperative learning, in which students carry out joint projects for a shared grade, based on an average of individual scores or on a group score (Johnson and Johnson 1975). This is similar to team sports, where players must perform well together in order to win.

In any test, stress is a factor. Test results reflect not only knowledge or skill, but also a person's ability to perform under pressure. Students need to learn test-taking skills in order to meet these challenges successfully.

Study Skills for Test Taking

Test taking consists of two phases: preparing for the test and taking the test. Some study skills apply more heavily before the test, others during the test, and many come into play during both phases. In this section, we identify the skills that are important to test taking in the broad sense and examine how they apply both before and during the test.

Because test taking represents a culmination of student learning, all the study skills discussed in previous chapters will help students with tests. Similarly, since students generally know in advance that they will be tested on their learning, their test-taking skills should have a reciprocal effect on how they carry out other study tasks—for example, how they listen in class and how they approach the task of reading textbook assignments.

Figure 8.1 summarizes the study skills presented in this chapter.

Figure 8.1

Study Skills for Taking Tests

CONTENT REVIEW SKILLS

1. Reviewing Assigned Readings
2. Reviewing Class Notes and Reading Notes
3. Testing Yourself
4. Using Mnemonic Techniques
5. Forming a Study Group
6. Using Self-Monitoring to Determine Test Readiness

TIME MANAGEMENT SKILLS

7. Recording Test Dates
8. Planning Time for Test Preparation
9. Avoiding Cramming
10. Planning to Arrive Early
11. Keeping Track of Time During the Test

TESTWISENESS SKILLS

12. Determining What the Test Will Cover
13. Determining the Question Format
14. Determining the Importance of the Test
15. Bringing Items Needed for the Test
16. Sitting in a Good Location
17. Reading Test Directions Carefully
18. Answering Easy Questions First
19. Using Appropriate Answering Techniques

PSYCHOLOGICAL COPING SKILLS

20. Using Relaxation Techniques
21. Using Positive Thinking
22. Expressing Feelings of Anxiety
23. Overlearning the Material

Content Review Skills

Some teachers denounce test-taking skills as gimmicks to help students score better on tests even when they lack knowledge of the material on the test. In fact, the most critical test-taking skills are precisely those that help students *review* the curriculum content.

STUDY SKILL 1
Reviewing Assigned Readings

Most courses have assigned texts or assigned readings, and tests generally cover the information in them. The best strategies for review depend heavily on the characteristics of the student, the nature of the readings, and the nature of the test itself.

We recommend that students balance their test review by scanning the text, reviewing their reading notes, and asking themselves questions (Gall and Gall 1988a). Scanning is most useful if the text has numerous headings, highlighted terms, and illustrations that cue the reader to important information. If students have not taken extensive reading notes, they may need to rely more on self-testing (see Study Skill 3) to enhance their cognitive processing of the text.

Anderson and Armbruster (1984) examined the research on underlining (or highlighting) text and concluded that underlining is no more effective than other techniques for reviewing important information. They suggest, however, that underlining can improve test performance if students do not highlight indiscriminately but take time to read closely and decide which parts are most important.

STUDY SKILL 2
Reviewing Class Notes and Reading Notes

Not only does the act of taking notes improve test performance (see Skill 20 in Chapter 5), reviewing notes can help as well. Students should read their notes, highlight the most important information, and then use their notes to test themselves. The Cornell method of taking notes, described in chapters 5 and 6, facilitates this type of review.

STUDY SKILL 3
Testing Yourself

Textbooks increasingly are being designed to include end-of-section questions. In research reviewed by Anderson and Armbruster (1984), students read materials that included text-related questions which they were required to answer as they read. The availability of these questions improved learning from the text, and the most improvement occurred when the text included the actual questions that later appeared on the test.

For encouraging deep processing and developing independent study skills, self-questioning is even more beneficial than answering provided questions. Research reviewed by Anderson and Armbruster (1984) generally supports the value of student-generated questions as a test preparation method.

Practice tests are another way for students to quiz themselves. Many study skills texts (e.g., Gall and Gall 1988a; Pauk 1989) recommend that students use copies of teachers' old tests to review for an upcoming test. To prepare for a standardized achievement test, students probably can find a book that provides guidelines and sample items from the test. Commercial coaching programs are also available; the Stanley H. Kaplan Educational Center, for example, prepares more than 100,000 students annually for the SAT, law and medical boards, and other academic entrance and professional certification tests (Deutsch 1988).

Research on the value of taking practice tests has produced mixed results. In a meta-analysis of 40 studies, Kulik, Kulik, and Bangert (1984) found that test scores generally improved as a result of students' taking practice tests. Gains were greater for high-ability students than for low-ability students, and the size of gains was related to how closely practice and test items matched and how many practice tests were given.

Not surprisingly, the designers of standardized achievement tests report lower gains from practice than do commercial coaching companies. The Educational Testing Service, which publishes and administers the SAT, cites average gains of 34 points from coaching. By contrast, Stanley Kaplan, head of the Kaplan Educational Center, claims that his students improve their scores by an average of 100 points (Stickney 1984).

STUDY SKILL 4
Using Mnemonic Techniques

Many test questions require students to recall specific items of information in rote fashion; even essay questions usually require the recall of many facts. To ensure accurate recall, students need to learn and use memorization skills, or what researchers call *mnemonics*.

Rohwer and Thomas (1986) found that only 11 percent of college students at an elite university reported using memory strategies regularly, even though such strategies improve test performance. The mnemonic key-word method, for example, has been successfully used to help secondary students acquire foreign language vocabulary (Raugh and Atkinson

1975). First, the foreign word is recoded into a familiar concrete noun (a key word) based on similarities in acoustic and orthographic properties. For example, the Spanish word *huevo* (pronounced *wave-oh*), meaning egg, might be recorded as the familiar English word *wave*. Next, a mental image of the object denoted by the English code word (wave) and the English equivalent (egg) is formed. For example, students might imagine an egg bobbing on the crest of a wave. When they are tested on the meaning of the word huevo, they can recall the meaning by using the acoustic and visual associations described above.

Jones and Hall (1982) cite a number of experiments in which students successfully used the key-word method for learning both Spanish and Russian nouns. In one study, eighth graders were taught to apply the key-word method to two common school tasks: recalling definitions of specialized technical terms (e.g., medical definitions) and associating names and facts (e.g., inventors and inventions, explorers and discoveries, authors and books). The students who received key-word training scored significantly higher when tested on these types of items than did students in a control group.

Various mnemonic techniques have been developed to help students with different memorization tasks. Some are described in the classic text *The Memory Book* (Lorayne and Lucas 1974). The authors' basic mnemonic rule is that "in order to remember any new piece of information, it must be associated to something you already know or remember *in some ridiculous way*." Other mnemonic techniques are presented by Gall and Gall (1988a), Orr (1986), and Sherman and Wildman (1982). Belezza (1981) describes a set of criteria for selecting appropriate mnemonic techniques for different learning purposes.

Memorization is most useful during the test preparation phase. Standley (1987), however, describes the Splashdown Method, a memorization technique that students can use during the test itself. As soon as they receive the test, they turn it over without looking at it. Then,

> on the back of the test paper, or on a piece of scratch paper if it's permitted, "splash down." Splashing down means simply writing as fast and as furiously as you can all of the terms, phrases, initials, abbreviations, and little memory joggers you can think of. If you are about to take a math test, jot down a few formulas or procedures, or work a quick problem. This splashdown should take no more than one or two minutes (p. 118).

Students then begin answering the test and use the splashdown information to help recall information. Standley claims that the Splashdown Method reduces tension and gives students a ready source of information they can use during a test.

STUDY SKILL 5
Forming a Study Group

In study groups, students can share study strategies and quiz one another before the test. Effective study groups have a group norm of striving to do one's best. Students tend to conform to peer group norms in their patterns of achievement (Wigfield and Asher 1984), so if the group values achievement, its members are likely to work hard; conversely, if the group does not value achievement, students are likely to do less than their best in order to be accepted by the group.

Students often view test taking as a competitive situation, and many believe that it is not in their best interest to help one another in study groups. Nevertheless, instructional approaches like peer tutoring and cooperative learning, which allow students to discover how they can benefit both from giving help to and receiving help from other students, are becoming popular in more and more classrooms.

Johnson and Johnson (1975) reviewed research comparing the cognitive outcomes of cooperative, individualistic, and competitive goal structures (study groups exemplify a cooperative goal structure). For complex tasks like problem solving, they found that cooperation produced higher achievement than did competition, particularly for low-achieving students. The Johnsons also found that cooperative goal structures "promote the cognitive beliefs that the subject matter area is important, that the student can affect his achievement in the class, and that the material is not too difficult to master."

Slavin (1986) concluded from his review of research that cooperative learning enhances student achievement only when it includes both individual accountability and group rewards. For most students, working closely with peers who are facing the same challenge (the test) provides emotional support, which is rewarding. In the end, however, each student must take the test alone.

STUDY SKILL 6
Using Self-Monitoring to Determine Test Readiness

Proficient students monitor their comprehension and progress as they study to help determine what steps to take next—for example, whether to rehearse difficult material, try another learning strategy, or get help (Armbruster and Anderson 1981). Proficient students also monitor their test anxiety; if it is too uncomfortable, they take steps to alleviate it. Davies (1986) describes a number of self-report scales that students can use to measure their level of test anxiety.

Although students may not automatically monitor their own behavior, most can be taught to do so. Brown, Campione, and Barclay (1979) found that mentally retarded students could be taught strategies for learning lists and a self-monitoring strategy for recognizing their readiness to take a test on the memorized information. Their skills were maintained for as long as a year after training and transferred to the study of prose passages.

Time Management Skills

General time management skills for effective studying were discussed in Chapter 4. Test taking involves some unique time management skills also, and they are reviewed below.

STUDY SKILL 7
Recording Test Dates

Because teachers often announce test dates only a week in advance, students should record test dates in their class notes, on a weekly schedule, or on an assignment sheet as soon as they are announced, so that they can plan their study sessions.

STUDY SKILL 8
Planning Time for Test Preparation

Study skills experts recommend that when students record a test date, they work back from that date and schedule time to prepare for the test. Students who have spent sufficient time on their initial study of material will need less review time right before the test. Review is also helpful, if it builds on a base of effective initial processing.

STUDY SKILL 9
Avoiding Cramming

Like other study skills experts, Pauk (1984) recommends that students avoid cramming. He reviews two lines of research that support this recommendation. In the first, rats that learned to run a maze under the pressure of hunger took much longer to learn the maze than rats that learned under noncrisis conditions. The rats also performed less well in choosing an alternate route when the learned route was blocked. In the second line of research, people responding to an unexpected fire alarm took two to three times as long to learn the escape route as they did under noncrisis conditions. Pauk surmises that in crisis situations, "the thinking mechanism is overstimulated and too jammed with unorganized thoughts, each of which counteracts the previous one, causing jerky, panicky reactions."

Orr (1986), while discouraging cramming, notes that occasionally it is necessary and suggests several strategies for getting the most value from cramming, such as: concentrating on the task of review; standing and breathing deeply when negative thoughts arise; writing "I CAN DO IT" on a card and keeping it handy; taking frequent short breaks; focusing on and writing down major points from notes or text; avoiding stimulants; and accomplishing specified goals before going to sleep.

Kesselman-Turkel and Peterson (1981) advise against cramming, but do recommend intensive review—what they call "prepared cramming"— the evening before the test, and getting at least six hours of sleep that night.

STUDY SKILL 10
Planning to Arrive Early

Most tests are scheduled during class time; special tests like the SAT, however, fall outside students' normal routine. It is to their advantage for students to arrive early, rather than just on time. They can choose a seat rather than take whatever seat is left, and they can settle in, arrange their materials, and relax for a few moments before the test starts.

STUDY SKILL 11
Keeping Track of Time During the Test

Because most school tests must fit into one class period, students need the ability to apply their knowledge of the content quickly and accurately. Poor students often find tests so unpleasant, however, that they go through them too quickly, rather than taking all the available time and trying to do a better job. Davies (1986) found that a high percentage of British high school students reported panic reactions during important tests: switching back and forth from one question to another, continually checking and rechecking their work, and dizziness and fainting. Other students reported proceeding too slowly, thus forfeiting the opportunity to respond to all of the questions or to check answers for careless errors.

Effective use of time during a test requires planning at the outset. Gall and Gall (1988b) discuss a procedure to help students allocate time to: (1) plan a schedule for the test, (2) attempt every question, (3) take quick rest breaks, and (4) check and correct answers. Once the test begins, students need to keep track of time and make sure that they are on schedule. This is easily done by writing time notations in the margin of the test paper (Standley 1987).

Testwiseness Skills

Testwiseness is the ability to use the characteristics of tests and test-taking situations to increase test scores. Testwiseness is logically independent of students' mastery of the content being tested (Millman, Bishop, and Ebel 1965). For this reason, teachers traditionally have not taught testwiseness skills, preferring to view tests as measures of students' mastery of the curriculum rather than of testwiseness.

Sarnacki (1985) observes, however, that "low test-wise examinees are penalized for lack of [testwiseness] abilities, especially when normed against students high in testwiseness." To be fair, all students should be taught testwiseness skills. Tests would then be more likely to measure knowledge or ability, and less likely to reflect students' different levels of testwiseness.

A meta-analysis of 24 studies in which elementary students were taught test-taking skills revealed that students trained in strategies for taking standardized tests had higher scores than did control groups, but that the average effect size was small:

> An effect size of that magnitude would raise a child's score on a standardized achievement test from the tenth to the twelfth percentile, or the fiftieth to the fifty-fourth percentile. Such differences are not sizable and should raise questions about the generally proclaimed benefits for such training programs (Scruggs, White, and Bennion 1986, p. 79).

The reviewers observed, however, that longer training programs (over four hours) were more effective overall, particularly for students in the lower elementary grades and for those from low socioeconomic backgrounds.

Ritter and Idol-Maestas (1986) found that sixth graders who were taught a set of test-taking strategies called SCORER performed significantly better than untrained students on a measure of testwiseness skills and on various achievement tests. The training particularly benefited students with low reading comprehension. SCORER includes six strategies: S, schedule your time; C, use clue words; O, omit difficult questions; R, read carefully; E, estimate your answer; and R, review.

Dreisbach and Keogh (1982) provided training in the specialized test vocabulary and response procedures of a standardized test to Spanish-speaking elementary students. Trained students scored significantly higher than untrained students on an achievement test used to determine school readiness, even though they received no content instruction. Improvement was greatest when the children first learned test-taking skills with Spanish language instruction and then relearned them with English instruction.

Scruggs, Mastro-pieri, and Tolfa-Veit (1986) taught learning-disabled and behaviorally disordered elementary students how to use a practice test booklet and answer sheet for the Stanford Achievement Test. Students were also taught to (1) work quickly and carefully, (2) check answers if time permits, (3) answer all questions, (4) eliminate answers known to be incorrect, (5) incorporate prior or partial knowledge, and (6) respond to subtest format demands. The researchers found that trained students scored significantly higher than untrained students on several subtests of the Stanford Achievement Test.

The following are testwiseness skills that can be used to prepare for tests.

STUDY SKILL 12
Determining What the Test Will Cover

Anderson and Armbruster (1984) found in their review of research that "when the criterion tasks [e.g., tests] associated with studying are made explicit . . . students spend more time and effort on the relevant segments of texts and learning outcomes generally improve" (p. 675). It is to students' advantage to learn as much as possible about the content of the test ahead of time. Some teachers tell students in general terms the content that will be tested; good listening skills are important for gathering this information. Students can make useful inferences about test content by studying the teacher's testing habits. Teachers tend to be fairly consistent from one year to the next, and from one test to the next. Examining previous tests can give students a good idea of what kind of information the teacher thinks students should learn—for example, dates in a history course, formulas and names of chemical compounds in a science course.

Sherman and Wildman (1982) suggest several other techniques for determining what will be tested: getting to know the teacher, meeting with the teacher outside of class, and using extra help opportunities, including review sessions provided by the teacher.

STUDY SKILL 13
Determining the Question Format

Students differ in their test performance not only because of their ability to retrieve information from memory, but also because of their ability to use reasoning appropriate to different types of test questions. Generally speaking, teacher-made tests use objective test questions (true-false, short-answer, matching, and multiple-choice) to test lower-cognitive objectives (knowledge, comprehension, and application) and they use subjective test questions (essay and performance) to test higher-cognitive objectives (analysis, synthesis, and evaluation) (Bloom 1956).

If students know the types of questions that will be on a test, they can focus their preparation on those types of questions. For example, they can spend more time memorizing vocabulary definitions and factual information if the test will emphasize objective questions, and more time asking themselves higher-cognitive questions if it will emphasize subjective questions.

Students who study as if all tests were essay tests generally do better, regardless of the types of questions the test actually contains. In a series of classic studies, Meyer (1934, 1935, 1936) found that students who anticipated essay and constructed-response exams performed generally better on all types of tests than students who anticipated true-false and multiple-choice types. Meyer also found that students studying for an essay exam wrote more summary statements, while students studying for an objective exam did more random note taking and underlining.

STUDY SKILL 14
Determining the Importance of the Test

Knowing how much weight a test has in determining the course grade can help students set priorities and allocate time and energy among their various study tasks. Some teachers provide this information in advance; others will give it to students if asked.

For tests that are not part of a course, such as the SAT, students should consider the outcomes or opportunities that may result from obtaining a high, average, or low score. They should evaluate the importance of the test results in relation to their goals and study accordingly.

The testwiseness skills we have described above are used when preparing for a test. The testwiseness skills described below are used during the test itself.

STUDY SKILL 15
Bringing Items Needed for the Test

Test performance can be affected by remembering to bring needed items to the testing room—for example, well-sharpened pencils, erasers, and pens. Math and science tests may require a calculator, ruler, or protractor; foreign language tests may permit the use of a translation dictionary; and so on. If students fail to bring needed or allowed items, they may lose valuable test-taking time trying to borrow them from others, becoming anxious and hurting their performance in the process.

STUDY SKILL 16
Sitting in a Good Location

If students are allowed to choose their seat, they should select one that will maximize their comfort, hearing, and view of anything relevant to the test (e.g., test directions on the blackboard). Orr (1986) and Kesselman-Turkel and Peterson (1981) also recommend avoiding seats near a heater or a window if it is noisy outside or very sunny; sitting away from friends and noisy students to avoid distraction; and sitting near a light if the room is dim.

STUDY SKILL 17
Reading Test Directions Carefully

Millman and Pauk (1969), in their classic book on how to take tests, devote an entire chapter to reading directions and questions carefully. They cite research conducted at the University of Chicago showing that

> the most distinguishing characteristic of poor test takers was their tendency to *mis*read directions and questions. Answers were often "off target" because these students jumped to conclusions about what was being asked. The sad part was that many points which should have been earned were lost even though these students really knew the material (Millman and Pauk 1969, p. 24).

Knowing how to record answers is an important aspect of following test instructions. A separate answer sheet is provided when students take standardized tests. Some teachers also use a separate answer sheet for class tests because it simplifies scoring. If students do not fill in these sheets correctly, they can lose points or fail the test entirely.

STUDY SKILL 18
Answering Easy Questions First

Students should try to answer the easiest test questions first in order to build their confidence and momentum and increase their chances of answering more questions correctly. Generally, easy questions appear first, but students' mastery of the content ultimately determines which ones are easy. Students need to develop the ability to flag difficult questions and quickly skip around on a test so that they can correctly answer as many questions as possible (Kesselman-Turkel and Peterson 1981).

STUDY SKILL 19
Using Appropriate Answering Techniques

Study skills experts recommend special techniques for answering the wide variety of test questions that students encounter in school. We consider here some of the more common types and techniques for handling them.

Sarnacki (1985) observes that "the majority of testwiseness research has centered around the recognition of secondary item cues that occur in flawed multiple-choice items" (p. 5211). For example, one item fault known as "absurd options" allows the testwise examinee to eliminate one or more of the alternatives because of their logical inconsistencies with the stem. If the stem asks, "The Golden Gate Bridge is located in which state?" and one alternative response is "San Francisco," the testwise examinee can eliminate this alternative because it is not a state. This flaw is a secondary item cue because it is independent of the content area being tested.

Another strategy is called "Guess before you choose" (Kesselman-Turkel and Peterson 1981). Crocker and Schmitt (1987) studied the effectiveness of this strategy, which they termed *response generation*. It involves making up an answer *before* looking at the multiple-choice options. The strategy improved the test performance of low test-anxious students, but hindered the performance of high test-anxious students.

Some techniques that study skills experts (e.g., Tuttle 1986; Pauk 1984; Standley 1987; Gifford and Fluitt 1981; Sherman and Wildman 1982) recommend for answering essay questions are: (1) read the question carefully; (2) jot key words and phrases next to the question and use them to outline the answer; (3) make the answer appropriate in length; and (4) review the answer for clarity, grammar, and spelling.

There are other techniques for specific types of content, such as preparing for and taking laboratory examinations:

> Carefully examine the complete range of laboratory specimens to familiarize yourself with all types, sizes, and perspectives of the material.
> Start your review early, so as to avoid inconvenience and crowding in the laboratory in the days prior to the examination.
> If you believe the tag on a specimen has been altered during the examination, summon a supervisor immediately (Orr 1986, p. 119).

In a research study described above (see Study Skill 17), Scruggs, Mastro-pieri and Tolfa-Veit (1986) coached elementary students in techniques for responding to tests in different content areas:

> The second and third sessions consisted of training in reading subtests. For the reading comprehension subtest, students were taught to refer back to the passage for recall questions, to use deductive reasoning strategies for infer-

ence questions, and to look for similarities between phrases or words in the passage and answer choices. For the word study skills subtest, students were taught to attend to appropriate cues and sounds, rather than letter similarities in stem and option. The fourth and fifth sessions covered strategies appropriate to math subtests. For the math concepts subtest, students were taught to attend carefully to specific format demands. For the computation subtest, students were taught to carefully recopy problems on scratch paper in the most familiar form. Finally, on the word problems subtest, students were taught to attend to command words in the problem and work problems carefully on separate paper (pp. 38-39).

Scruggs and his colleagues found that trained students outperformed control groups on word study skills and mathematics concepts subtests. The authors concluded that without training in test-taking skills, tests that have more complicated formats may prove differentially difficult for mildly handicapped students, thus obscuring students' true ability. Training for the subtests on reading comprehension and math word problems, which contain more obvious format demands, resulted in smaller effects.

Psychological Coping Skills

Since tests require concentrated preparation and a high level of performance under special conditions, anxiety may become associated with both anticipating and actually taking tests. Anxiety as an *emotional state* may be experienced by any individual under certain circumstances.

Text anxiety has also been studied as a stable *personality trait*, based on written self-report measures. Individuals high in the trait of text anxiety experience test anxiety more often and to a higher degree than other people.

Test anxiety produces two main types of difficulty for students. First, it may cause emotional arousal, signaled by sweaty palms, shortness of breath, and other symptoms that are upsetting to the students. Second, it results in worry, or negative cognitions, that interferes with concentration. These difficulties are assumed to prevent high test-anxious students from demonstrating their full knowledge or ability on a test. For example, Culler and Holahan (1980) found a negative relationship between test anxiety and school performance in a study of college freshmen.

Researchers have investigated approaches to reducing test anxiety that involve both treatment administered to students and strategies students can use themselves. One approach is simply to devalue the test. Rheinberg (1982) observes:

Of course, you can reduce anxiety dramatically by cutting through all instrumental connections between outcome and incentive valued consequences. But if you are completely successful in doing so you have ruined motivation to learn and prepare for the test as well (p. 135).

Accordingly, Davies (1986) notes that strategies that devalue the test should be used only with anxious students who are highly motivated. For other students, the same strategies are likely to lower performance. In fact, the present authors have observed the devaluing strategy used among many seemingly discouraged students, who handed in their tests after a short time without even trying to answer the questions.

A second approach to coping with test anxiety is to increase one's study efforts to make up for the negative effects of anxiety. Quantity of study, however, does not equate with quality of study. Benjamin, McKeachie, Lin, and Holinger (1981) found that high test-anxious college students reported more study hours than low text-anxious students, especially in the week before an exam, yet had lower exam performance. Similarly, Culler and Holahan (1980) found that high test-anxious college students reported more hours of study than their low test-anxious classmates, but had lower grade point averages.

The third approach to test anxiety is to treat its major symptoms, emotionality and worry. Below we will discuss one study skill directed at each of these symptoms. Finally, the fourth approach to test anxiety is a combination approach to the problem—treat the anxiety but also provide study skills instruction (Culler and Holahan 1980).

We believe that skills for coping with test anxiety are themselves study skills, but we concur with Culler and Holahan's recommendation to treat test anxiety with a combination of psychological coping skills and other study skills. All students need to improve their content review, time management, and testwiseness skills (what other authors refer to as "study skills") so that they can handle the tasks of test preparation and test taking more effectively. In addition, all students, particularly those who score high on test anxiety measures, need to reduce their anxious feelings and cognitions. We will discuss two study skills for dealing with test anxiety, the first focused on the emotionality aspect of test anxiety and the second on the worry aspect.

STUDY SKILL 20
Using Relaxation Techniques

Objectively, the emotional tension component of anxiety does not appear to hinder students' performance during a test (Covington 1985). Wine (1980) found that although high test-anxious students reported high levels of physiological arousal (sweating and increased heart rate) during a test, autonomic measures of their actual physiological arousal were no higher than those of low test-anxious subjects. High-anxious students *subjectively* believe themselves to be hampered by feelings of anxiety in taking tests, however.

Systematic desensitization is a common approach to treating feelings of anxiety. First students are taught progressive muscle relaxation—alternately tensing and relaxing each major muscle group in the body. Then the relaxation procedure is combined with an anxiety hierarchy—a set of statements representing scenes that stimulate test anxiety. Morris and Kratochwill (1983) reproduce a 20-item test anxiety hierarchy that has been used with junior high school students. Items are arranged from lowest ("You are attending a regular class session") to highest ("You are in the important exam. The teacher announces 15 minutes remaining, but you have an hour's work left") in their anxiety-provoking potential.

In traditional systematic desensitization, students are instructed to relax while items from the hierarchy are presented and to signal when they experience disruption in their relaxation. At this point, the stimulus is removed and students are instructed to return to a state of relaxation, at which point the procedure of presenting items from the anxiety hierarchy is resumed. Morris and Kratochwill (1983) describe variants on the traditional approach and summarize the research support. They note that despite limited evidence of effectiveness with children, systematic desensitization is the most widely used form of treatment for children's fears and phobias.

Denney and Rupert (1977) conducted a study of high test-anxious college students in which they introduced two changes in the traditional approach. First, some subjects received a *self-control* version of systematic desensitization. In this procedure, students signaled when their relaxation was disrupted, but were instructed to continue imaging the anxiety-provoking scene while trying to relax away their feelings of tension. The second change involved providing either an active-coping rationale or a passive rationale for the treatment. Students in the active rationale group were told that they would be learning a voluntarily controlled coping response that they could apply on their own to anxiety-provoking conditions at any time, whether in or outside of a counseling situation. Students in the passive rationale group received a description of the treatment that emphasized its automatic physiological effects and were advised to practice relaxation exercises only during anxiety-free times.

Denny and Rupert found that students in the self-control active-coping rationale condition scored lower than any other group in both a subjective and a performance measure of test anxiety following treatment; they also had a higher grade point average in the school terms following completion of treatment. These findings demonstrate that relaxation is most effective in reducing anxiety when students are taught to use the technique in anxiety-provoking situations.

STUDY SKILL 21
Positive Thinking

Covington (1985) hypothesizes that worry (i.e., negative cognitions), rather than tension or emotionality, is the predominant source of test-taking interference. He reasons that when students worry they are diverted from the task of preparing for the test and that worry may also inhibit answering questions during the test. Other research supports this hypothesis. Hunsley (1987) found that test anxiety among college students was strongly related to frequent negative thoughts during exams, and that students high in test anxiety had lower overall examination performance.

Worry may also interfere with students' ability to learn and review material when they prepare for tests (Covington and Omelich 1987). Thus, high test-anxious students would score lower on a test because they would not be as well prepared as low test-anxious students. Culler and Holahan (1980) cite the significant positive correlation between grade point average and scores on a study habits scale to support this interpretation.

In a review of research on treatments for test anxiety, Denney (1980) classified studies in three categories. Two categories treated only the emotionality aspect of test anxiety: (a) relaxation training and (b) self-control oriented systematic desensitization, both of which were described above. More positive results were found for treatments involving not only relaxation and self-control, but also (c) cognitive copying techniques, in which the cognitive-worry component of anxiety was addressed by having students substitute positive and rational self-statements for negative self-statements. Thus it appears that positive self-talk is the most potent component of treatments to reduce text anxiety.

Other research suggests that the benefits of positive thinking result not only from positive self-talk but also from positive *imaging*, or visualization. Kostka and Galassi (1974) found that students could be trained to imagine making nonanxious responses in a test situation and to imagine reinforcing stimuli (e.g., holding a test paper with a high grade on it) immediately afterwards. Training in this covert positive reinforcement method was as effective as a lengthier and more complex systematic desensitization treatment in reducing test anxiety and led to improved test performance.

Besides replacing negative self-thoughts, positive thinking can help students maintain attention by screening out distracting stimuli. For example, we have observed that students can become distracted in the test situation by what other students are doing (Gall and Gall 1988a). They may notice that other students are finishing the test and may feel pressured to speed up. Students can learn to ignore other students and stick to their own game plan. Using positive self-talk in this situation, a student might say, "I am going to use all the time available so I can get the highest possible score on this test, and I am sticking with it." Dansereau, McDonald, Collins, Garland, Holley, Diekhoff, and Evans (1979) taught students to monitor their moods and counter distractions by using relaxation in combination with positive self-talk or self-coaching. The training improved students' test performance under both nondistracting conditions and conditions in which students were distracted by noise.

<h2 style="text-align:center">STUDY SKILL 22
Expressing Feelings of Anxiety</h2>

Expressing anxiety to another person is a useful coping skill. It allows students to feel the emotion, thus avoiding neurotic stress reactions based on repression. And sharing feelings with a trusted confidante enables students to discover that others have similar feelings (Gifford and Fluitt 1981). By reducing feelings of isolation and uniqueness, students can move from shame or embarrassment to actively coping with their emotions.

This approach was investigated by Sarason (1975), who found that listening to a model who was high in test anxiety but able to successfully cope enhanced the performance of high test-anxious individuals. Alcoholics Anonymous and other self-help recovery programs successfully use a comparable approach in which members share their experience, strength, and hope with others who have similar problems.

Pauk (1989) presents ten strategies, recommended by the National Association for Mental Health, for handling stress. The first is the technique described above, which he labels "Talk It Out": "When something worries you, talk it out. Don't bottle it up. Talking to a friend will bring the worry into the open, where it can be dealt with rationally" (p. 20). Another strategy that Pauk describes is doing something for others: "Be a good listener. People with worries need someone with whom they can share their trouble. Don't criticize or give advice, just listen and show that you care" (p. 9).

Sharing feelings, then, involves finding a trusted colleague or confidante who can listen without judgment, and honestly expressing feelings rather than complaining or seeking advice.

<h2 style="text-align:center">STUDY SKILL 23
Overlearning the Material</h2>

Davies (1986) claims that overlearning is a useful technique for reducing test anxiety:

> A further step in the management of stress is to ensure that the subject matter or the skilled activity has been thoroughly learned—overlearned, in fact—

which means learning far more than is necessary for one correct answer or performance. . . . [Overlearning] serves to reduce anxiety because the candidate now perceives the examination as being less difficult (p. 77).

Similarly, we include overpreparation as one of six recommended techniques for controlling test anxiety (Gall and Gall 1988a). Overpreparation builds confidence, which in turn helps prevent test anxiety. Of course, overpreparation requires extra study time, so students who want to use this technique must manage their time carefully.

Methods of Teaching Test-Taking Skills

In this section we describe various methods that can be used to teach students the study skills involved in taking tests. These methods are listed in Figure 8.2.

Figure 8.2
Methods for Teaching Test-Taking Skills

CONTENT REVIEW SKILLS
1. Teach students to review the assigned readings by highlighting important information.
2. Teach students to review notes by using the two-column method.
3. Have students test each other as a class activity or in out-of-class study groups.
4. Prepare students for important tests by giving them practice tests and informing them of available resources.
5. Teach students to use self-monitoring to determine test readiness.

TIME MANAGEMENT SKILLS
1. Teach students a method of recording test dates.
2. Teach students how to manage time during tests.
3. Provide activities to compare the effectiveness of massed and distributed practice.

TESTWISENESS SKILLS
1. Provide systematic training in testwiseness skills.

PSYCHOLOGICAL COPING SKILLS
1. Provide training in positive self-talk and visualization.
2. Provide training in relaxation.

Content Review Skills

Teach students to review the assigned readings by highlighting important information. The teacher can do this by giving the class a section of text to highlight or underline using a special highlighter marker, pen, or pencil; if students are not permitted to write in the text, the selected phrases and sentences can be recorded as notes. Then the teacher can ask students to give a rationale for the text they selected, and give them feedback on their rationale.

Teach students to review notes by using the two-column method. Techniques for taking notes on what the teacher says in class and on reading assignments are presented in Chapters 5 and 6, respectively. The techniques generally involve writing key phrases or questions in the left margin of the note page and details or answers in the right margin, so that students can review their notes by quizzing themselves on cues in the left margin, and then checking their answers against the notes in the right margin. Methods for teaching students how to take two-column notes are described in Chapters 5 and 6.

A related method, called "Solitaire Lay-Down Cards," is described by Standley (1987). In this game, students make up 3" x 5" cards listing questions about information from their class notes (or directly from their textbooks). They then play "Solitaire" with the deck of cards, answering out loud the questions and checking their answers in the notes or textbook. Standley provides examples and practice exercises to aid students in learning this note-taking and review method.

Have students test each other as a class activity or in out-of-class study groups. Teachers can help students learn self-testing skills in preparation for a test by having them form testing pairs during the class period. One student generates a question about the text or other curriculum material, and the other student tries answering it. Students then switch roles. Adams, Carnine, and Gersten (1982) and Gall and Gall (1988a) have developed lesson plans and units that involve this teaching method. Also, Standley (1987) describes four ways in which the "Solitaire Lay-Down Cards" game mentioned above can be adapted to classroom group activity. Students can also use the questions at the end of units or chapters in the text.

Older students can be advised to form study groups outside of class to prepare for tests. Because this method is time-consuming, teachers should recommend its use primarily for tests that count heavily toward a course grade and that cover a lot of material. Kesselman-Turkel and Peterson (1981) recommend several rules that a study group should follow to get good results, including: "One hour spent with everyone's mind on the subject is worth four hours of work with time-outs every few minutes for fun and games."

Prepare students for important tests by giving them practice tests and informing them of available resources. Practice tests are an excellent way to help students review for tests. They also allow students to learn test-taking skills related to time management, testwiseness, and anxiety reduction.

Teachers can help students prepare for the SAT and similar tests by recommending pertinent reading material. Two booklets from the Personal Efficiency Programs (Reed 1983, 1985), for example, answer ten of students' most common questions, such as how to register for these tests and where to get study materials. Teachers also can tell students that when they register for the SAT, the College Entrance Examination Board will provide them with a booklet called *Taking the SAT*, which includes suggestions for preparing for the test, sample questions with explanations, and a sample test with answers, scoring directions, and data on the percentage of students answering each question on the sample test correctly. Another helpful book is *10 SAT's Plus Advice from the College Board on How to Prepare for Them, 3rd edition* (College Entrance Examination Board, 1988).

The *Video SAT Review* (Random House, 1988) provides a two-hour VHS cassette and practice booklets covering the math and verbal sections of the SAT, anxiety reduction techniques, a sample SAT-type test, and pretest suggestions for parents. Video instructors take students through three math tutorial sessions and four verbal tutorial sessions.

SAT Complete (Spinnaker Software, 1984) is a computerized SAT preparation program for use with Apple or PC computers. According to the catalog description, "The entire program is phased and controlled by the student to suit personal study habits, strengths, and weaknesses." The program also includes the book *SAT Success (revised edition)*, as well as mock SATs and a user manual.

Coaching programs are offered by companies such as the Stanley H. Kaplan Educational Center and the Princeton Review Service. A prominent feature of these programs is having students take practice versions of the test for which they are preparing.

Teach students to use self-monitoring to determine test readiness. Divine and Kylen (1979) developed an 18-question Readiness Checklist that students can use to determine if they have prepared adequately for a test. Students are ready if they can answer "yes" to such questions such as: Have I reviewed properly for the test? Have I learned to overcome test anxiety? Do I know the forms of the questions? and Do I know the total time allowed for the examination?

The checklist touches on all four categories of test-taking skills reviewed in this chapter—content review, time management, testwiseness, and psychological coping. Teachers can show students how to fill out this checklist, or they can develop a similar checklist specifically for their course.

Time Management Skills

Teach students a method of recording test dates. The teacher can review with students their current method of recording test dates and other important dates (e.g., due dates for assignments). If students do not have a method of their own that works, the teacher can teach one. Gall and Gall (1988b) present a lesson for teaching students to record test dates and other information on an assignment sheet that can be kept in a three-ring binder (see also the first activity under Teaching About Time Management in Chapter 4).

Teach students how to manage time during tests. Teachers can help students learn to manage time during tests by giving them practice tests, so that students can focus on skill development without the anxiety of having their test performance count toward the course grade.

The teacher can distribute the practice test and review with students the tasks they need to carry out: reading the test directions, scanning the test to get an overview of it, deciding the amount of time to spend on each set of questions, answering the questions, and checking answers. Next, the teacher can have students estimate the amount of time to spend on each of these tasks. Finally, students can take the test and find out whether their estimates were on target.

Davies (1986) describes several instructional procedures that teachers can use with practice tests. For example, he recommends giving students a series of practice tests so that they gradually build skill and confidence in dealing with testing demands. And he recommends increasing the pressure in subsequent practice test situations by reducing the time limit or by providing incentives of various kinds.

Provide activities to compare the effectiveness of massed and distributed practice. To demonstrate the advantages of planning sufficient, appropriately spaced time for test preparation (Study Skill 8), teachers can provide simple in-class learning activities using massed and distributed practice. For example, students can be asked to memorize a set of vocabulary definitions, seven-digit numbers, or word lists, using two sets of items matched for difficulty. Students would learn the first set in a massed practice session—for example, 15 minutes straight. They would learn the second set in a distributed practice session—for example, 5 minutes of practice followed by a 10-minute break or other activity; 5 more minutes of practice followed by another 10-minute break or other activity; and 5 more minutes of practice. On another day, distributed practice would precede massed practice, to control for order effects in learning.

Performance under the two conditions can be compared, and students can also be encouraged to observe their feelings and behavior under the two conditions. Generally speaking, performance should be superior under distributed practice, which will help demonstrate the disadvantages of cramming. The feelings that students experience under massed practice will probably be similar to those described by Orr (1986) as characteristic of cramming:

> Your general pace of living increases sharply and you find that you have difficulty sitting down calmly to do some studying.
> You experience pronounced thumping of the heart and your breathing rate is noticeably accelerated.
> Time slips away quickly and panic sets in (p. 89).

Feelings like these may motivate students to space their test preparation to avoid such feelings in the future.

Testwiseness Skills

Provide systematic training in testwiseness skills. The testing procedures to which students must respond are somewhat different for each class, depending on the teacher's personal testing style. A simple but effective way to teach testwiseness skills is to show students sample tests that are typical of those that will be given in class. Teachers can walk students through the sample test, and as they do so, suggest testwiseness techniques that students can use to enhance their test performance. Teachers might comment on:

1. The kinds of information they expect students to remember. For example, terms and definitions might be important to a science teacher, and names of key people and dates of significant events might be important to a history teacher. If teachers consider it important for students to understand and be able to apply principles relating to the subject taught, they can let students know that understanding and application of information will be tested.

2. The number of questions of each type they typically include on a test, and suggestions for responding to each. For example, if students are to answer essay questions, the teacher could suggest that they underline key words in the essay question (like *analyze*, *compare*, *define*, or *summarize*) before writing their response. If students are to answer multiple-choice questions, the teacher could suggest eliminating obviously wrong choices before selecting their answers.

3. The number of points that each test is worth, or the weight of the test in the student's course grade, and a suggested amount of study time that corresponds to the test's importance.

4. Hints for doing their best on any test (e.g., having extra writing supplies handy, sitting in a good location, and reading test directions carefully.)

5. A reminder to answer first the items that seem easy. The teacher can ask students which questions seem easy, and point out that students select different items depending on their knowledge of the subject or their preference for different types of questions. The teacher can also give suggestions for determining and marking the easy items, and for allocating time to make sure that all easy items are attempted.

Teachers also might want to teach the test-taking method called SCORER, developed by Ritter and Idol-Maestas (1986):

S – *Schedule your time.* Write a schedule on the test, indicating an appropriate length of time to spend on each part.

C – *Clue words.* Underline important words in the directions.

O – *Omit difficult questions.* Place a "+" or "++" beside difficult questions and attempt those questions only after answering the easier questions.

R – *Read carefully.* Write "P" beside the directions with more than one part.

E – *Estimate your answer.* Mark an "E" beside difficult questions for which you have estimated the answer.

R – *Review.* Write an "R" on the test, indicating that you have reviewed the test before handing it in.

These six learning strategies should be taught in order, with each introduced and practiced over a two-day period. Students learn the name of each strategy and the steps it includes, and then discuss how they would apply it. The teacher demonstrates the strategy and then students apply it by completing practice problems, after which they are given the correct responses to the problems. Students then receive a sample test and are asked to apply the SCORER strategies without actually taking the test. They are also asked to write from memory the name and major steps of the strategy studied that day. Each group session ends with a short review including both the strategy studied that day and those previously studied. Every student is questioned individually either once or twice over the 12 days of instruction and asked to describe the strategy studied that day. After instruction on each strategy, students apply them to several sample tests.

To ensure that the entire SCORER procedure has been mastered, each student is asked to describe all six strategies in writing. Students then take practice tests controlled for reading level, with directions to apply SCORER when taking the test. Mastery is defined as application of SCORER strategies on three out of four sample tests with 83 percent accuracy.

Psychological Coping Skills

Provide training in positive self-talk and visualization. The *Coping with Tests Program* (Thoresen et al. 1986) is a computer program that includes a Test Attitude Inventory to help students estimate the frequency and intensity of their anxiety and arousal in relation to an upcoming test. Its purpose is to give students immediate feedback about how their test anxiety compares with other students'. Depending on how they score, students can determine their need to use the other components of the program. One of these components is a diskette on success rehearsal that teaches students to imagine that they have a new set of positive thoughts, actions, and feelings in a test situation.

Davies (1986) recommends that students learn how to use positive self-talk by drawing up a list of positive statements to suit their individual needs and periodically repeating these statements until they become automatic. In this way, students can readily replace negative thoughts with positive thoughts when worries arise.

Orr (1986) provides a brief chapter on thinking positively, listing ten positive steps that teachers can teach students to help them towards examination success, including:

Ask yourself what is the single most interesting fact from each lecture or class.
Place a card in front of you on your desk with a meaningful positive message, such as, "Success is the product of positive thinking." Or make it more personal . . ."Jeremy Wilson will study daily and pass his exams."
Analyze your situation. If there's no real reason why you should not pass, then count on passing and work to that end (p. 86).

Orr's chapter on learning how to relax also includes instructions for giving positive self-suggestions. Gall and Gall (1988a) present a similar lesson in which students are taught to write and repeat self-affirmations that are stated positively, in present tense, and in personal terms. An example of a self-affirmation to alleviate test anxiety would be, "I am calm, confident, and well prepared as I enter the test."

Provide training in relaxation. Two components of the *Coping with Tests Program*, described earlier in this section, are an audiotape on learning how to relax, and diskettes on how to cope, relax, and concentrate.

The *Video SAT Review*, described earlier under Content Review Skills, includes a practice booklet that shows students how to evaluate their SAT goals, relax, and concentrate.

Orr (1986) and Davies (1986) provide detailed instructions for students to use, on their own or with a guide, to learn how to relax. Orr has developed a checklist of signs and symptoms associated with stress when thinking about or taking an examination (e.g., "Does your heart thump with exaggerated beats at an accelerated rate?"). It includes an eight-page description of relaxation training that students can teach themselves, or that teachers can use to teach students. Eleven steps are described in detail: (1) practice every day; (2) expect to relax; (3) find a quiet spot; (4) make yourself comfortable; (5) focus on your breathing; (6) focus your attention; (7) use positive self-suggestion; (8) come back slowly; (9) note how you feel; (10) plan your next relaxation session; and (11) draw up a daily practice chart. Detailed procedures are also described for using systematic desensitization to reduce the anxiety experienced in anticipating examinations, and for relaxing quickly in the examination itself.

Davies (1986) describes another procedure for systematic desensitization to test anxiety. Students are asked to imagine each item on a 20-item list. For example, the least anxiety-provoking item (#20) might be a pencil, a moderately anxiety-provoking item (#10) might be an untimed mock examination, and a highly anxiety-provoking item (#5) might be the morning of the examination. Students progressively learn to relax in the presence of the more anxiety-provoking items on the list. Davies also describes a detailed procedure for progressive muscle relaxation, and for the use of biofeedback to assess progress in learning how to relax.

Another useful resource is *The Relaxation and Stress Reduction Workbook* (Davis, Eshelman, and McKay 1982). It includes detailed instructions, illustrations, and activities for methods of reducing stress, including progressive relaxation, meditation, breathing, and numerous other approaches.

References

Adams, A., D. Carnine, and R. Gersten. (Fall 1982). "Instructional Strategies for Studying Content Area Texts in the Intermediate Grades." *Reading Research Quarterly* 18, 1: 27–55.

Anderson, T. H., and B. Armbruster. (1984). "Studying." In *Handbook of Reading Research*, edited by P.D. Pearson. New York: Longman.

Armbruster, B., and T. H. Anderson. (November 1981). "Research Synthesis on Study Skills." *Educational Leadership* 39, 2: 154–156.

Belezza, F. S. (Summer 1981). "Mnemonic Devices: Classification, Characteristics, and Criteria." *Review of Educational Research* 51: 247–275.

Benjamin, M., W. J. McKeachie, Y. Lin, and D. P. Holinger. (1981). "Test Anxiety: Deficits in Information Processing." *Journal of Educational Psychology* 73, 6: 816–824.

Bloom, B. S., ed. (1956). *Taxonomy of Educational Objectives*. New York: McKay.

Brown, A. L., J. C. Campione, and C. R. Barclay. (1979). "Training Self-Checking Routines for Estimating Test Readiness: Generalization from List Learning to Prose Recall." *Child Development* 50: 501–512.

College Entrance Examination Board. (1988). *10 SATS Plus Advice from the College Board on How to Prepare for Them*. 3rd edition. New York: College Entrance Examination Board.

Covington, M. V. (1985). "Test Anxiety: Causes and Effects Over Time." In *Advances in Test Anxiety Research*, vol. IV, edited by R. Schwarzer, H. M. Van Der Ploeg, and C. D. Speilberger. Hillsdale, N.J.: Erlbaum.

Covington, M. V., and C. L. Omelich. (1987). "'I Knew It Cold Before the Exam': A Test of the Anxiety Blockage Hypothesis." *Journal of Educational Psychology* 79, 4: 393–400.

Crocker, L., and A. Schmitt. (1987). "Improving Multiple-Choice Test Performance for Examinees with Different Levels of Test Anxiety." *The Journal of Experimental Education* 55, 4: 201–205.

Culler, R. E., and C. J. Holahan. (1980). "Test Anxiety and Academic Performance: The Effects of Study-related Behaviors." *Journal of Educational Psychology* 72: 16–20.

Dansereau, D. F., B. A. McDonald, K. W. Collins, J. Garland, C. D. Holley, G. M. Diekhoff, and S. H. Evans. (1979). "Evaluation of a Learning Strategy System." In *Cognitive and Affective Learning Strategies*, edited by H. F. O'Neil, Jr., and C. D. Spielberger. New York: Academic Press.

Davies, D. (1986). *Maximizing Examination Performance: A Psychological Approach*. New York: Nichols.

Davis, M., E. R. Eshelman, and M. McKay. (1982). *The Relaxation and Stress Reduction Workbook*, 2nd edition. Oakland, Calif.: New Harbinger.

Denney, D. R. (1980). "Self-Control Techniques to the Treatment of Test Anxiety." In *Test Anxiety: Theory, Research, and Applications*, edited by I. G. Sarason. Hillsdale, N.J.: Erlbaum.

Denney, D. R., and P. A. Rupert. (1977). "Desensitization and Self-Control in the Treatment of Test Anxiety." *Journal of Consulting Psychology* 24, 4: 272–280.

Deutsch, C. (October 1988). "Standardized Testing Has Become Big Business." *The Register-Guard* (Eugene, Oreg.).

Divine, J. H., and D. W. Kylen. (1979). *How to Beat Test Anxiety and Score Higher on Your Exams*. Woodbury, N.Y.: Barrons.

Dreisbach, M., and B. Keogh. (1982). "Testwiseness as a Factor in Readiness Test Performance of Young Mexican-American Children." *Journal of Educational Psychology* 74, 2: 224–229.

Gall, M. D., and J. P. Gall. (1988a). *Making the Grade*. Rocklin, Calif.: Prima.

Gall, M. D., and J. P. Gall. (1988b). *Study for Success Teacher's Manual*. Eugene, Oreg.: M. Damien.

Gifford, C. S., and J. L. Fluitt. (1981). *Test-taking Made Easier*. Danville, Ill.: Interstate.

Hunsley, J. (1987). "Cognitive Processes in Mathematics Anxiety and Test Anxiety: The Role of Appraisals, Internal Dialogue, and Attributions." *Journal of Educational Psychology* 79, 4: 388–392.

Johnson, D., and R. Johnson. (1975). *Learning Together and Alone*. Englewood Cliffs, N.J.: Prentice Hall.

Jones, B. F., and J. H. Hall. (1982). "School Applications of the Mnemonic Keyword as a Study Strategy by Eighth Graders." *Journal of Educational Psychology* 74: 230–237.

Kesselman-Turkel, J., and F. Peterson. (1981). *Test-Taking Strategies*. Chicago: Contemporary Books.

Kostka, M. P., and J. P. Galassi. (1974). "Group Systematic Desensitization versus Covert Positive Reinforcement in the Reduction of Test Anxiety." *Journal of Consulting Psychology* 21, 6: 464–468.

Kulik, James A., C. C. Kulik, and R. L. Bangert. (Summer 1984). "Effects of Practice on Aptitude and Achievement Test Scores." *American Educational Research Journal* 21, 2: 435–447.

Lorayne, H., and J. Lucas. (1974). *The Memory Book*. New York: Ballantine.

Meyer, G. (1936). "The Effects on Recall and Recognition of the Examination Set in Classroom Situations." *Journal of Educational Psychology* 27: 81–99.

Meyer, G. (1935). "An Experimental Study of the Old and New Types of Examination: II. Methods of Study." *Journal of Educational Psychology* 26: 30–40.

Meyer, G. (1934). "An Experimental Study of the Old and New Types of Examination: I. The Effect of the Examination Set on Memory." *Journal of Educational Psychology* 25: 641–660.

Millman, J., C. H. Bishop, and R. Ebel. (1965). "An Analysis of Test-wiseness." *Journal of Educational Research* 25, 3: 707–726.

Millman, J., and W. Pauk. (1969). *How to Take Tests*. New York: McGraw-Hill.

Morris, R. J., and T. R. Kratochwill. (1983). *Treating Children's Fears and Phobias*. New York: Pergamon.

Orr, F. (1986). *Test-Taking Power*. New York: Monarch.

Pauk, W. (1989). *How to Study in College*, 4th edition. Boston: Houghton Mifflin.

Pauk, W. (May 1984). "Preparing for Exams." *Reading World* 23, 4: 386–387.

Random House. (1988). *The Video SAT Review*. Westminster, Md.: Random House Media.

Raugh, M. R., and R. C. Atkinson. (1975). "A Mnemonic Method for Learning a Foreign Language Vocabulary." *Journal of Educational Psychology* 67: 1–16.

Reed, M. E. B. (1985). "How to Pass College Entrance Exams." Seal Beach, Calif.: Personal Efficiency Programs.

Reed, M. E. B. (1983). "How to Pass Standardized Tests." Seal Beach, Calif.: Personal Efficiency Programs.

Rheinberg, F. (1982). "Reducing Anxiety in Classroom Settings: Some Theoretical Observations." In *Advances in Test Anxiety Research*, vol. I, edited by R. Schwarzer, H. M. Van Der Ploeg, and C. D. Spielberger. Hillsdale, N.J.: Erlbaum.

Ritter, S., and L. Idol-Maestas. (July/August 1986). "Teaching Middle School Students to Use a Test-Taking Strategy." *Journal of Educational Research* 79, 6: 350–357.

Rohwer, W. D., Jr., and J. W. Thomas. (1986). "The Role of Mnemonic Strategies in Study Effectiveness." Unpublished manuscript, University of California, Berkeley. Cited in Kiewra, K. A. (1988). "Cognitive Aspects of Autonomous Note Taking: Control Processes, Learning Strategies, and Prior Knowledge." *Educational Psychologist* 23, 1: 39–56.

Sarason, I. G. (1975). "Test Anxiety and the Self-Disclosing, Coping Model." *Journal of Consulting and Clinical Psychology* 43, 2: 148–153.

Sarnacki, R. E. (1985). "Test-wiseness." In *The International Encyclopedia of Education*, edited by T. Husen and T. N. Postlethwaite. New York: Pergamon.

Scruggs, T. E., M. A. Mastro-pieri, and D. Tolfa-Veit. (September/October 1986). "The Effects of Coaching on the Standardized Test Performance of Learning Disabled and Behaviorally Disordered Students." *Remedial and Special Education* 7, 5: 37–41.

Scruggs, T. E., K. R. White, and K. Bennion. (1986). "Teaching Test-Taking Skills to Elementary-Grade Students: A Meta-analysis." *The Elementary School Journal* 87, 1: 69–82.

Sherman, T. M., and T. M. Wildman. (1982). *Proven Strategies for Successful Test Taking*. Columbus, Ohio: Merrill.

Slavin, R. E. (1986). "Cooperative Learning: Engineering Social Psychology in the Classroom." In *The Social Psychology of Education*, edited by R. S. Feldman. New York: Cambridge University Press.

Spinnaker Software. (1984). *SAT Complete*. Cambridge, Mass.: Spinnaker Software.

Standley, K. E. (1987). *How to Study* . Palo Alto, Calif.: Dale Seymour.

Stickney, J. (January 1984). "Acing the SATs." *Money*, 121(4).

Thoresen, C. E., P. M. Insel, W. T. Roth, W. Ross, and M. F. Seyler. (1986). *Coping with Tests: A User's Guide*. Palo Alto, Calif.: Consulting Psychologists Press.

Tuttle, F. B. (1986). *How to Prepare Students for Writing Tests*. Washington, D.C.: National Education Association.

Weinstein, C. (1982). "Learning Strategies: The Metacurriculum." *Journal of Developmental & Remedial Education* 5, 2: 6–7, 10.

Wigfield, A., and S. R. Asher. (1984). "Social and Motivational Influences on Reading." In *Handbook of Reading Research*, edited by P. D. Pearson. New York: Longman.

Wine, J. D. (1980). "Cognitive-attentional Theory of Test Anxiety." In *Test Anxiety: Theory, Research, and Application*, edited by I. G. Sarason. Hillsdale, N.J.: Erlbaum.

Index

learning process, 26
learning task, 26, 28
teacher-as-mediator, 24-25
Motivation
attribution theory, 23
causal attributions, 24
external, 23
importance of, 11, 23-24, 34-35, 74
internal, 23
social learning theory, 24

N

NAESP, 7
NASSP, 7
Note-taking skills
how to teach, 101, 105-107
list of, 92
Notes
abbreviations in, 98
and SQ3R, 124
Cornell method, 100
effectiveness of, 118
importance of, 118
labeling and dating, 99
legibility of, 98
organizing, 118
paraphrase, 98, 117
percentage of students who take, 105
reviewing, 100
revising, 99-100
skeletal, 105
storing, 99
when to take, 88-89, 96-97, 117-118

O

Organizing
home study space, 64, 74, 76
how to teach skills for, 74-76
list of skills for, 62
materials and space, 63-64, 74
using a binder, 63
using subtasks, 66
Outlining
definition of, 154
effectiveness of, 119
when to teach, 119

P

Parents
involving, 57, 76, 78, 81, 83
Participation skills
for discussion, 104-105
how to teach, 101, 103-105
list of, 92
Positive self-talk
See Positive thinking
Positive thinking, 71, 192, 200

Practice
massed vs. distributed, 198
Praise-Question-Polish method, 170
Primary-Secondary Education Act, 87
Priorities
setting, 65-66
Procrastination
definition of, 64
overcoming, 65
Programs
A Guidebook for Teaching Study Skills and Motivation, 53
Cognitive Learning Strategies Project, 51
developed by associations, 51-52
developed by private publishers, 53
developed by school districts, 52
Effective Study Strategies, 53
hm Study Skills Program, 51
hm Study Skills Program, Level B, 51
Learning Strategies Curriculum, 51
Learning Strategies/Study Skills Program, 36, 52
Skills for School Success, 53
STEPS: Study Skills Scope and Sequence K–12, 52
Study for Success Teacher's Manual, 53
Study Power, 52
Teaching Study Skills: A Guide for Teachers, 53
Progressive muscle relaxation, 69

Q

Question-answer relationships
types of, 137
Question-answering skills
look-back strategy, 137
teaching, 135-137
use of, 122-123
Question-generating skills
teaching, 135-137
use of, 122-123
Questioning strategies, 90
Questions
importance of answering, 95, 178
importance of asking, 96
types of, 104

R

Reactive statements, 71
Readability levels, 112
Reading
cue words, 129
deep processing, 114-115
elements of, 110
elements of effective, 122-123
explicit vs. implicit instruction, 138
how to teach skills for, 127
in lower grades, 111
in upper grades, 111
initial instruction, 112
reciprocal teaching reading strategy, 125

LB 1049 .T64 1990

Tools for learning

DATE DUE			
DEC 17 1990			